PAYNE VC

Mike Colman is associate editor of *The Courier-Mail*, Brisbane. He has written over a dozen books, including bestselling biographies of rugby league's Paul Vautin, *Fatty: The Strife and Times of Paul Vautin*, and Gorden Tallis, *Raging Bull*. His biography of Eddie Gilbert, *Eddie Gilbert: The True Story of an Australian Cricketing Legend*, written with Dr Ken Edwards, won the Australian Cricket Society's Jack Pollard Award for the best cricket book of 2003. A member of the News Limited Olympic reporting team since 1992, he covered his fifth Olympic Games in Beijing, 2008. He lives in Brisbane with wife Linda and children Matilda, Amelia, Isabelle and William.

Other books by Mike Colman

Fatty – The Strife and Times of Paul Vautin (1992)
Super League – The Inside Story (1996)
Show Me the Money (2000)
Eddie Gilbert (with Ken Edwards, 2002)
Raging Bull (2003)
1500: The Story of Australia's Race (2004)
Blood in the Water (2006)

PAYNE VC

The story of Australia's most decorated soldier of the Vietnam War

MIKE COLMAN

Foreword by
General Peter Cosgrove, AC, MC (Ret'd)

ABC
Books

The ABC 'Wave' device is a trademark of the Australian Broadcasting Corporation and is used under licence by HarperCollins*Publishers* Australia.

First published in 2009 by ABC Books
for the Australian Broadcasting Corporation
Reprinted by HarperCollins*Publishers* Australia Pty Limited
ABN 36 009 913 517
harpercollins.com.au

Copyright © Mike Colman 2009

The right of Mike Colman to be identified as the author of this work has been asserted by him in accordance with the *Copyright Amendment (Moral Rights) Act 2000*.

This work is copyright. Apart from any use as permitted under the *Copyright Act 1968*, no part may be reproduced, copied, scanned, stored in a retrieval system, recorded, or transmitted, in any form or by any means, without the prior written permission of the publisher.

HarperCollins*Publishers*
Level 13, 201 Elizabeth Street, Sydney, NSW 2000, Australia
Unit D, 63 Apollo Drive, Rosedale, Auckland 0632, New Zealand
A 53, Sector 57, Noida, UP, India
1 London Bridge Street, London SE1 9GF, United Kingdom
2 Bloor Street East, 20th floor, Toronto, Ontario M4W 1A8, Canada
195 Broadway, New York NY 10007, USA

National Library of Australia Cataloguing-in-publication data

Colman, Mike
  Payne VC: the story of Australia's most decorated
  soldier of the Vietnam War/Mike Colman
  1st ed.
  ISBN 978 0 7333 2488 8 (pbk).
  Includes index
  Payne, Keith
  Vietnam War, 1961–1975 –Veterans – Biography
  Vietnam War, 1961–1975 – Psychological aspects
959.7043092

Editing by Jean Kingett
Index by Puddingburn Publishing Services
Cover design by Luke Causby/Blue Cork Designs
Typeset in 11.5/15pt Bembo by Kirby Jones
Front-cover photograph of Keith Payne, Australian War Memorial (LES/69/0593/VN);
  helicopter and soldiers, Corbis
Back-cover portrait of Keith Payne, Australian War Memorial (ART27773)
Project management by Richard Smart Publishing

To Flo Payne and Linda Colman
They also serve who only stand and wait
– John Milton

Photographs
Forty, between pages 110 and 111

A khaki wedding
Training prior to secondment to
　US Special Forces
Don Taylor
Barry Tolley
Gerry Dellwo
Kev Latham and Ray Simpson
　VC
Supervising Montagnards'
　training
Sharing a meal with Yards in the
　field
Remains of Special Forces HQ,
　Pleiku
The hill near Ben Het where the
　VC action took place
Anastacio Montez and Paul
　Auriemma
Back to the Highlands with
　Derek Payne and Ray Martin
Flo rings her congratulations on
　the VC
Greeting the little 'cobbers'
'Show us your medals, Dad'
Welcome home from Flo and
　the boys
A 'photo op'

Off for a day's fishing
The keys to the city of Brisbane
The VC pinned on by Her
　Majesty the Queen
Flo and the boys meet the
　Queen
The lunch menu aboard the
　royal yacht *Britannia*
A previous meeting with the
　Queen
Receiving RSL life membership
Two old soldiers
The opening of Keith Payne Park
The first beer pulled at the Keith
　Payne Recreational Club
A record-breaking snapper
A professional fisherman
Flying the flag
Off to Korea
In Korea
In Malaya
Off to Oman
Receiving the Cross of Gallantry
　with Bronze Star
Awarded the Distinguished
　Service Cross
An elder statesman

Contents

Acknowledgements	ix
Foreword	xi
Prologue	1
1 Wild Colonial Boy	3
2 The Recruit	14
3 Cold as Hell	23
4 Flora and Fauna	31
5 Army Wife	41
6 Konfrontasi	48
7 Warrant Officers' Corps	61
8 Escape Route	69
9 The Team	77
10 In Country	84
11 Operational	98
12 Anzac Day	111
13 'Simmo'	124
14 Ben Het	132
15 Officer Payne	140
16 'Oh Shit, Sir'	152
17 Coming Home	165
18 'Yes, Ma'am'	175

19 In the Service of the Sultan	186
20 Collateral Damage	196
21 Fighting Back	211
22 A Cross to Bear	225
Glossary	*233*
Index	*240*

Acknowledgements

The seed for this book was planted a few days after Anzac Day 2006. I was returning from a trip to Gallipoli, where I had followed the footsteps of my grandfather and great uncle, both of whom went ashore on the first day's fighting on 25 April 1915. Like so many Australians, Kiwis, Brits and Turks who have visited this monument to man's stupidity, it proved a deeply emotional experience, one that made me want to further explore the motivation and thought-processes of ordinary men who find themselves in extraordinary situations in time of war.

On the way back to Brisbane, during a two-hour stopover in Singapore, I sat at a computer and accessed the citations of Australia's Victoria Cross recipients. After reading about Keith Payne's actions near Ben Het, Vietnam, on 29 May 1969, I knew I had my man. What Keith did that night, returning to enemy territory time and time again to rescue men, many of whom he had first met only hours earlier and whose language he did not speak, seemed almost unbelievable. But, as I researched this book over the next couple of years, I found it was only a small part of the story.

After giving me their trust, Keith and Flo Payne opened their home and their hearts. Nothing was off-limits. Forty years on Keith found it hard to speak about what happened at Ben Het, but he did, many times, as I pressed him for details. He never flinched when speaking of that terrible night – or of those that followed.

To many people Keith Payne is a hero for what he did in uniform. To his family he is a hero for the way he overcame the demons that followed him from Korea, Malaya and Vietnam. It was not easy being a veteran in Australia in the 1970s and 1980s. It was even harder with the letters VC behind your name. And it was particularly difficult for Keith, Flo and their sons Ronald and Derek, who spoke on behalf of their three brothers, to relive those years. I can't thank them enough for doing so.

Acknowledgements

Likewise my deepest thanks go to Keith's comrades-in-arms, most especially the remarkable Gerry Dellwo, Don Taylor and Gus Breen, whose contributions were invaluable. I am indebted to Brigadier Russell Lloyd (Ret'd) for all his help. It is not hard to realise why he was – and still is – so respected by Keith and other members of the Team. Thanks also to General Peter Cosgrove (Ret'd) for agreeing so readily to write the book's Foreword, and for doing it so wonderfully well.

Where I have used excerpts from other published sources it has been noted in the text, but I would like to thank the publishers and copyright holders for granting permission for their use. They include the Australian War Memorial, the Australian Department of Defence, News Limited, Barry Petersen and Fred Kirkland. While I did not quote from it, I would like to acknowledge Stan Krasnoff's book *Where To? For Valour* (Shala Press, 1995) which was a valuable reference source.

The majority of photographs in the book came from Keith and Flo Payne's private collection; many were presented to Keith in 1970 by his Korean War contemporary Eric Donnelly on behalf of Brisbane press photographers. Other photographs, including the one of Keith Payne taken by Darren England at the Queensland Museum, were kindly provided by News Limited. Cover photograph credits are on page iv.

This book could not have been written without the help and support of two 'transport officers', Flo Payne and Linda Colman. I would also like to sincerely thank my editor Jean Kingett and publisher Richard Smart for their professionalism and patience.

Finally, I would like to thank Keith Payne VC and all the other ordinary men and women who find themselves in exceptional situations, and react in extraordinary ways.

Mike Colman

---

* The academic citation for the back-cover portrait of Keith Payne reads as follows:
Shirley Bourne, *Warrant Officer Class II Keith Payne*, Duntroon ACT 1972
Oil on canvas, 76.2 x 61cm, Australian War Memorial (ART27773)

Foreword

ORDINARY MEN DO EXTRAORDINARY things: it's a modern cliche. Yet in warfare it has always resonated, and still does. Warfare of any nature, and particularly in South Vietnam, is so extraordinarily convoluted and deadly that all of the protagonists are swept along in its inexorable and vicious tide.

Battlefields often provide instances of a kind of 'crazy courage' where, in the blink of an eye, men or women do something remarkable. During Australia's long modern military history there have been plenty of examples, and there is an element of it in the remarkable actions of Keith Payne. However, it is important to remember that Keith also endured mortal danger over many hours with one thought in mind, to protect and save the men under his command.

While many Australian soldiers I know have had similar beginnings and experiences as Keith Payne – the digger, the junior NCO, the sergeant and the warrant officer – what sets him aside, apart from his remarkable courage while in deadly danger, is his profound acceptance of the responsibility of a leader – a responsibility that knew no bounds.

For very obvious reasons, Victoria Cross winners are not pre-selected, nor are they amenable to being kept in cotton wool after the event. The actions of the legendary 'Diver' Derrick after he received his Victoria Cross during World War II testify to that – he threatened to go AWL unless allowed to return to his men in the front line.

Foreword

Keith's long battle with his personal demons, coupled with the unexpected and unwanted celebrity status, will strike a special chord. As with so many soldiers, I suspect Keith would probably say that the best part of his life was not his career in uniform, spectacular and exciting though it was, but the strength and love of his family, Flo and the boys. Keith, to all of us you seem to have won your inner struggles; you are much admired for the dignified, compassionate and likeable man you are today.

Many readers have taken delight in Mike Colman's insightful and entertaining prose. Good journalists, and Mike is one of the best, have a special ability to give life to a story while never drifting away from the truth. Mike, congratulations on this vivid and often gripping tale of a great warrior. It is a testament not only to your writing skill but also your rapport with Keith and his family.

In 2001, when I was the Chief of the Australian Army, a celebratory 100th anniversary dinner was held in Canberra. In the dining hall about 1600 soldiers loudly greeted the various notable guests, but without doubt the loudest cheers were reserved for our three surviving Victoria Cross winners, Roden Cutler, Ted Kenna and Keith Payne. It was not unlike like the roar of an AFL grand final crowd at the MCG.

The Australian Army has always had great respect, indeed reverence, for its paladins, always will have. And, as an old soldier, I am delighted to welcome this fine story of a very brave man, Keith Payne, VC.

General Peter Cosgrove, AC, MC (Ret'd)

Prologue
24 May 1969

PAYNE WAS THE LAST man out. A few metres in front he could see his medic Dellwo catching up to two others. Through the smoke and his own pain he made out Sergeant Montez, commander of the other company, and Montez's medic, Auriemma. The two medics were either side of Montez, half-dragging him along. Payne jogged to catch up.

'What's going …?' he started to ask, then stopped, as he took in the situation. The bottom half of Montez's face was gone, shot away. The big American looked at him through shocked eyes. Payne slipped his shoulder under Montez's arm and helped pull him around the bottom of the hill.

The journey was painfully slow. They only had 100 or so metres to travel, but Montez was very heavy, and Payne was starting to feel weaker. His head throbbed from the wound in his scalp and the pain where he had been shot in the hand and arm seemed to intensify with every step. Finally they reached the others. Payne left the medics to look after Montez and the other wounded and looked around. Men were lying and sitting around in the long grass, bareheaded and stunned. A few were still armed but most were without weapons.

Is this all, he thought, doing a quick headcount. He looked back up at the hill, then again at the men, barking orders, pointing, getting them to secure the perimeter. Some looked at him dumbly at first, not comprehending, not caring. He gave the order again, calmly but more forcibly. They got to their feet and took up their positions.

Payne saw Kev Latham and the young American lieutenant away to the side. The lieutenant was on the radio. As Payne walked over he could hear him speaking. He was calling in a napalm strike on the hill. Payne quickened his stride.

'Countermand that order,' he said sharply. The lieutenant stopped mid-sentence.

'Our men are still up there.'

Payne turned to Latham.

'Someone's got to go back up there and get 'em mate,' he said. 'And it's going to have to be me.'

He picked up a radio and some ammunition and checked his rifle. At that moment he thought of his family back in Brisbane – Flo and the five boys. He saw their faces as they had waved him goodbye, and knew he would probably never see them again. Then he thought of his men still up on the hill. He slung the radio strap over his shoulder and headed out.

Halfway up the hill he heard it. Single shots echoing around the valley.

The bastards were executing his men.

1

Wild Colonial Boy

IF THE PATH THAT leads to a man being awarded his country's highest award for valour could be said to start at a specific time and place, for Keith Payne the time was 1939 and the place Ingham, North Queensland. He was six years old, and it was the day he first got his hands on a rifle. To his mind there was nothing unusual about a boy so young being given a firearm – in his case a bolt-action .22 calibre BSA. It was a matter of survival then, and it would be a matter of survival for the rest of his life.

Payne's father Henry was born in Ingham, 120 kilometres north of Townsville; his mother Remilda – better known as 'Millie' – in nearby Halifax of an Italian mother and English father. Together they would produce thirteen children, one of whom, John, would die soon after birth. The rest would survive through tough times: the Depression, World War II and the many natural predators from snakes to crocodiles and wild pigs that were a day-to-day part of growing up in country Queensland at the time.

Henry Payne was a grocer who did his best to provide for his ever-growing family but he couldn't do it alone, especially during the Depression when, for several years, he lost his shop because customers couldn't meet their credit. Until times improved and he could get another job, the mainstay of the Payne family diet was bags of two-day-old bread that could be purchased for a shilling. As soon as the children were old enough to bake a loaf of bread or shoot game they were expected to pull their weight. At first it might be collecting old bottles to claim the refund or picking potatoes and putting them in bags for resale in the shop; later it would be literally putting food on the family table. Keith was the fourth child, the second son, born twelve months behind his brother Toby. The two boys were doing a man's work before they started school. One of Keith's first memories is of cutting fence posts with a crosscut saw when he was five or six.

A year later he was shooting wild turkeys and ducks and, along with Toby, learning the basics of fishing and bushcraft from a local fisherman named Grassy Crisp. A few years older than Henry Payne, Crisp had a son Billy who was Keith's age. A future Queensland buckjumping champion, Billy and another local lad, Arthur Levis, teamed up with Keith and Toby to form a tight gang. Under the not-so-watchful eyes of Henry and Grassy, the boys became proficient at hunting and fishing. Henry was a keen pig hunter and duck shooter who took his two sons along on his trips into the bush. Grassy would go fishing from Saturday to Thursday. The boys would walk for a few hours to his hut after school every Friday to help repair his traps and nets and soak up his knowledge over the weekend.

They were pretty wild kids, larrikins not averse to making mischief. Finding empty soft-drink bottles and returning them to local shops to claim the deposit money was a steady stream of income – as was pinching them back and selling them again. The boys loved shooting 'muddies' – freshwater cod – at night. Walking along the river bank with a torch, one boy would pick out the pink eyes of the fish in the shallows, as another would aim and fire. They made their own canoes using corrugated iron, bits of kerosene tins and tar 'liberated' from the council work yard. The craft were used for fishing, pulling nets across the creeks and, during floods, for floating around Ingham shooting snakes that had wrapped themselves around fence posts. When the boys were older, a flagon of cheap homemade Italian wine would be a compulsory provision for overnight camping trips and if any of them got into a fight it was a case of one in, all in. Another mate was Arthur Brackenbridge, an Aboriginal lad whose younger brother, fighting under the name of George Bracken, would become one of Australia's most popular and successful boxers. George's trainer, Tommy Quetta, rounded out Keith's education when he taught him and the others how to box.

Roaming the bush around Ingham, setting traps and nets in the creeks and estuaries, their free time became a constant routine of finding food to help feed their families. No opportunity was missed. When he began walking to and from school at the age of seven, there were times when Keith would carry his schoolbooks in one hand and his .22 calibre rifle in the other, in case he spotted a scrub turkey or pig on the way.

The young Payne soon developed into a natural bushman with two particular talents: he was a deadly shot and he could crawl through the bush without making a sound. He and his mates learned to track game and spent hours alone in the bush at night. They became totally at home in the darkness, as comfortable and confident as if it was broad daylight. These were all skills that would help him hunt birds in the early 1940s, and save his life and the lives of his fellow soldiers some twenty-five years later.

There was another talent that Payne discovered he possessed in his early years, and again it was one that would prove useful in a theatre of war. He was a water diviner. 'Some people can do it, some can't,' he says. 'Toby and I used to play around with forked branches when we were kids and it turned out that I could find water. I'd hold the stick under my chin and if there was water under the ground it would start shaking so hard that sometimes I could hardly hold it. Even when we were considering buying the block of land to build our last house in Mackay I said, "I'll check it out and if it's got water on it we'll buy it". I got the stick out and sure enough there was water under the ground. We've got a bore out the back.'

In his early years Payne never contemplated a greater use for his bush skills than hunting or fishing. To be truthful, the importance of helping out the family was secondary to the fun of being with his mates, waiting for Grassy to come back from a fishing trip or sitting around a campfire telling fishing and shooting stories.

But things changed in 1942 when Keith was nine. Everything suddenly became more serious. Henry Payne was going to war.

Keith recalls: 'He'd tried to enlist right back at the start of the war but they wouldn't take him because he had such a big family – five kids and number six on the way. By the time he tried again in 1942 they weren't so fussy. By then it was a case of one eye, one finger, one bum – okay, you're in. He went into engineering. He was pretty good with his hands. His father had been a wheelwright who had served in World War I. One of my vivid memories is watching my grandfather putting the rim on a wooden wheel, making sure it was perfectly straight and pulling the spokes in. Anyway, Father joined up. First he went into the militia with my older cousin Frank – I remember them practising their slope arms drill in the shed with broomsticks. Frank got into the army first and went to the Middle East. By the time Father was accepted, Japan was in the war and he went to the Pacific. I remember him leaving. He was in his uniform and he said goodbye, then he walked through the horse paddock alongside our house to catch the train. When the war started everyone was supposed to hand in their rifles but Father wouldn't do it. He said, "We're going to have to fight the Japs right here". We never had to do that, but we sure put those guns to good use. Father's train hadn't left town before we had the rifles and nets out. He came home on leave before he went overseas and stayed a bit too long. He had to go back and face the beak. He got confined to barracks and loss of pay. Military pay wasn't great to start with. That just made it worse for a while.'

Not that the Payne boys were too concerned. With their father away their hunting took on more meaning, and soon there was another element added to the mix. The US Army began deploying large numbers of troops to North Queensland, especially in Townsville and Thuringowa, 60 kilometres south of Ingham. When they had time to spare the Yanks were looking for entertainment and for the Paynes that meant money.

'Ammo was hard to come by during the war but the Yanks had heaps of it. At first we used to meet the troop trains when they passed through and sell them fruit – one price for the Yanks and free for the Aussies – but once they started heading down on weekend leave, that was another matter. They wanted to go wallaby shooting and for a price we were happy to take them. They'd pay us for our time and give us all the ammo we needed. Shotgun cartridges, .22 shells, they had it all. The Yanks would head back to base, we'd skin the wallabies we'd shot, dry and salt the hides ready for sale and give some of the meat to the dogs. When we were in the bush for a few days we'd shoot wallabies and eat the meat ourselves and use it in our crab pots and fish traps. Back then anything we could eat we'd hunt. We had a lot more food on the table from off the land than from a shop. Scrub hens, turkeys, ducks, pigeons, pigs, fish, crabs, you name it. And firewood. We were always collecting firewood. We needed fires for cooking on wood stoves and for heating up the coppers for washing the clothes. We burned a lot of damn wood. Father had an old Model T Ford we'd drive when he was away. At the end of a weekend we'd be driving back home with a dead wallaby hanging down between the mudguard and bonnet on one side, a hobbled pig hanging down the other side and a pile of firewood on the back.'

Not all the boys' attempts to provide for the family were as successful as the American soldiers' wallaby safaris. Late in the war fourteen-year-old Toby came up with a plan to enter the live animal supply business and talked Keith into helping him trap a crocodile to sell to Townsville Zoo.

'The wet season had just started and we waded across Trebonne Creek to take our net across. After a while we caught one, about 3 metres long, pulled it out and tied it up with belts and ropes and nets. We strapped it to a log and picked it up and carried it on our shoulders up the bank. Toby was taller than me so he was down the back with its tail. I was up the front at the bitey end. Its jaw wasn't tied tight enough and it was snapping away right behind my shoulder. Toby was pushing me forward up the slippery bank and telling me to hurry up and this thing was snapping away behind me. It wasn't the most comfortable position but we finally got it to the truck and back home. Townsville Zoo said they'd buy it but we had to deliver it. Toby's plan was that we'd put it in the back of the Model T and he'd drive it up there but because of the rainy season all the roads were blocked. We had that thing in our backyard for about six weeks.

'We tied it to the mango tree and fed it wallaby meat and fowl but Mum and the girls weren't too impressed. Every time they went out into the backyard it looked like it wanted a piece of them. When the sun came out we had to keep it wet so we'd put damp sacks on its back which it didn't like much. Finally we ended up making a crate for it and Toby took it to Townsville on the train. It was more trouble than it was worth in the end but when you've got mouths to feed you'll try anything.'

And the number of mouths to feed just kept on growing. As Keith puts it, 'Every time Father came home on leave Mum would get pregnant again. It was like we had three families. There were those of us from before the war, then those during the war and those after the war. I got two new sisters between when I joined up and when I got back from serving in Korea. People always thought we were Catholic but we weren't. Mum was Catholic but Father was Church of England. There are some of us who are Methodist, some C of E, three Salvationists. Mum couldn't make up her mind what she wanted us to be. It's a funny sort of thing. The older ones never really got to know the younger ones. I had a brother Frank who was only four years younger than me but I never got to know him as someone I got around with, like I did with Toby. It wasn't until much later that our ages all seemed to equal out more but by then we'd all gone our own way.'

The feeling of a family growing apart was one that greeted Henry when he returned from the war in 1945, after serving at Balikpapan on Borneo and the island of Moritai. As the head of such a large family he was one of the first to be discharged. He returned to an Australia about to enter a long period of prosperity and was quickly offered a good job with a large grocery chain. Money was no longer such a problem but he found that the two young sons he had left behind were no longer boys.

'We'd seen Father a few times when he'd come home on leave but for three long years we'd been the ones providing for the family while our older sisters Gwenda and Merle helped Mum look after the house. Now Father's back and he's in charge. It was awkward. When he'd left we were kids and now we were young men. We were only thirteen and fourteen but for years we'd been the providers, the ones supplying the family with food. Toby had already left school and I was just about to. All of us older ones left school at fourteen. It was only the younger ones who went on to secondary school. Toby was an apprentice plumber and I was going to start an apprenticeship as a cabinetmaker so it was hard for Father and hard for us too. He never talked about the war. It was only later, when I'd been away to war, that we could sit down and talk about it. It was only then that we could both understand.'

As Keith neared his fourteenth birthday his mother approached a local cabinetmaker who agreed to take him on as an apprentice. Millie, having endured the deprivation of the Depression, was determined her children would have a trade behind them. A regular income would also top up the family coffers. Keith earned 17 shillings and sixpence a week, of which 10 shillings went straight to his mother. He also caught and sold fish on the weekends to add to his earnings.

It didn't take Keith long to realise cabinetmaking was not for him. Overnight he went from being a carefree youngster who walked to school with a rifle over his shoulder and spent every spare moment roaming free in the bush, to working long hours in a noisy factory. There was one saving grace. At fourteen Keith was old enough to join the regimental cadets. At the time there were two types of army cadets: school cadets similar to those still operating today, and regimental cadets that were open to anyone aged between fourteen and eighteen. Almost as soon as he was eligible, Keith joined his local battalion, the 31st.

'Having grown up through the war years and seen uniforms of all nations passing though Ingham, it just seemed like a natural thing to do. Plus there was another bonus. They issued you with a .303 rifle.'

With the war just over and ammunition for the army issue .303 now readily available, Keith was like a kid with a new toy. The powerful rifle gave him greater potency as a hunter, and also saw him rise in status above his older brother Toby.

'I remember one night Toby and I went fishing and we had to put a net across the creek. He told me to swim across and let the net out while he covered me with the .303 but I wasn't letting go of it so he grabbed the end of the net and started wading in. He'd just started across when I saw the pink eyes of a big crocodile in the torchlight. I started firing on either side of it to keep it away. I reckon Toby swam across that creek in ten seconds. I'd never seen him move that fast. He wouldn't swim back though. He walked all the way around, back to the old bridge crossing and then back to our camp. It took him hours.

'The .303 was good for shooting wild pigs. Some of the big ones we'd come across you could hit with a .22 and it wouldn't even slow them up. The three O would bring them straight down. That was the Payne staple diet in those days, cold pork.'

But the regimental cadets gave Payne far more than a uniform and a bigger rifle. It introduced him to a whole new world. A world to which he found himself perfectly suited. The more he realised that the life of a tradesman wasn't for him, the more he realised that a soldier's life was. He found himself drifting further away from his real family and moving closer to a new family: the army.

'I started to go around with older blokes who were in the unit. When they were old enough some of them joined the CMF – the Army Reserve – and when I turned sixteen and a half, I joined too. You were supposed to be over seventeen, but I got in early.'

Now, instead of spending every weekend hunting and fishing with Toby and his mates, Payne was more likely to be on a cadet or CMF camp. He was a natural soldier. It was as if everything he had done prior to joining the part-time army had been a stepping stone towards it. He could shoot, survive in the bush and, unlike some of his fellow recruits, had no fear of the dark.

'That was one thing which I found funny at first. A lot of blokes were afraid of the night. They totally lost their bearings and were spooked by the noises. To me it was second nature. Growing up, we'd spent night after night hunting pigs in the bush, sometimes alone. We'd split up and arrange to meet at such and such a place at such and such a time and have to set out alone and get there on time. We knew all the different sounds: curlews, crocs, dingoes. We didn't just survive in the dark, we utilised it to our advantage.'

The cadets and then CMF were an extension of the outdoors life Payne and his mates had lived for as long as he could remember. If joining the cadets seemed the natural thing to do, making a life in the regular army seemed even more obvious. When he turned seventeen he approached his boss and asked to be released from his indentures so he could enlist. At Millie's urging the employer refused, making Payne work out his final six months. If Millie thought the extra time in the factory would make him change his mind, she underestimated her son's determination.

On 13 August 1951, Keith Payne caught the train to Brisbane and joined up.

For a young man somewhat naively hoping to experience adventure and see foreign lands, Payne's timing couldn't have been much better. In June 1950 the so-called Cold War had erupted in a place which few Australians had ever given much thought to: Korea.

A peninsula in East Asia, Korea is bordered by China to the north-west and Russia to the north-east, with Japan across the Korea Strait to the south-east.

A monarchy which had remained isolated from the rest of the world for much of its early history, Korea was forcibly occupied by Japan in 1910 and remained under Japanese rule until Japan's defeat at the end of World War II. In 1945 the country was divided in accordance with a United Nations arrangement, to be administered by the Soviet Union in the north and by the United States in the south. The Soviets and Americans were unable to agree on joint trusteeship, leading in 1948 to the establishment of two separate governments, each claiming to be the legitimate government of all Korea. The geographic and ideological line dividing the two countries was known as the 38th parallel.

The fragile peace on the peninsula was shattered on the night of 25 June 1950 when eight divisions and an armoured brigade of North Korean soldiers, some 90,000 in total, crossed the 38th parallel and invaded South Korea. The South Koreans were no match for the battle-hardened invaders, many of whom had served with Chinese and Soviet forces in World War II, and the capital Seoul was soon overrun.

The next day the United Nations Security Council directed the United States to help South Korea and a force under the leadership of US general, Douglas MacArthur, was hastily assembled. Two Australian warships and the RAAF 77 Squadron were sent to join the campaign from Japan where they had been part of the British Commonwealth Occupaton Force. At first the Australian government planned to limit military involvement but as the situation worsened and the UN forces were driven back to the port of Pusan on the south-east corner of the peninsula, MacArthur sent out a call for reinforcements. At the time the Royal Australian Regiment 3rd Battalion (3RAR) was in Japan and, although they had been trained as an occupation force rather than for combat, the men were asked to volunteer for service in Korea. They arrived on 17 September 1950. Two days earlier MacArthur had succeeded with an audacious amphibious landing at Inchon in which US and South Korean forces came ashore north of the enemy and liberated Seoul.

MacArthur then continued to drive north, back across the 38th parallel, even though the further he went the greater the risk that China would enter the conflict. On 25 October UN forces met stiff resistance from Chinese units virtually across the entire front line. Within a month as many as 300,000 Chinese troops had entered North Korea and MacArthur called on his commanders to pull back. Over the next seven months the UN forces lost all the ground they had taken and in April MacArthur was recalled and replaced by General Matthew Ridgway.

Ridgway, in charge of a UN force made up of troops from sixteen countries, favoured a more tactical approach of assault and counterattack aimed at keeping the enemy off-balance and minimising casualties. Under his leadership the Chinese Army was pushed back to an area close to the Imjin River near the 38th parallel. And there it stayed for the next two years, the fighting bogging down into what was termed a 'static' war.

By the time Payne joined up fourteen months after the start of hostilities Australia was fully committed, with 3RAR about to launch an assault that would become known as the Battle of Maryang San. The objective was a hill codenamed Hill 317. It was a place Payne would come to know very well. In just over a year he would be climbing up a road towards it, the sound of exploding artillery shells ringing in his ears, and wondering what the hell he'd let himself in for.

But that was still a long way off. As he signed his enlistment papers that day in Brisbane, raised his right hand and swore to 'well and truly' serve his country, all that Payne knew about Korea was all that he wanted to know: that ceasefire talks had failed and Australian reinforcements were needed.

Like his father and grandfather before him, Keith Payne was going to war.

2

The Recruit

THE AUSTRALIAN REGULAR ARMY of 1951 was something of a hotchpotch, made up of soldiers who had served in World War II, those who felt it was their patriotic duty to serve in Korea and youngsters, like Payne, starting a career in the service. His time in the cadets and CMF had introduced Payne to men of different ages and backgrounds but the regular army was something else again.

'There were blokes from the city and from the country; there was a vet surgeon, a Pommy remittance man, shearers, journalists. There was a photographer named Eric 'Bluey' Donnelly who ended up being taken prisoner and was knocked around a hell of a lot. There were blokes who had served in World War II and some who had never worn a uniform in their lives. It was all quite different for a kid from Ingham. Some of those city blokes could talk a bit but I worked them out pretty quick.'

Some things Payne didn't have to work out. They came naturally. His initial enlistment was for six years, but he trained alongside recruits who had joined K-Force, the army formed specifically to serve in Korea. Their two-year period of service was made up of six months administration and leave, six months training, and twelve months active duty. Payne and his fellow inductees were placed in a recruitment company at Enoggera army base in Brisbane's west where for three months they learned to march, salute and fire a weapon. He then went to Puckapunyal in Victoria as a member of the 2nd Battalion Royal Australian Regiment.

The Recruit

2RAR was a reinforcement battalion, preparing soldiers to be sent to Korea to support the 1st and 3rd battalions, which were rotating in the front line. At Puckapunyal the recruits were placed in platoons of around thirty men and trained in patrolling and other infantry basics. From there the men moved to Site 17, an area opposite the School of Infantry at nearby Seymour, and finally back to Puckapunyal and an open area known as Scrub Hill where they were trained to patrol and use their weapons in simulated battle conditions.

It was in this stage of training, known as Draft Priority 3, that Payne stood out. Already he had distinguished himself at Enoggera when a weapons instructor had asked the recruits, 'Anyone know anything about the Bren gun?' When Payne answered in the affirmative, the instructor had pointed to the weapon and barked, 'Load'. Without missing a beat Payne dropped to his knees, loaded the gun in seconds and stood to attention, bringing a nod of approval. But that was nothing in comparison to his competence in the field. It was as if everything he had done in the bush around Ingham had been a dress rehearsal for his time in the army. He wasn't a large man, standing around 175 centimetres and weighing 76 kilograms, but he was wiry and fit, without an ounce of fat, the perfect build for carrying packs and scaling hills. As he puts it: 'I took to it like a duck to water'.

Not everyone was as lucky. There were a number of casualties as the recruits were put through a tough training regime, learning to use mortar and Bren guns, traversing rough terrain and crossing creeks on rope bridges.

All too soon the training was over and Payne's company was sent to Ingleburn army base outside Sydney to wait for deployment to Korea. When the time drew closer for embarkation, Payne was given leave to return to Ingham and farewell his family, just as his father had done nine years earlier.

'It took me ten days by train to get there and ten days back,' he recalls. 'I said goodbye to my family and my mother said, "Where are you going now?" I said I was going to Japan and then Korea and she didn't believe me. She said, "Oh, you're not going to Korea at all". I just said, "Righto Mum, bye". It wasn't an emotional farewell for me. Truth is, in my mind I'd already left the day I went down to Brisbane to join up. There was nothing to keep me in Ingham. Toby and I and my other mates had all drifted apart; there was a girl named Betty Roberts who I had taken out a bit but it was nothing serious. I felt like from the moment I'd gone down to Brisbane, and then Sydney, so much had happened to me and so much more was about to happen. Then I went back to Ingham for that leave and looked around at the blokes I'd gone to school with and my family and old friends and nothing had changed one bit. Even when I came back from Korea and went back for a few days I thought, Jesus Christ, these people haven't grown up at all. I felt like we had nothing in common any more. War can do that to you.'

It was back to Sydney for inoculations and final processing, then Payne and the rest of his company boarded a Qantas flight that took them to Jackson Airstrip in Port Moresby and on to Manila where they celebrated a last night of freedom the way soldiers have through history. 'It was a wild old night,' Payne laughs, shaking his head at the memory over half a century later.

The next day the company flew to Iwakuni in Japan, caught a boat to Kure and went into a reinforcement holding camp in Hiro. Ask Payne what he remembers about his time in Hiro and he will answer in one word: 'Hills'.

'That's where we learned to climb hills. It was hills, hills, hills. That was the sort of terrain we were going to face in Korea and Japan's got a lot of them too. It was hard work and pretty monotonous but it was good training and a chance to learn the tactics we'd use in Korea. What we'd learned in Australia had been a mixture of desert and jungle warfare but this was different. My platoon sergeant was a bloke named Tim Daly who had been with a machine-gun platoon in the Battle of Kapyong so he knew what we'd be up against and he put us through our paces. He had us doing patrols belting up and down those hills, day in, day out.

'Being the age I was it didn't worry me. It was all part of the big adventure. Just being in Japan was an eye-opener. They were just coming out of the war years and Hiro had been bombed during the war. You could still see the burnt-out buildings.'

As he hadn't yet turned nineteen, under Australian military regulations Payne was not old enough to be deployed to the war zone and stayed behind in Hiro while those he had joined up with were sent to the front as replacements. He was keen to go but the army made sure the extra time in Japan was well spent, putting him through a machine-gun course and additional training. Two days after his nineteenth birthday Payne was sent to Korea. The great adventure was about to get serious.

He sailed from Kurai on a ship called the *Esang*, and landed at Pusan. 'It wasn't very nice,' he says in classic understatement.

'The Allied forces had been pushed a long way down and Pusan was full of refugees. The place was a complete mess. People were living everywhere, finding shelter wherever they could. Most of the dwellings were made from flattened beer cartons and old rations boxes. It was absolute squalor. It was early autumn and still hot so the cold wasn't a problem then, but it would sure become a problem later.'

Payne and his fellow replacements were taken to an old school where they slept on wooden floors before catching a train for a two-day journey to Seoul. Once again they were forced to sleep on the floor but this time they were luckier. There were no seats in the carriages, just hard benches down either side. These went to the officers and NCOs, while the enlisted men stretched out on their kitbags, finding they made comfortable beds.

There was nothing comfortable about Seoul. The South Korean capital had been captured by the North Koreans, then recaptured by UN forces and had been completely devastated in the process. All bridges across the Han River had been blown up by the retreating communists, the only possible links to different parts of the city being across army-built prefabricated Bailey bridges. As in Pusan, there were homeless and refugees everywhere, but battered as Seoul might have looked to the young Payne, it would seem like a holiday camp in comparison to where he was headed.

Within days of arriving in Korea in early September 1952 he was sent up to brigade headquarters at Uijeongbu to await deployment to a forward unit. From there he went to battalion headquarters, some 10 kilometres behind the front line. At the time 1RAR was the battalion in the line, with 3RAR having its turn in reserve. Payne was put into B Company, 1RAR, and spent an anxious night waiting to head to the front.

'That was when I started to feel apprehension. Not so much about what might happen to me, but whether I'd be able to do my job and not let anyone down. There was that worry: when it comes down to it will I be able to do what I'm supposed to do? Do I know enough? I'd learned all I could back in Australia and in Japan but this was different. Now I was in Korea and I had to learn everything all over again. You can do all the training you like but it's not until you get into the real situation that you learn how things work. Just everyday things like the different patrol formations; recon patrols, standing patrols, ambush patrols and snatch patrols where we'd try to get a prisoner – everything was new. Waiting to go up there was pretty daunting.'

Payne didn't have to wait long to find out just how daunting. It was all about hills. Each was numbered in relation to its height in metres above sea level. One side would take a hill and hold it. The other would try to take it back. At the time Payne joined the action all the Australian units were in defensive mode. They had taken dominant ground from the Chinese and dug in. Their assigned task was to keep that ground as the Chinese tried to take it back. Every night up to 240 artillery shells and mortars were sent in by the Chinese. Every now and then a self-propelled rocket would be fired at the UN lines and roar across the valley. B Company was holding Hill 317.

On the reverse side of the hill was a road used by the Allies to send supplies and reinforcements to the front line. It was known as the 'Crazy Half Mile', with the Chinese guns trained to pick off the trucks as they came into range. With the trucks providing such an easy target, Payne was dropped off at the top of the road and told to walk the final 2 kilometres to company headquarters. Walking that road, toting his own gear as well as urgent supplies and hearing mortar fire landing on the Australian positions, Queensland had never felt further away.

Payne got into position just on last light. It was a period the Aussies called 'solemn time', the last few moments of comparative peace before the enemy barrage started for the night. It was also the time when the evening patrols set off. In the warmer months they would stay out all night. Once winter set in it was so cold they could last only two hours before being forced back to the defensive position.

'I was straight into it,' Payne recalled. 'That first night, with the artillery coming in, was bloody frightening. It was a constant barrage, boom, boom, boom, all night. Forget about sleeping. Those were the two worst things about Korea. The cold and the lack of sleep. Whenever and wherever you got a chance to sleep you took it but those chances didn't come along often. We learned to sleep through the shelling when not on duty but you'd be lucky to snatch four hours sleep in twenty-four. There was always so much work to do. Even at full strength it would have been hard but we were never at full strength.

'I was put in 4 Platoon of B Company. There were supposed to be thirty of us but there wouldn't have been more than twenty-two at any one time. There were always blokes sick, wounded, on leave, doing courses or on detention. A section was supposed to be ten men but you'd be lucky if there was six or seven.'

Usually there were three companies of around a hundred men each in the line and one in reserve. The soldiers in the front line would spend most of their daylight hours in trenches, crawling around and keeping their heads low. The enemy was doing the same. The closest Payne came to 'him' – or 'he' as he calls the enemy – in that situation was 100 metres. At night there was more freedom to move about, but with the added dangers of the incessant enemy shelling.

Each afternoon there would be a meeting of officers and NCOs at which the orders for the night patrols were passed on. These were mainly of three types: fighting patrols out of the line, wiring parties to repair the defensive concertina wire set up in front of the Allied lines, and protection parties to support the engineers. Those not on patrol were rotated on sentry duty, which brought its own challenges and dangers.

'It was a strange thing trying to see what was going on at night. It was an artificial light. There would be mortars exploding and flares going up all night. It messed up your eyesight. The trick was to shut one eye. You'd have one eye for when it was dark and the other one for when the lights were going off.

'The worst thing was the incoming artillery. You'd be ducking when a shell was coming but you never heard the ones that landed close. What we were most fearful of were the ones that landed just in front of you; they were real bad news.'

Within a day Payne had fallen into the routine of life in the trenches as if it was the most normal thing in the world. The constant pounding of artillery, the lack of sleep, the endless work ... there wasn't time to think about things too much, just get in and do your bit.

'I always felt we were kept pretty well informed as to what the overall picture was, but we never got a real detailed picture of what was happening in our own unit. It was like the poem, ours was not to question why, ours was just to get stuck in. We concentrated on our job and we knew that everyone else was working just as hard. If there was a bludger in our midst he'd get sorted out pretty quick. When you talk about it now it sounds like a bit of shambles but it wasn't really like that. We were all utterly focused on what we were doing and everything was well organised within the constraints of war.'

Having arrived as a replacement late in the unit's time in the front line, Payne had only ten days on Hill 317 before they were moved back into reserve. After two weeks they were back at the front to relieve the Australians stationed on a position known as 'Holiday Hill'.

Known to the Koreans as Yong Dong, Holiday Hill earned its nickname because it was a relatively quiet post, but it was across the valley from one of the most tactically important features of the entire campaign, a crescent-shaped ridge known as 'the Hook'. Holding the Hook was of vital importance to both sides because it dominated the Samichon Valley, offering a perfect position from which to open up an invasion route to Seoul. Four times the Chinese tried to take it in major assaults and four times they were forced back, once by US marines, once by the British Black Watch, once by the Duke of Wellington's Regiment and finally in the very last action of the war, just two days before the ceasefire, by a combined force of the 2nd and 3rd Battalions RAR. But as well as those four major battles the Chinese threw tens of thousands of troops at the Hook in attempt after attempt to gain the tactical stronghold. To Allied troops positioned on hills across the valley, the almost daily assaults on the Hook provided chilling viewing. While stationed on Holiday Hill Payne witnessed such a show.

'There was a British battalion stationed on the Hook and they were attacked by a huge force of Chinese. I've never seen anything like it. The Poms were totally outnumbered. We couldn't do anything to help because we were too far away. We just had to sit there and watch. We always felt sorry for the Poms. We were getting paid 2 pound 10 shillings a week; they were getting 1 pound 8 shillings. We used to say we wouldn't go outside the wire for that.

'The build-up to that battle started late in the afternoon and increased through the night. First the Chinese artillery pounded away at the British positions and then the attack started. The flares went up and we could see thousands of Chinese swarming across the valley. I remember thinking, Gee, I hope those Poms have got plenty of ammo, because there was no way anyone could get any to them if they ran out. You'd have to cross the valley and with that sort of bombardment going on you'd never make it. The whole place was lit up. There were flares and half the regiment's artillery giving it to the Chinese. The artillery was all New Zealanders and they did a bloody good job too. The Chinese took the hill and then the Poms took it back. I don't know how many men the Poms lost but it must have been 10 or 15 per cent. You couldn't count the Chinese. There were stacks of them lying all over the hill where they fell.'

The next feature Payne's unit was positioned on was Hill 355, known to the soldiers as 'Little Gibraltar'. By now he had been in Korea for three months. He felt he had settled in pretty well. He knew the routine, was becoming an experienced hand and had fitted in well with his fellow soldiers. 'This is okay,' he said to himself. 'I'm on top of it.'

And then a new enemy arrived. One that nothing Payne had experienced before could possibly equip him to handle. Winter.

3
Cold as Hell

ANYONE WHO THINKS THAT hell is a hot place hasn't been to Korea in December. The Korean winter is one of the coldest and most bitter on earth. For a nineteen-year-old plucked from tropical North Queensland and thrown into the desolate surroundings of a battlefield locked in stalemate, it was a numbing experience. What had been uncomfortable suddenly became, with the change of season, almost unbearable. The Chinese were an enemy the Australians could cope with. The cold was another matter altogether.

'When winter started to fall we got our first bit of winter gear – smocks, winter boots, mittens – but we still had no idea what was going to come. People can warn you, they can tell you "Just wait until winter. It gets bloody cold", but until you've been through it you can't even imagine it. At first it wasn't too bad. It was cold but nothing we couldn't handle, and then it started to snow. The water froze overnight. It was a whole new world, a whole new way of having to do things.

'Going on patrols became awkward. The water in the paddy fields would be all frozen over. You'd be trying to creep around quietly but when you walked on the ice it would crack and make a noise that would echo all over the valley. If the order came to go to ground you'd be throwing yourself face down in frozen water. It was bloody miserable.'

If patrolling was a nightmare, living in the line was even worse. To escape the conditions the men burrowed underground, living in bunkers carved into the rock-hard ground. Heat came from homemade stoves, known as 'choofers'. Fashioned from 25-pound artillery shell casings, the choofers served two purposes. Burning petrol or aviation fuel, they heated the bunkers and produced a black sooty residue the men used to blacken their faces for night patrols. The crude but effective heaters kept the men from freezing, but they were not without risks. They could easily be knocked over. One man in Payne's platoon was badly burnt when his bunker caught fire. Also the lack of washing facilities saw the men break out in rashes and blisters as the soot they rubbed on their faces became ingrained in the folds of their skin. A condition known as 'choofer neck' was a common complaint.

'It was so cold we'd have our balaclavas on the whole time. The only part of your body you could wash was your face. When we were on the line we wouldn't get a change of clothes for two and a half months. We'd be wearing the same string vest and long johns the whole time. Hygiene sergeants would come around with the medics and check our boots and feet. They'd get us to open the tops of our shirts and trousers and spray for lice.

'When we went into reserve we'd finally get a shower. We'd throw all our clothes into a pile and they'd be taken off and washed and we'd just pick up another set from the clean pile. These days they'd call that recycling. Sometimes when we were on the line we might try to wash some clothes but when winter came it wasn't much use. You'd put it on some concertina wire to dry and it would freeze stiff as a board, so that was the end of that.'

There was another reason not to leave clothes lying around unattended. Theft. A member of the unit was caught stealing clothes. The company commander turned a blind eye as the men dished out their own punishment, then sent the man to the military detention centre for fourteen days.

'They had him cleaning his mess tin so much that you could have used it as a mirror to shave with. He was a changed boy when he got back.'

The soldiers weren't the only ones to seek shelter during winter. As Payne put it, 'We lived underground like rats'. And big rats they were.

'The rats were as big as bandicoots. I'd scored a US .45 pistol somewhere along the line and I used it to shoot rats in our bunker. I remember thinking how bad off the Koreans were in Pusan when I first landed. I didn't know I was going to spend the next seven months of my life living the same way.'

The routine continued. Months in the front line, weeks in reserve. Given the choice, the soldiers preferred to be in the line. They might not get to bathe, but at least they were active. In army-speak the time in reserve was 'make and mend'. In effect it was polish boots, clean weapons and practise drill – all the tedious duties normally carried out in barracks. The time at the front brought its own tedium – the endless patrols (as Payne put it: 'We crawled all over their hills and they crawled all over ours'), the shocking living conditions and the danger, but that was soldiering. When he left Ingham to join up Payne had fantasised of faraway places and adventure. He got both, but not as he had dreamed. Still, terrible as Korea was, it provided Payne with memories, some shocking, some humorous, some downright frightening, that would stay with him forever.

There was the time he was in position on Holiday Hill watching as a flight of Allied fighter-bombers, probably US Corsairs or Douglas Sky Raiders, hit Chinese positions on a feature in front of the Hook. As they peeled off after dropping their load they were fired on by Chinese machine guns set up in front of Payne's position.

'One was hit. He tried to get over the saddle between us and the next feature. As he went past he was at eye level with me. I saw the pilot in the cockpit, trying to pull it up. He just went straight into the side of the hill and exploded.'

Even more frightening was the time he almost shot acting platoon commander Sergeant John 'Mac' McNulty.

Sergeant McNulty, a dapper little Englishman, had taken over temporary leadership after platoon commander Lieutenant John Seaton was killed while leading a fighting patrol on the night of 12 November 1952. McNulty took two others and went back into enemy territory to retrieve his body.

Seaton was one of many officers wounded or killed while leading the patrols. His replacement, Gus Breen, says there was no pattern to it. The Chinese weren't specifically targeting the officers; it was just the luck of the draw.

'There were plenty of diggers wounded and killed too,' he said. 'That's just the way it happened.'

One officer who was badly wounded while leading a patrol was Breen's Duntroon classmate, Colin 'Genghis' Khan, who was commanding 5 Platoon. An outstanding officer who would reach the rank of brigadier, Khan would receive the Distinguished Service Order (DSO) for his actions in Vietnam commanding the 5RAR 'Tiger' Battalion. In the early hours of Armistice Day 1952 his fighting patrol came into contact with the enemy. During the ensuing battle he was hit by machine-gun fire. The word was quickly relayed back to Little Gibraltar.

'Whenever there was a firefight headquarters would immediately send out a "flying patrol" with stretchers to bring back the wounded and reinforce the troops,' said Payne. 'When Genghis Khan was hit I was part of the reinforcements. We got down to the valley and he'd been shot in the chest. It would cost him his lung. Years later I ran into him and he said, "I remember you, you were one of the stretcher bearers who brought me back up the hill". He was close. I wasn't a stretcher bearer but I did help to carry him out, as well as provide protection.'

The next day it was Seaton's number that came up.

With Gus Breen awaiting orders in Japan, Sergeant McNulty took over the platoon for almost three weeks. It nearly cost him his life – at the end of Keith Payne's Owen machine carbine.

'Mac had gone back to headquarters for a briefing one night. When he got back, for some unknown reason he decided he'd inspect the picketline. Well, you just don't do that. If you want to check how things are going there are walkie-talkies and telephones in the Bren-gun pit. You don't just go walking around in the dark, there's no need for it. Anyway, I'm on picket and I'm carrying an Owen gun. It wasn't unknown for Chinese snatch patrols to sneak around at night trying to grab a prisoner so you'd always be on your toes. I've stepped out of the pit and there's the shape of a bloke in front of me – right where he shouldn't be. I'm just about to pull the trigger and a flare has gone up and I see who it is. Another half-pound of pressure on that trigger and I would have cut him in half. There was some pretty choice words said. It's a frightening thing to nearly shoot one of your own and I didn't hold back. Nobody swears like an Australian. It was "You bloody idiot, you let people know if you're bloody well coming in. You were bloody close to being bloody history." Mac was a very good soldier but he wasn't thinking too well that night. Like most of us, he was over-tired.'

Sergeant McNulty's short time as platoon commander ended with the arrival of Breen who, like Colin Khan, had graduated from Duntroon in December 1951. He would have an extraordinary time in Korea, being seconded to the US Air Force as an aerial observer for which he was awarded the US Distinguished Flying Cross and Air Medal. A former private school boy from Sydney's Waverley College, Breen soon learned that the front line in Korea was a long way from Sydney's eastern suburbs.

'His batman was a tough World War II veteran, a huge man named Sammy Small,' Payne said. 'Pretty soon after he arrived Gus told Sammy to clean his pistol. Sammy picked it up, pointed it at the ground, shot off a round and handed it back. "There you go boss," he said. "She fires." He was a character, Sammy, and by Christ you needed characters out there.'

Another character who has gone down in the folklore of 1RAR was the soldier on guard duty on Pintail Bridge across the Imjin River. A Chinese prisoner broke free and started to run across the bridge, hoping to get back to his own lines. The Aussie knew exactly what to do in the situation. He had been trained for it over and over again; instructors had barked the orders at him so many times that he could do the sequence on automatic pilot. Which is exactly what he did – except for one thing. He shouted out the orders as he did them, as loud as any instructor back at Puckapunyal. 'Lying – Load – Aim – Fire!'

Still, at least he got the opportunity to put his hard-learned drill into practice. For all the months Payne spent in the line, all the patrols and sentry duty, the only thing he ever got to shoot at during his tour of duty in Korea was rats.

'All that time I only had one contact. We patrolled and patrolled, but I never got to fire my weapon directly at the enemy. Not that it wasn't dangerous out there. Apart from contacting the enemy, there were two things that worried you most on patrol. What was really scary was the risk of being down in the valley and another friendly patrol getting lost and coming into your area. Firing away at your own men isn't what you want to happen. The other was coming into a minefield during winter. With all the snow you never knew what you were walking into.'

Payne's one enemy contact came late in November 1952 when the platoon was in reserve behind Hill 355. There were three outposts on the hill, named by the Canadian troops who held it before the Australians as Calgary, Vancouver and Halifax. To avoid confusion, patrols would always leave and return through the same outpost. They were seen as a doorway to the outside. Manning the outposts was a hazardous occupation as they were closest to the enemy and furthest away from the main body of friendly troops. When Payne's platoon was supplying standing patrols of six men on Calgary it was hit by a Chinese snatch patrol. One Australian was killed and another taken prisoner.

The units in reserve were used for the largest patrols as they were better able to prepare for the specific objective. At this time Payne and seventeen others were briefed for a fighting patrol which left through Vancouver and headed down into the valley in the standard formation: four diamonds made up of four men each, forming one large diamond, the signaller and officer commanding in the centre.

The nicknames for Calgary, Vancouver and Halifax weren't the only legacies left by the Canadians who had been stationed on Little Gibraltar. Their supply dumps and bunkers were left in a poor state, with old food boxes and empty cans littering the area. One of Payne's mates found something else that had been left behind – a snub-nosed

Bren gun which he passed on to Payne. It was this weapon that he carried as he followed his mates out into the darkness.

'The grass was all icy and we were slipping all the way down, then we started patrolling through these paddy fields which were all iced over. We were making a lot of noise but you just couldn't avoid it. The grass was all frozen and it made cracking noises every time you took a step. We were down below Calgary and we either bumped into or were ambushed by a small patrol of Chinese. I reckon there were about five of them but the others always felt there were more.'

As the Australians and Chinese began exchanging heavy fire, Payne brought the Canadian Bren up to the firing position, but never had the chance to pull the trigger.

'I was at the rear of the group and didn't get to fire a shot. It was all over pretty quickly. We had one enemy killed, one wounded and the rest got out of there. Our main objective was to get the two Chinese back up the hill to our intelligence people. The wounded soldier looked about sixteen to me. He had very Mongol-type features. The dead one could have been anywhere from nineteen to twenty-five. We would always try to take any bodies back with us. You can tell a lot from looking at a body. The intelligence people could work out what unit they were from, but just by looking at them you can tell how the enemy is travelling. Is he well fed, well uniformed? Does he have good equipment, plenty of ammo? You're always hoping that they'll have some paperwork on them but they were like us, they never carried anything.'

While Payne didn't get to fire his weapon during that skirmish, only a matter of days later he played a part in a major operation undertaken by B Company.

The aim of the operation – to capture an enemy prisoner – was simple. The procedure was anything but. It required intricate planning, hard training and precise execution. In the end, in terms of the stated objective, it was not strictly a success but in terms of a well-drilled unit demonstrating discipline, initiative, courage and even humour under fire, it was a perfect example of what Australian soldiers are all about.

Along with other platoon leaders Lieutenant Gus Breen was briefed by B Company commander, Major A.S. 'Joe' Mann, on the morning of 9 December 1952. They were told B Company was to raid a Chinese position on an enemy-held hill known as Flora, some 1000 metres behind enemy lines, snatch a prisoner and return to the Australian positions. The mission was codenamed 'Operation Fauna'.

4

Flora and Fauna

GUS BREEN HAD BEEN in charge of 4 Platoon for only ten days when he was ordered to lead the assault. He had led a couple of patrols and knew most of the men by name, but he had no idea how they would perform under combat conditions.

'I have to say I'd been very well trained,' he said. 'I'd had four years at military college and technically this was pretty much a routine exercise. I knew exactly what I had to do and what the fellas had to do. My job was to keep everything moving. That's the key to an operation like that. You can't get bogged down. Once you stop, you've had it.'

Breen led the platoon out at midnight on 10 December, exactly twenty minutes after 5 Platoon had left to set up a forward base close to the Chinese line. The men had been preparing all day, cleaning and checking weapons and being taken two at a time to the forward trenches to be shown the route they would be taking in darkness later that night. At 4 p.m. A Company arrived and took over the company's position. The men were fed, had church services and moved forward, ready to go, all the while running over in their minds what they had to do. To ensure nothing was left to chance the company had been pulled from the line a day earlier and taken to a feature which closely resembled Flora. There, under the watchful eye of brigade commander Brigadier Tom Daly, they carried out a complete dress rehearsal of the operation. 'Not good enough,' growled Daly. 'Do it again.' A third rehearsal was held at night. For Payne the dry-run was more than an opportunity to learn the lie of the land. It gave him a first opportunity to experience the full firepower of the UN force in action.

'That rehearsal was the first time I'd heard all the company's weapons fired at once. You'd hear a platoon firing their weapons but never something like this, where there were about a hundred of us all firing at once. It was just awesome. Preparing for something like Fauna was pretty daunting. The main thing was to get to the objective undetected and that was a pretty big ask, so there were concerns. To see the company all working together at those rehearsals and knowing that we had the Kiwi artillery to back us up certainly made us feel better about things.'

As Breen led the platoon out, followed by Company Headquarters, one section of the Assault Pioneers Platoon and 6 Platoon, there was another thing that pleased the Australians. For the previous two nights the South Korean division stationed about 800 metres to the east of the Australian emplacements had been attacked by massed Chinese forces. The architects of Fauna were hoping the attacks would continue for a third night, diverting attention from the Australian operation. They did, with the Chinese artillerymen concentrating on supporting their own offensive, totally unaware of the single line of soldiers slipping and sliding down the ice and barbed wire-covered hillside towards Halifax outpost.

Once through the gap in the minefield outside Halifax, progress was painstakingly slow – and noisy. The sound-deadening snow the Aussies had hoped for had not arrived. Every footstep over iced and frozen grass crackled and popped like a child playing with bubblewrap. Just 700 metres were covered in the first hour, with 3000 still to go.

As they neared the forward base set up by 5 Platoon there was a short burst of machine-gun fire. Breen and his men threw themselves to the ground and froze. Ten minutes later the order came through from Major Joe Mann to keep going. The fire had come from a 6 Platoon scout after a challenge had gone unanswered. The 'enemy' turned out to be a fellow Australian who was slightly wounded. Despite the noise, somehow they remained undetected and continued on their way between two Chinese-held hills. The aim was to go past the objective and swing back, attacking from the rear. It was a plan with no margin for error. Go too far before turning back and the small Australian assault force would walk straight into the main Chinese defences. Turn early and they would miss Flora altogether.

Two hours behind schedule, but still with the element of surprise in their favour, Breen turned his men back towards the target. He knew they were in the right place because of two things: a deep communication trench that was a key indicator on intelligence maps, and the distinctive aroma of Chinese cooking.

The communication trench, a link between fighting pits, was long, deep and empty. The Australians approached warily in an extended line, knowing it would be part of an underground tunnel system which could fill with heavily armed men in minutes. They crept closer and closer, to within 40 metres of the enemy line before the Chinese finally realised they were under attack.

With calls of *Choh, choh* – 'Beware, beware', the Chinese poured into their trenches and opened fire with Type 50 submachine carbines – nicknamed 'Burps' by the Australians, 'potato-masher' hand grenades on a stick and concussion grenades. Pushing forward, some dropping to their knees, the Aussies fired back. With the action underway the Australian artillery forward operations officer John Salmon sent the codeword 'Capstan' back to the New Zealanders on 355 and they sent out a barrage to six targets to the sides and rear of the Australians, effectively cutting off any hope of the Chinese sending reinforcements to Flora.

With all hell breaking loose around them Payne's section leader, Corporal Ron Porto, yelled at Keith and the soldier nearest to him, Albert Charfield, to get into the communications trench and 'clean it out'. It was a case of jumping into the darkness, knowing neither the depth of the trench, nor what might have been in it, waiting.

Gus Breen rates the actions of Payne and Charfield as among the most outstanding of the operation.

'I've said all along that it took plenty of guts to do what they did. You think about it. It's the middle of the night, it's pitch black and freezing. You can't see what's in front of you and you're told to drop into a bottomless pit. We knew the pit was there but we didn't know how deep it was. What we did know was that any reinforcements were going to come through those tunnels. It was a honeycomb down there, you wouldn't believe how those Chinese could dig.'

Payne and Charfield dropped into the trench expecting it to be a metre or two deep. It was closer to 3 metres below ground level, with entrance holes to connecting tunnels regularly spaced out along the walls. The two men quickly moved along, dropping grenades into the holes.

'We had six grenades each,' Payne recalled. 'Three concussion grenades and three normal grenades. The concussion grenades didn't have any shrapnel in them but they gave off a tremendous explosion. The holes could have led to sleeping bays or shelter bays or been part of a tunnel network between a whole lot of trenches. We weren't thinking about it at the time, just worrying about getting the job done and getting out.'

Payne later told Breen the holes ran so deep that he couldn't hear the grenades explode. Breen has no doubt they did their job.

'I'm sure they would have knocked a few off down there. In an enclosed area like that, with a grenade exploding, it would have been good night nurse.'

The trench secured and no enemy encountered, Payne and Charfield now had another problem – getting out of the pit. Porto came up with a solution which still gives Payne nightmares more than fifty years later, instructing other members of the section to lower their rifles, bayonet first, into the trench and pull up their mates.

'You don't think about it much at the time, there's plenty happening and you just act instinctively,' Payne said. 'But later on, you can't help thinking, How bloody stupid. You've got blokes under attack with one round up the spout and the safety catch off and there we are hanging off the front of their rifles.'

Payne and Charfield were extracted safely and rejoined their section as they met up with the main force charging towards the enemy trenches. The position was overrun by the Australians as the Chinese retreated into the tunnels, taking their wounded with them.

While retreating the Chinese continued to lay down covering fire. A potato-masher grenade thrown from a Chinese bunker landed in the middle of the Company Headquarters group, blowing Major Joe Mann off his feet and wounding artillery officer John Salmon. As Mann stood up and started to pull Salmon to safety another grenade landed in front of them. Again Mann was knocked over and Salmon further wounded. Climbing to his feet, Mann charged the Chinese bunker. A few bursts from his Owen machine carbine ended the Chinese resistance.

With their own forces now safely underground, the Chinese began mortaring what had been their defensive position only minutes earlier. The Australians received the order to withdraw to their own lines around 4.20 a.m. For Breen it was an arduous, dangerous, but ultimately successful end to the operation.

'We didn't get our prisoner, which was the objective, but in retrospect that was always virtually impossible. The Chinese didn't leave their wounded lying around above ground. They were dragged back down and taken to their casualty centres. All that was left was dead bodies and there were plenty of them around. The way they could reinforce an area through their tunnels I've got no doubt there were a lot more Chinese on that hill at the end of the operation than there had been at the start.'

Having regrouped 30 metres past the Chinese trenches, Breen did a quick headcount before heading back. The platoon was missing two men and another three were wounded. Corporal Ron Porto pleaded with Breen to be allowed to go back and search for the missing men. One, Ron Rootes, was the brother of his girlfriend.

'I wouldn't let him go,' Breen said. 'I didn't have any option. I had two men missing; if I'd let Porto go back it would have been three men. I have no doubt Rootes was killed in the initial contact when the Chinese opened up on his section from about 30 metres. His family contacted me fifty years later. They wanted to know what had happened to him, and that's what I told them. There was nothing to be gained by letting Porto go, we had to get off that hill and back to our lines.'

The platoon set off back towards Hill 355 a section at a time with Breen and his batman Sammy Small bringing up the rear. John Salmon, although hit with at least twenty pieces of shrapnel in the grenade attack, continued to coordinate a covering artillery barrage as he was helped back by his Kiwi assistant John Bright and radio operator John Burgess. John McNulty – the platoon sergeant Payne had almost shot a few weeks earlier – stayed back to help Sergeant Kavanagh of 6 Platoon who had been wounded while protecting 4 Platoon from counterattack. McNulty's conduct during Operation Fauna saw him awarded the Military Medal. Joe Mann was awarded the DSO.

The Chinese attempted to pound the Australians with mortar fire as they made their withdrawal but were once again outsmarted. Predicting correctly the enemy would shell the western side of 355, the Aussies headed back up the eastern side. It was safer, but harsher terrain and the final part of the trek, with the Chinese realising their mistake and laying down mortar fire, was excruciating. All members of 4 Platoon took a turn in carrying their wounded mate Bob Auhl, strapped unconscious onto a stretcher with rifle slings. The last brutal metres to safety were travelled on their hands and knees.

Finally, six and a half hours after they had left, Breen brought his platoon back through the Australian forward defensive line. When he had taken over the platoon just ten days earlier Gus Breen had known nothing about his men or their capabilities. Now, after a true baptism of fire, he knew plenty.

'I never knew John Seaton but I could tell from the way the men handled themselves that he must have been a very good soldier. I was also very lucky with John McNulty. He was very helpful from the moment I arrived. Some people don't bother. They think, Let him work it out himself, but Mac went out of his way to help from day one. He was a friend of mine until the day he died many years later.

'As for the men, they knew their jobs and they did them. What Keith Payne and Albert Charfield did in jumping into that trench was a good example. I always thought they should have earned recognition for that; been Mentioned in Dispatches at least, but that's how it is sometimes.

'I remember where I was when I heard about Keith's VC. I was out of the army by then and I was at Albury Airport, waiting for a flight to Sydney. There was a poster at the papershop saying "Aussie VC Winner" so naturally I went over to have a look and I saw the photo and thought, God, it's Payney. I hadn't seen him since Korea at the time — we met up years later — but I'd always thought of him as just a typical ordinary digger. Anyone who served with him in Korea would tell you that. I patrolled with him in no-man's-land, we gumshoed around the scrub and he was a good solid fella. You didn't look at him and think, There's a VC winner, but that's the thing. It was like Ron Porto wanting to go back out to look for Ron Rootes that night; they were all just ordinary blokes. It was how they reacted in certain situations which made them special, and until you are put in those situations yourself you never know what you will do.'

After Operation Fauna 1RAR was taken out of the line and in March 1953 headed back to Australia. Breen, who had been in Korea only a few months, was posted to 2RAR as a platoon commander before being seconded to the US Air Force. Over the next three months he flew seventy-six missions as an observer with the Americans before returning to 2RAR. He was on the Hook on 24 July when the Chinese made their final assault on the feature. It was to be the last battle of the war. Two days later the truce was signed.

Like Breen, Payne didn't have the chance to return to Australia with his 1RAR mates.

'I was a bit pinged off that I couldn't go back with them. I would have liked to have come back with the battalion and the blokes I had been through so much with but because I'd been a replacement and hadn't served my full twelve months I had to stay behind. I was put into 28 Brigade escorting vehicles and ammo trucks up to the lines.'

The war might have been coming to an end but there was no let-up in the hostilities. Quite the opposite. To build up their bargaining power at the negotiating table, the Chinese stepped up their attempts to take territory held by the UN forces. Stationed behind the line Payne found himself with the luxury of six hours sleep a night and temporary corporal stripes on his sleeve, but no reduction in workload or danger. In late April, escorting a water truck back from the line, his luck ran out.

'Our side had built these giant spotlights on a feature we called "Searchlight Hill" at the back of 355. The hill was useful for two reasons – it was the supply route for 355 and the searchlights shone across the valley on to the Chinese-held Hill 227. We had a giant 6 inch naval gun on Searchlight Hill that pounded the rear of the enemy lines. The lights were very necessary for that but they also gave the Chinese guns a bearing when we were using the supply road. One night I was coming back down the hill in a water truck with a driver named Matthews; there was an explosion and we went off the road. I thought I'd been hit by artillery but in my records it says I was injured when the truck rolled. Either way, my face was severely smashed up and my leg was buggered as well. I crawled out of the wreck and got to the brigade officers' mess. I called out and a couple of blokes came out. I didn't know how bad I was but I knew I was in big trouble. I told them that Matthews was still up on the hill and then I think I must have passed out. Next thing I knew I was in an Indian field hospital, then on a plane being evacuated out to Japan.'

On the same plane was Bluey Donnelly, the former press photographer who had joined up with Payne in Brisbane two years earlier. Donnelly was one of twenty-nine Australians taken prisoner during the war. On the night of 13 January 1953 he was shot in the leg and captured while trying to help a dying comrade during a patrol on the enemy-held Hill 227.

In time Donnelly would write of his experiences in a memoir, which was a combination of horror and humanity. He would tell of mateship under the most gruelling conditions, of cruelty and of kindness encountered in the most unlikely places. The most poignant moment of his time in captivity came ten days after his capture. Refused medical treatment for his shattered leg by the Chinese until after he was interrogated, Donnelly finally underwent crude surgery. It was 28 January 1953, his twenty-third birthday, and Donnelly was lying in the back room of a makeshift hospital, confused, depressed and trying not to cry out in agony as the effects of a spinal injection wore off. Then, as Donnelly wrote:

> In the early hours of the following morning, when the pain was at its worst, a Chinese soldier came over and sat beside me. He looked at me for a little while and watched as I tried to control the pain I was experiencing and then he reached down and cradled my head in his arms. He began to sing in perfect English, the old Paul Robeson spiritual, 'Swing Low Sweet Chariot, coming for to carry me home'. This is one of the most moving experiences that I will always remember. The soldier could not speak English to carry on a conversation, but I found out later that he had attended an American missionary school when he was a child. This was the turning point in my imprisonment. The next day, the pain in my leg eased a bit and I started to regain my spirit. ('Eric Donnelly, I Was a Prisoner in North Korea', in *Korea Remembered: The RAN, ARA and RAAF in the Korean War of 1950–1953*, comp. & ed. M.B. Pears and F. Kirkland, Wancliff, Isle of Capri, Qld, 1996)

For the next four months Donnelly was shifted to a succession of caves, farmhouses and makeshift compounds, surviving in appalling conditions, before being handed over to UN forces in a prisoner swap known as 'Little Switch'.

Payne and Donnelly were taken to the UN hospital in Kure, Japan: Donnelly for quick treatment before repatriation to Australia, Payne for a longer stay.

'I had an operation a day or two after I got there. I'd smashed my jaw and had a giant gash under my lip. They stitched that and wired up my jaw and every six weeks I had to go back into theatre so they could change the dressing. Also I was in a wheelchair with my leg in plaster. I was there for more than two months. It was pretty boring but we made our own fun. We used to have wheelchair races in the spare ward. One night we all went to the officers' ward to watch a movie. There was a ramp outside which went over one of those Japanese fishponds. No prizes for guessing who ended up in that.'

As he slowly recuperated there was a question mark over whether Payne should be sent back to Australia or return to active duty. The ceasefire ended that debate. He was home for his twentieth birthday, a year to the day since he had arrived in Korea. The first great adventure in Payne's life had come to an end but he was determined it would not be the last. As far as he was concerned, his life's course had been set. He was a soldier.

5

Army Wife

THE MOMENT PAYNE KNEW he was really out of the war zone was when his flight home landed at the US army base in Guam and he was given real milk.

'All the Australians got stuck into it. We made pigs of ourselves. That's my main memory of the trip home, the taste of that milk. From there we got a flight to Sydney and then on to Brisbane. When I was at the personnel depot at Yeronga I bumped into my old platoon sergeant. He told me we'd lost about four of our initial recruitment platoon in Korea. It was sad to think of those young blokes not coming back and in a way it seemed like we were the only ones who cared. They call Korea the Forgotten War, and that's exactly what it was. There were about 1500 casualties over there, more than 300 killed. What 3RAR did in the Battle of Kapyong was one of the gutsiest actions in Australian military history but these days no one seems to mention Korea at all. What happened was we were getting home at the same time as the soldiers who had been part of the Japan occupation force. To be honest everyone at home was sick and tired of war. There was no animosity like there was to the Vietnam veterans. Australians knew the complexities of the Cold War and we had national service at the time, so the threat of communism was always there in the back of people's minds. That was where they wanted it to stay, right in the background. Everyone just wanted to get on with their lives. We came home, got different campaign medals and different coloured shoulder patches to what the World War II veterans got, but no one took much notice.'

Payne had accrued ninety-six days leave and headed home to Ingham. Some things hadn't changed at all since he had been away and some things had changed too much. A few mates had moved away, others seemed stuck in a time lock. His high-school sweetheart Betty Roberts had sent a 'Dear John' letter soon after he arrived in Korea.

'After two weeks I just said, "Stuff this", and headed to Brisbane. I had no one to talk to in Ingham, no one who would understand what I'd been through. Back in Brisbane a lot of blokes were coming back from Korea. We stuck together because we could talk. We spoke the same language.'

After his leave ended Payne was posted as a corporal storeman/driver to the 4th Cadet Battalion in Townsville. It was to be a fortuitous posting. The battalion was in charge of a number of high-school cadet units and Payne was soon assisting the instructors as they worked with the student cadets. Within a short time he was giving his own lessons, which took him into the instructional sphere of the regular army, his main direction for the rest of his career.

Another major life change was just around the corner. In June 1954, less than a year after his return from Korea, Payne was ordered down to Brisbane to do a driving course at the Trade Training Centre at Enoggera. By chance at the same time the centre was holding a clerical course attended by a WRAAC named Florence Plaw from Wacol army base.

Flo Plaw had been in the Women's Royal Australian Army Corps for just over a year. Born in Goondiwindi and raised in Brisbane, she came from a service background, with her father a former sailor in the British merchant marine. After attending boarding school at Clayfield, Flo's first choice had been to join the navy. When her enlistment was held up, she turned instead to the army and was posted as a typist-receptionist to Wacol where she processed the intake of national service recruits. One of the first decisions she made after joining up was that she would never marry a soldier. It took Keith six weeks to change her mind.

'He was doing his course and I was doing mine and we'd all get together at meal times,' she recalled. 'He was living in at Enoggera while he was doing the course and I was at the WRAAC barracks at Chelmer. There was a place with a jukebox not far from the base at Enoggera where we'd go after the course finished for the day. Sometimes Keith would escort me back to Chelmer. On the last night of the course we were standing against the fence outside the barracks and he asked me if I'd consider marrying him and I said "Yes". It was as simple as that.'

Keith remembers it even more simply: 'I cast my eyes on this young chick and she looked pretty good to me. I started chatting to her and we were engaged by the end of the course. Oh, we were pretty smart dudes, us.'

At the end of the course Keith went back to Townsville to his duties and Flo went back to hers at Wacol.

'Flo put the engagement notice in the paper which was how Mother found out,' Keith said. 'Flo was working on the paperwork for the "nashos" and there was a bit of downtime between intakes so she came up to Ingham to meet the family. The first thing Mum said to her was, "Has Keith told you about Betty Roberts?", so it wasn't the greatest start but after that they got on alright.'

But not without some work on Flo's part. Remilda Payne was a strong-willed woman, as is her daughter-in-law. Flo developed her own system for avoiding confrontation.

'I never let her get to me. I made sure every time I bought something for my own mother — for her birthday or Christmas or Mother's Day — I'd buy exactly the same thing for Keith's mother. That way there could never be any argument.'

It was a short engagement and the newlyweds moved into army-subsidised housing in Townsville. Due to regulations prohibiting marriage between army personnel Flo, now also a corporal, was forced to resign and give up work.

'I signed my marriage certificate on a Saturday and on the Monday I had to go in and sign my discharge papers,' Flo said. 'I was little bit sad having to do it, but that was just the way it was then. I enjoyed what I was doing but I'd made the decision and that was it. I must admit about five years later when I read that they'd changed the regulations I thought, Why couldn't they have done that before I got married? Another twelve months or so in the army would have been good for me but I wouldn't swap what I did for anything. In the end it was good that I had been in the army because it prepared me for what was to come with Keith.

'That's why I thought I would never marry a soldier, because the time I had in the army opened up my eyes to things. At the same time it clued me up. When I was working on the switchboard at Wacol wives would ring up and they'd tell me things, and then I'd put them through to their husbands and the husbands would tell me things, so in a way I was getting a look at married life in the army from both sides.

'I was never under any illusions. I knew that in Keith I was marrying a very dedicated soldier. Even today the soldier in him is still there. I sometimes think he doesn't realise he's taken off his uniform. He still takes an interest in what's happening in the army and he loves to see the school cadets in their uniforms. So I knew what I was getting into and it was a good thing too. Even today I'm walking on edge and I will until the day I die because of everything Keith's been through and how it has affected him. That's why I would tell any girl who was marrying a soldier to make sure she really knows what she's doing because it's not an easy life. If she hadn't had anything to do with the services I'd tell her to find out everything she could about service life before taking the final step, or to walk away and find someone else. It's a wonderful life but for every good thing that happens there's a bad one. When your husband is away you've got the children by yourself; you're left to do all the packing up. When a married quarter becomes available you get the call to "Pack up and get here". From 1953 until the day we moved into our own home in Mackay that was my job. Even when we moved for the last time in 1993, we slept at the house for the first night with everything we owned in packing boxes all around us on the floor and when Keith woke up he was straight out the door to catch a plane to do a TV documentary in Vietnam. I waved him off and looked around at all that unpacking ahead of me and thought, Well things haven't changed much in the last forty years, have they?'

Keith and Flo were married in December 1954. The couple's first son, Ronald James, was born ten months later.

In 1956 Keith was posted to 11 National Service Training Battalion at Wacol as a corporal instructor, where he stayed until it was closed at the end of national service in 1959. During that period he studied for his sergeant's stripes – along with other courses.

Brigadier Tom Daly, by then the officer in charge of Northern Command, which took in all of Queensland, had changed little since the day he oversaw his troops' rehearsal for Operation Fauna and said, 'Not good enough. Do it again.'

'Tom Daly didn't believe in having troops sitting around with nothing to do,' said Payne. 'He wanted us busy and fit and that meant doing courses. During those three years I did just about every course you could think of: parachute, signals, diving and infantry-armour cooperation. I did my central instructors course and jungle training out at Canungra.

'Tom didn't realise it at the time – he thought he was just keeping us on our toes – but what he was doing was preparing us for Vietnam. We were the ones who would train the blokes who went over, and in a lot of cases we went over ourselves, so without really meaning to, he was putting the groundwork in place for what was going to come.'

Which could also be said for the entire national service program.

Nashos began in 1951 with the onset of what would become known as the Cold War. From the start of the blockade of West Berlin by the Soviet Union in 1948, the world had lived with the spectre of nuclear war. Throughout Europe, Asia and the Middle East, communist and US-allied forces had been locked in a dangerous stalemate. As hostilities threatened to escalate on two occasions the Australian Liberal government of the day – with bipartisan support – had instigated a program of compulsory military training for all males over eighteen.

The first National Service Scheme was brought on by the start of the Korean War. It continued through Australia's involvement in

Malaya before ending in 1959. During that time 227,000 young men were enlisted in fifty-two intakes. They didn't see active duty but were obliged to serve six months, followed by another five years in the Army Reserve. The second scheme, which ran from 1965 to 1972, involved two years full-time service integrated into regular army units, with deployment to Vietnam where required. While Payne's first nashos did not serve overseas, they received full training and, according to Payne, a solid grounding which would stay with them throughout their lives.

'It was great for them and it was great for the country. When they came in they were all pissed off about being there but three weeks later they were proud of what they'd achieved. Even today I bump into recruits I trained at 11 Battalion and they'll say "National service made me". They wouldn't be saying that when they arrived. We'd go down to the railway station to pick them up and they'd be a rabble. We'd take them back to camp and throw them into barracks, give them their gear and then take them down to the barber to get shorn. That was when they really knew they were in the army.

'In the first platoons I had there were blokes that were older than me but we worked it out. My policy was to be firm, fair and friendly – I never threw out too many charge sheets – and it was very satisfying to see them come together. We were the busiest training battalion in the country, with up to 1500 recruits at a time at our peak. To see a battalion of 1500 men marching onto the parade ground and their bayonets hitting the same piece of sunlight together, you know things are working.'

While Payne was training nashos at Wacol for action they would never see, the Cold War continued to heat up in South-East Asia. Since the end of World War II communist cells had been active throughout the region, with regular attacks on police stations and government buildings by groups known as communist terrorists – CTs – in Malaya, Thailand, Vietnam, Laos and Indonesia.

The area of most concern to Britain, and thus Australia, was Malaya. Previously a protectorate of Britain, Malaya had been occupied by the Japanese during World War II. At the end of the war the British returned, promising eventual independence, but local communists had other ideas. In June 1948 three expat British plantation managers were murdered by CTs and the Malayan Emergency was declared. Australia became involved in 1950 with the arrival of RAAF aircraft and personnel to support British and Malayan government forces as they attempted to put down the insurgents. In October 1951 the situation worsened when the British High Commissioner Henry Gurney was assassinated but by the time the first Australian ground troops from 2RAR arrived in Penang four years later, the communists were very much on the back foot.

2RAR engaged in a lengthy mop-up operation for almost two years, patrolling the main areas of communist activity, guarding plantations and generally protecting British interests. In October 1957 they were replaced by 3RAR who in turn were replaced by 1RAR in October 1959. The Malayan Emergency was officially declared over on 31 July 1960, although 1RAR would stay for another year before being replaced by 2RAR. For Payne, drilling nashos back in Wacol, the thought of his former battalion engaged in active duty was frustrating. By now he was a husband and father of a rapidly growing family – Ron had been followed by Greg, Colin and Ian, and Derek was on the way – but he was also a professional soldier who yearned to be in the action.

'I kept asking but they wouldn't let me go. By now there was a changeover in the training ranks. The World War II blokes were being phased out and the blokes from Malaya were just coming back. I was sort of stuck in the middle.'

The landscape changed in November 1959 when national service ended and 11 Battalion was disbanded. Payne was posted back to 3RAR, for a short time as a section commander and then platoon sergeant. He and his men were sent to Canungra for training prior to embarkation for Malaya where the battalion was to take up a peacekeeping role. By now it was 1962 and there was another region in South-East Asia which was starting to hot up and cause concern to international observers. It was a small country to the south of China, nestled beside Laos and Cambodia.

Vietnam.

6

Konfrontasi

THE HISTORY OF VIETNAM is that of a country torn apart for centuries by the attempts of foreign powers and opposing political factions to gain control. In the 1800s it was France that enforced colonial rule. The French remained in power until the country was invaded and occupied by Japan during World War II.

At the end of the war the communist Viet Minh, which had led the resistance movement against the Japanese, declared the country's independence and for nine years fought against the French who had returned with plans to re-establish a colony. In July 1954 the war between the Viet Minh and France ended with an internationally brokered agreement that granted Vietnam its independence but established two separate republics divided by the 14th parallel. In the north was the communist-run Democratic Republic of Vietnam and in the south the Republic of Vietnam, strongly supported by the United States.

Over the next twenty years this elongated S-shaped peninsula roughly the size of Italy became the site of the worst international conflict since World War II and saw over one million armed forces and up to four times that many civilians killed before Saigon, the capital of South Vietnam, fell in April 1975.

In time Vietnam was to become a major influence on Keith Payne's life but as he prepared to head off to Malaya with 3RAR it was just another Asian country under threat of communist domination.

Following the division of Vietnam in 1954 there had been low-key opposition to the rule of South Vietnamese leader Ngo Dinh Diem. This escalated to the point where in December 1960 the North Vietnamese government authorised the creation of the National Front for the Liberation of South Vietnam. Its principal objective was to seize political power through a popular insurrection, thus unifying the country and putting an end to US influence.

Throughout 1961 and 1962 Diem repeatedly pleaded with the United States to send military assistance to stem the threat of invasion from the north. Finally, in July 1962, the Australian government agreed to send thirty 'advisers' to help prepare the South Vietnamese armed forces for any attack. The advisers were brought together under the epithet of the Australian Army Training Team Vietnam (AATTV) but would become better known simply as 'the Team'.

Between 1962 and 1972, 992 members of the Team served in Vietnam. They lost 33 killed in action and 122 wounded. They were awarded 147 medals for bravery and meritorious conduct – including four Victoria Crosses and a US Distinguished Service Cross – and earned a reputation as the best of the best. And Keith Payne would become one of the proudest and most highly regarded of them all – but that was still a long way off and, as he underwent jungle training at Canungra in preparation for Malaya, the furthest thing from his mind.

The last time Payne had gone to war he had been eighteen years old and had to cool his heels in Japan until he was old enough to see action. By the time he left for Malaya in 1963 he was thirty, married and the father of five boys. He was very much a different person, and this was a different war. In fact, it wasn't even termed a war. It was a 'police action' and Payne didn't have to worry about how Flo and the boys would cope while he was away. He took them all with him.

'The British had always taken their families to Malaya with them and so everything was set up in terms of accommodation. Even when things were at their worst over there in 1954 and 1955, 2RAR had taken their families along so by the time we went over it was just accepted that they'd come. By that time we were used to being an army family. We didn't know anything different. It was like being part of a bigger family. You all lived together in married quarters and you looked after each other. When you moved into a new house there would be a cooked dinner waiting for the first night. When someone was away and his wife and kids were on their own everyone else would chip in. You'd mow the lawn or wash the car.'

In Malaya there was no need for such extra duties. For the first time in her life Flo found herself enjoying a perk of army life.

'We had a nice house opposite the beachfront at Terendak and I had two *amahs* – maids. I had a house amah and a children amah. One would help with the boys, the other would help with the house. I never had to worry about a thing. If I couldn't find the boys I knew they'd be down the road at the local village playing with the other kids and the amah would be looking out for them. It was quite an experience. I remember there was a water shortage when we were there and the army would have to deliver water but in the rainy season there would be a rain shower every day at exactly the same time. It was as if someone turned on a tap and down it would come and then it would stop, just like that. All of us Australians would put on our swimsuits and be waiting and we'd go out and stand in the rain and wash our hair. The boys loved it. The locals must have thought we were mad but it was a lot of fun. At the same time Keith would be out in the jungle doing his patrols. I knew there was an element of danger, but there was an element of danger in everything he did. I didn't think about it. If I had done I would have gone stark raving mad. I just kept my hair on and my fingers crossed. What else could I do?'

Flo was right in her assessment of the situation. There was an element of danger, but for the first few months that he was in Malaya Keith wasn't exposed to it. In fact, early in their stay it was Flo, not Keith, who had to call on her training to deal with an emergency.

Looking out the window of their house one morning she saw an elderly Malayan man riding his pushbike along the waterfront road. A large truck sped past and the gust of air it created picked the man up and threw him across the monsoon drain where he hit his head on the concrete. Grabbing a towel and bedsheet, Flo ran across the road and tried to administer first aid, calling to neighbours to phone an ambulance as she wrapped him in the sheet and tried to stem the flow of blood with the towel. It was no good. The man was dead. When the ambulance arrived the man was placed in the back, still wrapped in the sheet and towel, and taken away.

For Payne, at first anyway, there was no such excitement.

'I didn't see any action. We'd go off on patrols for weeks at a time but nothing came my way. In all the time Australians were over there they probably only had four or five contacts. One of the blokes in my recruit platoon for Korea was involved in the 'Pipeline Ambush' which was probably the biggest single action of the whole emergency.'

In June 1956, the action known as the Pipeline Ambush saw a five-man patrol from 2RAR ambushed by a large group of CTs lying in wait near a track which ran parallel to a water pipeline. Alerted by the noise other Australian patrols hurried to the area and fought off the terrorists but not before three Australians had been killed and another three wounded. In all some 11,000 civilians and service personnel were killed during the Malayan Emergency, including fifty-one Australians. Another twenty-seven were wounded. By the time Payne arrived the worst of the conflict was over, but that didn't mean it was always a comfortable experience. The CTs might have been thin on the ground but the natural predators such as snakes, red ants and, most of all, leeches, were a constant source of irritation.

For Payne it wasn't a communist bullet or mine that laid him up during the Malayan Emergency. It was a wasp.

'I was leading a patrol up on the Malay–Thai border. The only people we came across was a group of illegal timber cutters but they weren't what we were looking for so we didn't bother them and they didn't bother us. What did bother us was a swarm of wasps. They weren't even very big things but by crikey they had a sting. One of the buggers stung me in the face and I was gone. My face all swelled up and I couldn't see a thing. And the pain was incredible. The diggers had to lead me back to base. All that could be done was to put hot and cold poultices on my face for two days before the swelling went down. It was the worst injury I had the whole time I was there.'

Worse even than the broken ribs he suffered in the infamous Affiliation Parade.

'It all started back in Korea. When 3RAR was over there they had in support a squadron of tanks from the 8th King's Royal Irish Hussars, which later became the Queen's Royal Hussars. One day the commander of the Hussars marched into the tent that was 3RAR officers' mess, stuck a lance into the ground and said, "We are hereby affiliated". At the same time the 2nd Battalion of the King's Own Yorkshire Light Infantry was over there as well and they were affiliated with the 8th Hussars, which meant they were then affiliated with 3RAR too. They were both royal regiments, as was 3RAR, so the whole thing had to go back to England for all the paperwork to be done. Anyway, when we got over to Malaya it turned out that all three just happened to be there at the same time, so it was decided we had to have an affiliation parade. The King's Own, who we called the 'Koylies' – as in King's Own Yorkshire Light Infantry – were based near us at Terendak but the Hussars were set up in pretty grand quarters at Ipoh about 350 kilometres up north, so it was decided to hold the parade there.'

A company was chosen to represent 3RAR and as Sergeant Payne climbed aboard the train that would take them to Ipoh for a week of rehearsals, he and his fellow Aussies were determined to do their regiment proud. Flo and the wife of an Australian private decided to drive to Ipoh in the Paynes' new Fiat 1800 stationwagon late in the week to watch their men in all their glory.

'We were driving along late in the afternoon when we went down a steep incline and the interior of the car started filling with smoke,' Flo recalls. 'I couldn't stop where I was so when we got onto the flat I pulled over and turned everything off and tried to work out what to do. I saw two wires hanging down under the dashboard and wondered if they should be together but I wasn't game to do anything about it, so we just sat there. The locals were driving and walking past, looking at these two strange white women sitting in their car, and my companion and I were starting to get a little concerned. After a while a British Army Land Rover came past and I asked the soldiers to get word to Ipoh that we were there and could they send out a rescue party. When nothing happened and it was getting darker and darker, I took hold of the two wires and said to the other lady, "Well, here goes nothing". I twisted them together, expecting a huge explosion, but when I turned the key everything worked perfectly. I was pretty proud of myself and when we finally got to Ipoh and I told Keith what I'd done all he could say was, "Why didn't you check the fuse box?" Fuse box? I didn't know what a fuse box was. I still don't. I could have strangled him.'

Actually, given what he had gone through the previous week, it was a wonder Payne could say anything at all.

'When we arrived we saw they had an Olympic-sized swimming pool and it was full of ice and beer cans.'

Says Flo, 'By the time I got there it was half-full of empties.'

That night Flo was the only Australian woman in the sergeants' mess as the Australians took on their hosts in a game of indoor rugby. By the end of the match Keith had broken ribs and his company commander was sporting a generous black eye. Two days later they marched around the parade ground in perfect formation.

'Given what I saw I still can't believe they did it,' Flo says. The parade over, she drove the Fiat home without further drama, although the adventures weren't quite over for A Company, 3RAR.

'When they saw us off at the station the Koylies thought we hadn't drunk enough over the week so they put all the leftover beer on the train with us.'

But wasps and indoor rugby weren't the only threats to Payne's wellbeing in Malaya. The original reason for Australian troops being sent to Malaya was very much petering out. The CTs had been controlled and Britain was in the process of moving out of Malaya and Borneo, the two colonies then being combined – in the original plan along with Singapore and Brunei – to form the independent state of Malaysia. On face value it appeared a peaceful solution to a long-running conflict but if the powerbrokers in London thought it would bring stability to the region, they were very much mistaken. Plans to form Malaysia opened a Pandora's box and saw a new player, Indonesia, enter the game.

Like other Asian countries that had endured colonisation by a European power – in this case the Netherlands which named the territory the Dutch East Indies – Indonesia gained its independence after occupation by the Japanese in World War II. Where Indonesia differed to others in the region was the strong and long-term leadership of its first president, Sukarno.

The son of a Javanese schoolteacher, Sukarno became leader of a pro-independence party when it was formed in 1927. Arrested numerous times by the Dutch authorities over the next fifteen years, he was in prison when Indonesia was taken over by the Japanese in 1942. By then Sukarno enjoyed huge support among native Indonesians and the Japanese put him to good use recruiting local labourers and broadcasting propaganda messages through their radio network. At the same time Sukarno used his radio broadcasts to further the cause of independence and increase his profile. When the Japanese were defeated in 1945, Indonesia declared itself independent, demanded control over all former Dutch East Indies territory and installed Sukarno as its first president. For the next four years Sukarno led his country in conflict against the Dutch who had returned to reclaim control of their former colony. Finally, in December 1949 after trenchant criticism of the Dutch by the United Nations, Queen Juliana of the Netherlands acknowledged sovereignty to a federal Indonesian government. The following year Indonesia became the sixtieth member of the United Nations.

Sukarno's Indonesia presented a problem to both the superpowers. Sukarno was neither a US-style democrat nor a committed communist. Instead his vision for an independent Indonesia contained elements of both systems, as well as a firm belief in Muslim fundamentals. His system of government – which he called 'guided democracy' – included representation by a wide range of factions and agendas and inevitably led to power struggles from groups wanting total control. Sukarno survived numerous assassination and coup attempts, including one backed by the CIA in 1956. Throughout the 1950s Sukarno strengthened his ties to the communist parties and moved closer to North Korea and the People's Republic of China. He also accepted large amounts of military aid from both the Soviets and the United States, while trying to unite developing Asian and African countries into a non-aligned movement as a counter to the influence of the superpowers.

Not surprisingly, Australia kept a wary eye on this neighbour lying less than 1000 kilometres north of Darwin. After all, by 1960 the population of Indonesia had passed 100 million, around ten times that of Australia. Indonesia had the largest Muslim population in the world and the third largest communist party, behind only those of the Soviet Union and China.

Of particular significance was the fact that Indonesia had designs on part of Australia's closest neighbour, New Guinea.

Indonesia's claim on part of New Guinea had its roots back in 1828 when the Netherlands had formally claimed the western part of the island and named it Netherlands New Guinea. By 1884 Britain had claimed the south-eastern part of the island and Germany took the north-east. In 1906 Australia took over control of the British-held colony by then called Papua and in September 1914, with the first Australian shots fired in World War I, took over the German section as well. New Guinea was invaded by the Japanese in 1942 and became the battlefield where Australian forces, aided by local tribesmen, fought a desperate rearguard action to prevent invasion from the north. Less than twenty years later there were genuine fears that Australians would again be forced to draw a line in the Papuan sand.

In 1949 when Indonesia gained its independence from the Netherlands, the Dutch regained control of Western New Guinea. Throughout the 1950s the Dutch government moved towards granting full independence to the former colony and in December 1961 an elected council announced the renaming of Netherlands New Guinea as West Papua and unveiled a national emblem, anthem and flag, to be flown alongside the Dutch flag. Indonesia refused to recognise the new entity, saying it had been promised all Dutch East

Indies territory under the original treaty and mobilised its army. Backed by the Soviet Union, President Sukarno threatened a full invasion. The Dutch prepared for war but under strong pressure from the United States agreed to hand the territory over to the United Nations, which in turn gave control to Indonesia. The territory was renamed West Irian, and then Irian Jaya.

Having the region's largest and potentially most aggressive power move in virtually next door did nothing for the peace of mind of Australians and their leaders. The border between Papua and Irian Jaya would be a matter of dispute for years, but it was the confrontation between Indonesia and Malaysia that almost brought the region to flashpoint.

Needless to say, when Sukarno refused to recognise Malaysia, saying it was just a front for the British to exercise more control in the region, Australians took notice. When he mobilised his army and threatened to 'crush' the new nation, the whole world sat up and paid attention.

The Indonesia–Malaysia Confrontation – or *Konfrontasi* as it is known to Indonesians – was fought from 1962 until 1966. Sukarno's first action was to send small parties of regular and irregular soldiers to carry out terrorist and propaganda actions in Sarawak and Sabah, the former British colonies on Borneo. There were also fears the Indonesians would try to carry out commando raids on British ships anchored in Singapore Harbour.

For Payne, still serving with 3RAR in Malaya, it was a case of being the right man in the right place at the right time. Throughout his army career he had chased action around the world. Now a conflict had come to him.

'When the Indonesian Confrontation started I was patrolling on the Malay–Thai border. The word came through that I and a corporal named Black had to get back for a special assignment. Because we'd both done a diving course we were put on a plane and sent to Singapore. The British had regular army and Gurkha troops stationed there and the intelligence was that the Indonesians were going to carry out raids on the harbour. The idea was that they would get into the harbour on fishing boats and send divers down to put mines on the ships like the Aussies had done to the Japs with the Krait raid in World War II. They put us on HMAS *Terra* and our job was to go down and check out and clear the shipping.'

That short assignment over, Payne returned to the battalion in Malaya. The confrontation was hotting up and small parties of heavily armed Indonesian special forces were being landed on the Malayan mainland, their mission to recruit local sympathisers and coordinate anti-British activities. They also carried out guerrilla-style operations to disrupt local life and communications. While Keith was out on patrol looking for Indonesian units, Flo recalls how the seriousness of the situation was brought dangerously close to home for her and the boys.

'Our house wasn't in the confines of the barracks. We lived close to the waterfront in an area called Somerset Green. One night when Keith was away at the border and we were all feeling nice and sound at home, there was this almighty explosion. What had happened was the Indonesian infiltrators were trying to blow up power poles to bring down the communication lines. There was a big pylon about 1500 metres from our house and they had set charges on the four legs. Only three had gone off so the thing was still standing, but it was like the leaning tower of Pisa.'

With the Indonesians coming into the country by boat rather than on foot, the Australians were called back from the border and deployed to the Malacca Straits area. One night Payne was involved in the capture of a landing party.

'We had been patrolling a bridge in the area and two companies were sent down to intercept an Indonesian landing party which came ashore down the Muar River. I was back sitting up on a pipeline directing mortar fire while the capture party was down on the river bank waiting for the Indonesians to land. There were a couple of shots fired, they threw up their hands and it was all over. We confiscated their weapons and the local currency they had on them. The idea was that they'd recruit supporters who would rise up against the government, leading to a Bay of Pigs–type invasion.'

It never came to that but there were anxious times ahead for Australia. After repeated requests from the Malaysian government, Australian forces were sent to Borneo where they came face to face with Indonesian troops. The first Australian soldiers involved in the Borneo campaign were 3RAR who went straight there at the end of their two-year deployment in the former Malaya. The battalion had four contacts with Indonesian forces over the next two years, losing four men to mines, before being replaced by 4RAR in 1966.

By then Payne was long gone. He was called back to Australia six months before the battalion headed to Borneo, ending another chapter in his career and opening the door for the next.

If Korea is known as the 'Forgotten War', Malaya doesn't even get that amount of recognition. Unlike more recent Australian military involvements such as East Timor, there was no welcome home parade or media fuss when the Australians returned from Malaya, but for Payne the eighteen-month stint he spent in the Malayan jungle was both memorable, and invaluable. In fact, it was one more link in the chain that reached all the way from Ingham to Vietnam.

'It was the best training ground for Vietnam you could possibly have. All the lessons that we learned at Canungra: patrolling, jungle warfare, dealing with booby traps and mines, navigation and map reading – we took them into the jungle in Malaya and we did them until they were second nature to us. They were all arts of war we taught to the soldiers who were going to Vietnam and then used when we went ourselves. People have forgotten all about Malaya, but it kept a lot of Australians alive in Vietnam, believe me.'

Payne's battalion was posted to Malaya for two years but he didn't see out the period. After eighteen months he was called back to Australia to carry out a special duty. The situation in Vietnam was worsening and from November 1964 the Australian government re-instigated national service, this time with a difference. Unlike the original nashos of the 1950s who were restricted to locally based service, the young men conscripted in the second National Service Scheme were eligible for 'special overseas service' – a euphemism for deployment to Vietnam. All twenty-year-old men were required to register for national service and if selected were called up for two years full-time service in the regular army, followed by three years part-time service in the Army Reserve.

It was an issue that would divide the country. A whole generation of young men grew up with the spectre of conscription and possible deployment to a war zone. With the voting and legal drinking age at the time being twenty-one, they were not old enough to cast a vote or buy a beer, but their government deemed them old enough to be shot at and possibly killed in Vietnam. Opposition to conscription started slowly but grew to become a major political issue. Scenes of university students burning their registration papers and being bundled into police paddy wagons were a regular sight on TV news bulletins in the late 1960s. The anti-conscription movement was one of the first anti-establishment causes to bring together multi-generations in Australia. In 1965 a group of women in Melbourne formed the Save Our Sons movement and in 1970 five members were jailed for handing out anti-conscription pamphlets while on government land. But much as the opposition to conscription grew, the government of the day stuck by its commitment to its main ally, the United States.

Until the scheme was disbanded by the Whitlam government in 1972, over 63,700 young men were called up by ballot based on their birth date. Of these, 100 served in Borneo and 17,424 served in Vietnam. The remaining 46,366 served in support units in Australia, Malaysia and Papua New Guinea. The recruits received twelve weeks initial training at Kapooka or Singleton in New South Wales or Puckapunyal in Victoria.

There was also another group – 1500 in all – who were selected for officer training and sent to a specially formed facility at Scheyville in New South Wales. There they were trained by the army's best and most experienced instructors, hardened veterans of Korea and Malaya – Keith Payne was one of them.

Payne was one of eight 3RAR sergeants who were recalled to Australia to undertake warrant officer training prior to posting to Scheyville. In the Australian Army warrant officer is the most senior non-commissioned rank. Standing between the commissioned officer and non-commissioned officer such as sergeant and corporal, the warrant officer is recognised as the most experienced and highly trained of the ranks. They may be appointed to the position of regimental sergeant major (RSM), battalion sergeant major or company sergeant major. The name of the rank comes from the tradition of the warrant officer being appointed to the position and being presented with an actual warrant outlining duties and responsibilities, just as an officer is presented with a commission. The warrant officer is addressed as 'Sir' or 'Ma'am' by subordinates and 'Warrant Officer' or 'WO' by officers. The day he was given the right to wear the crown on his sleeve in recognition of his appointment as Warrant Officer Second Class (WO2) was among the proudest of Payne's life but before he and Flo left Malaysia they were to experience an equally memorable ceremony.

Flo recalls: 'All the senior sergeants who were heading back for their warrant officer training were farewelled at a formal dinner attended by their wives. All the men were dressed up in their mess kits, the band was playing, the regimental colours were marched in ... it was just a dream night. Regimental Sergeant Major Stanley was addressing everyone and in the speech he was talking about "your" colours. Then when the dinner was over he asked the men who were headed back home to leave the mess before "the" colours. That meant they were no longer part of the regiment. We all got up and walked out and the band was outside playing "Now is the Hour". It was one of the most moving things. On a night like that it's like you're in another world. We had probably two days to get packed up and move back to Australia and that was it. Our eighteen months in Malaya were all over.'

Once again it was time for Flo to pack up the house and move on – but not without a reminder of her Good Samaritan deed of over a year earlier. In a typical display of army efficiency, an inventory was carried out on the Paynes' home. It was found to be short one sheet and one towel. Sergeant Payne's pay was docked accordingly.

7

Warrant Officers' Corps

UNBEKNOWN TO PAYNE, AS he arrived in Malaya he had virtually crossed paths with another Australian soldier whose two years as a platoon commander had just ended. As Payne settled in to the routine of patrolling the Malayan jungle, the other man was being put through a series of courses in preparation for a special mission in Vietnam. The work he did and the success he had would indirectly have a huge influence on Payne's life. His name was Barry Petersen.

Like Payne, Barry Petersen was a North Queenslander, born and raised at Sarina just south of Mackay. Two years younger than Payne, Petersen had a similar upbringing. With his father away during World War II, Petersen spent long hours fishing with his grandfather. Like Payne he developed a love of the outdoors and an affinity with the tropics. He had entered the army as a national serviceman and then gone on to Officer Cadet School at Portsea in Victoria. By the time he left Malaya and began preparing for deployment to Vietnam as part of the AATTV – 'the Team', Captain Petersen was twenty-eight years old.

If Petersen had any illusions about what waited for him in Vietnam, they were soon shattered by the training courses he was put through in the months before his departure. He did the jungle-training course at Canungra, was briefed on the situation in South Vietnam at the School of Military Intelligence and trained to liaise with guerrilla forces behind enemy lines. Most telling of all though was a twelve-day course he undertook at the army's Intelligence

Centre at Sydney's Middle Head. There, along with thirteen others, he was subjected to the harshest forms of simulated capture and interrogation imaginable. The instructors and graduates of the course called it the 'School of Torture' and it lived up to its name. But for Petersen and others like him, it was entirely necessary. His was to be one of the most amazing stories of the Vietnam War. Like the storyline of a Hollywood film, he was headed deep into the heart of South Vietnam where he would recruit and lead an army of primitive mountain tribesmen known as Montagnards.

Petersen arrived in South Vietnam in August 1963 to join the Team's thirty-man force, but his mission was different to that of the other 'advisers' who trained and supervised units of the government-backed army, known as ARVN. He was directly under the control of the US Central Intelligence Agency, the CIA, which was funding a program to keep the Montagnards from turning to the communists.

'Montagnard' is a generic term given by the French to describe the many mountain tribes inhabiting the Indo-China peninsula. There were up to one million Montagnards from twenty-five tribes on the Vietnam peninsula at the start of the war and their relationship with the Vietnamese people and government was uncomfortable at best and downright hostile at worst. To the Montagnards, the original inhabitants of the area, the Vietnamese were interlopers. To the Vietnamese, the Montagnards with their darker skin, coarser features and nomadic lifestyle, were *moi* or savages. The Montagnards longed for independence from South Vietnam, while the South Vietnamese government saw them as little more than a nuisance and had no intention of giving them autonomy. When refugees from North Vietnam began flooding south following the country's division in 1954, the South Vietnamese government began a program of resettlement in the Highlands. While the Montagnards, or 'Yards' as the Australians would later call them, had no legal hold over the land, it had been their traditional home for generations. The feelings of animosity between the mountain people and the Vietnamese worsened but in the early 1960s the Montagnards suddenly found themselves very popular indeed. As the North Vietnamese began infiltrating south the Montagnards became a key element in the campaign. Their villages lay in the path between north and south. They could either provide shelter to the North Vietnamese as they moved further south, or form a defensive barrier for the South Vietnamese. In order to get the Montagnards on side the North Vietnamese dangled the carrot of future self-rule. The South Vietnamese, thanks to the support of the CIA, could offer something far more in the here and now: money.

In mid-1962 US advisers convinced the South Vietnamese government to recruit, train and arm Montagnard tribesmen. The plan was to form them into small platoon-strength units whose job it would be to protect their villages from the North Vietnamese. In time their duties would be extended to include fighting patrols and gathering intelligence about North Vietnamese movement in the area. They would be paid a daily rate, depending on the type of work they had done and the action they had seen. In effect, the CIA would turn these primitive mountain villagers into a mercenary army, and Captain Barry Petersen of Sarina, North Queensland, would become their commander-in-chief.

On arrival in South Vietnam in 1963 Petersen was flown the 265 kilometres north from Saigon by the CIA to Ban Me Thuot. It was a town of some 45,000 people in the province of Darlac that the CIA had chosen as the base of its Montagnard operation. Handed a bag of local currency, Petersen was told to make sense of a situation in which the CIA was outlaying large sums of money to pay for an army its advisers had never seen and local Vietnamese officials had little intention of producing. Over the next two years Petersen did much more than unravel a shambolic system of intrigue, local power-plays and double-dealing; he built a cohesive army, was adopted as a Montagnard chieftain and became a key figure in the Montagnard independence movement. Like Marlon Brando's fictional Colonel Kurtz in the film *Apocalypse Now*, he was seen as having become too close to the natives he was sent to lead and, he would later claim, he was marked for assassination by both local political figures and the CIA.

As Petersen was starting to organise the Montagnard tribesmen into military units similar to those which Payne and other members of the Team would one day command, Payne was completing his warrant officer course and moving to Scheyville to train the Vietnam War's first batch of nasho officers.

Located some 50 kilometres north-west of Sydney, Scheyville had a colourful history. Before World War I it was a training farm for English boys brought to Australia to start a new life on the land. During World War II it was an army training camp and from 1949 it was a migrant hostel, catering mainly for European families displaced during the war.

In 1964 with the numbers of national servicemen far outstripping the number of officers from Duntroon and Portsea, the Australian government reinvented Scheyville once again. It became the home of the Officers Training Unit formed to fast-track national service volunteers through a 22-week training course at the end of which they graduated with the rank of 2nd Lieutenant. When the first intake of potential officers came through the gates of Scheyville on 1 April 1964, WO2 Keith Payne was there waiting.

'When we got back from Malaya I headed straight to Ingleburn for six weeks to do my warrant officer training. There were no married quarters available so Flo and the boys were staying with her mother in the Brisbane suburb of Nudgee, which was just one of our problems. Everything was a bit of a mess. It was winter in Australia and I'd come straight from the jungle without any winter clothes and we also had a problem with the car we'd bought in Malaya. The taxation department ruling then was that if you bought a car overseas and didn't bring it into the country for two years you didn't pay any tax. Well of course we thought we'd be over there for more than two years but the army called me back early. So there was Flo, back in Australia with five boys and no car, because the customs people wouldn't release it until we paid the tax, which we had no intention of doing.'

Flo soon proved that Keith wasn't the only fighter in the family. She wrote letters directly to the Minister for Defence explaining in clear language that the only reason she and her family were in the country was because he and his generals had ordered them there. A few days later she received a phone call from a rather harassed-sounding customs official. 'Mrs Payne,' he said, the exasperation evident in his voice, 'would you please come and get your car'.

Not all the Paynes' problems were solved so easily. At first Keith was happy to be at Scheyville. The training program was outstanding, the recruits wanted to be there and were eager to do the work, and he himself was increasing his knowledge and skill daily, but a few hours away by plane there was a war on, and he wanted to be part of it.

'My job was to assess and train the officer cadets and it was a great training ground for me. It was a six-months course that covered everything they would have to know to command a platoon in Vietnam. By giving the course I was effectively taking it myself, so after two and a half years I'd taken that course five times. It would have made me one of the best-trained soldiers in Vietnam but the problem was, I couldn't get there. The day Scheyville opened there were about thirty of us there, officers, NCOs and warrant officers. We were all professional soldiers and we all wanted to be in the action but the job we were doing was seen as important and once we were there we couldn't get out. Every one of us was writing letters asking to be sent to Vietnam but we might as well have screwed them up and thrown them in the bin for all the good it did us.'

Between 1965 and 1973 Scheyville produced 1871 officers, of whom some 1639 were national servicemen. Of these, 328 served in Vietnam and about 270 transferred to the regulars after their national service. At least thirteen rose to the rank of brigadier. Many Scheyville graduates also made their mark in civilian life, the best-known being Jeff Kennett, who became Premier of Victoria, and Tim Fischer, who was Deputy Prime Minister of Australia. Eight were killed in action in Vietnam.

One of these was 2nd Lieutenant Gordon Sharp, a former television cameraman who was the only officer killed at the Battle of Long Tan. Lieutenant Sharp had been commanding the lead platoon of D Company, 6RAR, on the afternoon of 18 August 1966, when it encountered a small group of Viet Cong. After a short firefight in which one Viet Cong was killed, the Australians continued to patrol the area and encountered the main body of the Viet Cong's 275 Regiment. Heavily outnumbered and unable to call in air support because of poor visibility due to monsoonal rain, D Company held off up to 2500 enemy at the loss of seventeen of their men, until reinforced by A Company, 3RAR.

According to Sharp's platoon sergeant Bob Buick who took over command of the platoon and earned the Military Medal for his action at Long Tan, the young lieutenant had died instantly when shot in the neck while crawling around under fire trying to assess the situation. His last words, to Buick, were, 'Don't worry about me'. Sharp had been a member of Payne's first graduation class from Scheyville. 'He was a bloody good little soldier,' he said.

There were plenty of 'bloody good little soldiers' who came through Scheyville's intensive and gruelling program. As one graduate, Military Cross–winner Gary McKay, described it in his book *In Good Company* (Allen & Unwin, 1998), 'There was one standard and it was excellence'.

Which was hardly surprising, given the calibre of the men in charge of the training program. They were all outstanding soldiers who had two things in common. One: they were good at what they were doing, and two: they wanted to stop doing it. Soldiers they had served with and knew well were fighting and being killed in Vietnam, and they felt their place was there with them. To add insult to injury, two of the first members of the Team had returned from Vietnam and joined the instructors at Scheyville. Their tales of what was happening in Vietnam made those at Scheyville even more frustrated at being kept out of the action. As Keith put it, 'All me mates was goin' and I wanted to be goin' too.' Easier said than done. The official lines of command were closed to the warrant officers stationed at Scheyville; the army had them where it wanted them and nobody in charge was in any hurry to let them go. With the official doors closed the warrant officers did what they have always done: they sorted things out for themselves.

Warrant Officers' Corps

'There is an unofficial Warrant Officers' Corps. It's like a secret society. Officers have been trying to break it for as long as anyone can remember and they're still trying to break it today. It's like, "Where did you get this Sergeant Major?" "Don't ask, sir." At Scheyville we had an escape committee. If we couldn't get out one way, we'd get out another. We had one of our blokes, Pat Brennan, posted in the Director of Infantries office. Pat was our inside man. He looked out for us and when something came up, he made sure it came our way. Not that everyone was patient enough to wait. The first one of us to get out was a WO named Alex von Kurtz. Alex was a German who'd come out to Australia after World War II. He was a character. He had a photographic memory. The rest of us would be studying the manuals before taking our tests. Not Alex; he'd take one look and that would be it, he'd have it all locked away upstairs. Alex was with me in the first posting to Scheyville and he wanted to get out as much as any of us. The first time he got leave he headed straight up to the base at Enoggera and said, "I'm Alex von Kurtz. I'm not AWL, I'm here and I'm not going back. I want to go to Vietnam." What could they do, put him in irons? They sent him to Vietnam.'

Payne wasn't quite as forthright as the colourful German. He didn't go over the wall, so to speak, like von Kurtz; he tunnelled his way out – via New Guinea.

'New Guinea was one of our escape routes. We were involved in another police action over there and they needed NCOs. It was a lot easier to get to Vietnam from New Guinea than it was to get there from Scheyville. When a position for a warrant officer to go to New Guinea came through his office Patty Brennan grabbed it and offered it to Norm Goldspink who was teaching drill at Scheyville. Norm was a great soldier whose name was on the shortlist to be regimental sergeant major at Duntroon but he jumped at the chance to go to New Guinea because it meant a way to get to Vietnam. Then, before he had a chance to leave, word came through that he'd been chosen for the RSM job. Pat had to tell the higher-ups that Norm had already accepted the spot in New Guinea because he wanted to get to Vietnam so they said, "Okay, fast-track him to Vietnam for six months and then he can go to Duntroon". That got Norm to Vietnam but it still left the spot in New Guinea. Patty rang Norm and asked who else he could send. Norm said to me, "Hey Payney, do you want to go to New Guinea?" I said, "Mate, I just want to get out of Scheyville". He said "No worries", and that was that. I was back into the action and one step closer to Vietnam.'

8
Escape Route

MENTION THE TERM 'COLD WAR' to anyone born after 1970 and the defining image is black and white TV footage of US and Russian soldiers staring across strands of barbed wire in divided Europe, or perhaps Soviet tanks rolling into Budapest in 1956. More recently there is the full-colour vision of the Berlin Wall being torn down in 1989. An entire genre of literature was based on the shadowy world of Soviet, British and US spies. The pervading feeling is very much of a European standoff between the superpowers but to Australians in the 1950s and 1960s the Cold War was much closer to home. In fact, the only difference between the threat of invasion during the world war of the 1940s and the Cold War version a decade later was that the identity of the potential invader had changed from Japanese to communist.

It was a threat Australians took very seriously. The wording of the newspaper advertisements calling for volunteers to serve in Korea summed up the country's feelings of nationalism and fear of the 'red menace' perfectly. 'Two year enlistment in K Force for service in Korea,' one ad read. 'No previous experience necessary. Help stop the Communist thrust south. Apply any Army Recruitment Office …'

In Korea Payne and his fellow diggers had fought the North Koreans and the Chinese. In Malaya it had been the local CTs. In New Guinea the threat came not from local communist cells, but from a far larger and potentially more powerful force, Indonesian nationalists.

The Indonesia–Malaysia Confrontation had never escalated into full-blown conflict but it had come very close. Australian, British and other Commonwealth forces had all fired at and been fired upon by Indonesian troops. Both sides had suffered casualties. It was only lack of support from factions within the Indonesian government that stopped Sukarno from pushing ahead with his threat to crush Malaysia and push South-East Asia and perhaps the world superpowers to the brink of war.

The confrontation ended towards the end of 1965 when Sukarno was overthrown in a coup d'état and replaced by General Suharto. Due to this domestic conflict, Indonesian interest in pursuing the war with Malaysia declined, and combat eased. On 28 May 1966, at a conference in Bangkok, the Malaysian and Indonesian governments declared the conflict was over. The violence ended in June, and a peace treaty was signed on 11 August and ratified two days later, but when Payne landed in New Guinea that resolution meant little. As far as the Australian public was concerned, the Papua–Irian Jaya border was still as much a symbol of good versus evil as the wall in Berlin, and it had to be patrolled and defended just as vigorously.

In time the major reason for border patrols would be so Indonesian troops could stop oppressed Irian Jayans from 'defecting' to independent Papua, but in the mid-1960s the dispute was over just how far the border extended on either side. With potentially billions of dollars worth of mining rights at stake, it was an expensive argument that the Pacific Islands Regiment was given the responsibility of fighting on Australia's behalf.

The regiment, which Payne joined in 1966, had a relatively short but glorious history as a fighting unit. It was formed in November 1944 from an amalgamation of the Papuan Infantry Battalion and the 1st and 2nd New Guinea Infantry battalions. It was awarded Australian battle honours, the first of which was the Kokoda Track. It fought in ten of the eleven Papua New Guinea campaigns of World War II, the exception being Milne Bay.

By the time Payne joined, the regiment's role was to keep the peace in the Australian territory of Papua New Guinea and train indigenous soldiers so that in time they could carry out similar duties on their own. It also patrolled the border between Papua New Guinea and Irian Jaya to ensure Indonesian forces did not infiltrate Australian territory.

Before he left Australia Payne had to undergo psychological testing to assess his suitability to work with indigenous soldiers in New Guinea. His early days in Ingham spent knocking about with local Aboriginal families and in particular Arthur Brackenbridge held Payne in good stead. Despite prevailing attitudes of the time Payne had no problems whatsoever working with indigenous soldiers. Once again the unofficial training ground of his youth had hammered a link in the chain. It served him well in New Guinea and would again in Vietnam.

Payne was ordered to report to 2nd Battalion Pacific Island Regiment headquarters in the northern coastal town of Wewak, site of some of the fiercest fighting of the New Guinea campaign of World War II. Coincidentally, it was near Wewak, twenty-one years earlier, that Ted Kenna of Hamilton, Victoria, had earned his Victoria Cross.

On 15 May 1945 Kenna (then twenty-seven) and his unit, Company A of the 2/4th Battalion, 19th Brigade, 6th Division, were pinned down by three Japanese machine-gun posts high on a hill near the Wirui Mission. With several members of his unit hit, and unable to lift his Bren gun high enough to return fire, Kenna called on a comrade to throw him his .303 rifle. Standing in full view of the enemy only 50 metres from their bunkers – so close that he could feel the wind from enemy bullets as they passed by him – Kenna picked off three Japanese gunners with the rifle and cleared out a second bunker with his Bren gun. The third bunker was destroyed by a tank and the Australian advance continued.

There was another link between Papua New Guinea and the Victoria Cross for Payne. His first act on arrival at Wewak was to report to his commanding officer, Don 'Jock' Ramsay. Formerly of 1RAR, Ramsay would later be relieved by Russell 'R.D.F.' Lloyd who would in turn move on to Vietnam to take command of the Team. Some three years later it would be Lloyd who wrote the citation for Payne's VC.

Payne would see plenty of action between his arrival at Wewak and the circumstances leading to that citation, but his initial duties in New Guinea were anything but action-packed.

'Jock Ramsay appointed me Regimental Duty Warrant Officer at headquarters. My duties included acting as regimental sergeant major when he was absent, and running NCO courses for the PIs – the local indigenous 'Pacific Island' soldiers. I was stuck down in the quarter store area writing out these courses, filling out training schedules, making stores lists of the things we'd need like tents and other equipment and interviewing potential instructors. The only problem was that the courses never happened. I'd been there three weeks when I got a call from Pat Beale.'

Beale and Payne went back a long way. When Payne was instructing at Wacol in the late 1950s, Beale arrived as a 2nd lieutenant straight out of the academy at Portsea. He would eventually win the Military Cross in Borneo and the DSO in Vietnam while commanding Payne's old battalion. When he called Payne in New Guinea he was serving as an intelligence officer in the 2nd battalion 2PIR, organising units to patrol the Star Mountains along the Irian Jaya–PNG border.

'He thought he could put me to better use than planning training courses which never came off. He said "Forget that, you're going to Vanamo".'

It had taken a while, and a circuitous route, but Payne was back in his element. On patrol in some of the harshest territory on the planet.

'We were patrolling razorback mountains like you've never seen but I couldn't have been happier. If I hadn't been commanding a mortar platoon it would have been perfect. The worst thing I ever did was a mortar course. From that day on I couldn't get away from the bloody things. I never liked the things. I was the crankiest mortarman in the army.'

The role of the Australians in the Pacific Island Regiment was very similar to that of the instructors in Vietnam. They worked alongside the PNG soldiers, training and leading at the same time. Companies would be led by one Australian officer, along with three indigenous Papuan officers. It was in this way that George Ibo, the first indigenous general in the PNG Army and a future member of parliament, had his grounding in the services. Payne was appointed company sergeant major, serving alongside an indigenous company sergeant major.

'There were very little CSM duties. My role was really second-in-command to the company commander and to lead patrols. I was basically commanding a forward platoon for the entire time I was out there. I'd look after airdrops of food and supplies and keeping an eye on the border. Because we weren't at war with Indonesia we were under very strict rules of engagement. If we came across any Indonesian patrols we weren't allowed to shoot at them except under the most serious circumstances, but some of our indigenous soldiers weren't against having a crack at them with sticks. The Indonesians would shift the pegs marking the border, and we'd pick them up and put them back where they were supposed to be. A few days later we'd go over the same ground and the pegs would be moved again.'

It wasn't just the indigenous soldiers that Payne and the other experienced NCOs were expected to train. With New Guinea seen by the military as a good training ground for Vietnam, a steady stream of young officers had their first taste of real-life soldiering in the Star Mountains. One was Laurie Lewis who went on to become a brigadier. For Payne, who would find himself commanding another group of indigenous soldiers not too far down the track, it proved an invaluable time.

'I was there for about eighteen months all up and I enjoyed the whole experience. After patrolling the Star Mountains for six weeks I was given the job of transport officer. That went back to the time I'd spent as a driver/storeman at school cadet camps after Korea. That's the thing about the army. Everything you do is on your record, there's no escaping it. This was a good thing though. I really enjoyed the role. I worked well with the officers and I got along well with the indigenous soldiers. I found the indigenous sergeants and corporals particularly good. They had 'E' badges, meaning they spoke English but it was more that I spoke a bit of pidgin and we met in the middle.

I remember showing them how to change a battery and to work out which was the positive terminal; it was like, "Name belong this same as cross belong Jesus".'

Finding a way to get things done in difficult circumstances is what a soldier's life is all about and Payne had to use all his initiative – and call once more on the unofficial Warrant Officers' Corps – to get Flo and the boys to join him in Wewak.

'When I got over there I was pleased to see there were all these brand new houses for the married quarters but when I asked about them I was told my family couldn't come over until the water was connected. What had happened was they'd built this new water scheme on the Fly River and the new houses were supposed to be supplied by that but they'd put in these rigid steel pipes and every time there was a minor earthquake – and at Wewak there were plenty – the pipes would crack. After it had happened two or three times I was told new pipes were coming over by ship from Australia but after six months there on my own I decided to take some action myself.'

Chatting to a local motor mechanic named Jimmy Crawford, Payne learned there was an old water tank lying abandoned halfway up a hill near the public hospital. With some assistance from the troops Payne got the tank to his house and set it up on a low timber stand. With a bit of patchwork and the regular afternoon downpour, the tank was full. Now all he had to do was get the water into the house.

'I went over to the engineers and asked Lieutenant 'Bing' Crosby if he could make me up a pump. He said "No worries", and with a couple of bits from here and a part or two from there, they put together a pump and a generator. I went to the battalion 2IC Major Wally Campbell and told him I had the water on and needed a call forward notice for my wife and kids. Once I had that, it was over to the Warrant Officers' Corps. I went to Warrant Officer Rex Wiggans, the signals WO at Wewak. Two other WOs, Mick Gill and Don Watts, rigged up an antenna and Rex got straight on the radio to WO John Fuge, chief clerk at Scheyville. John, who was another one who later served with the Team, rang Flo at the married quarters at Riverstone and told her to get packed. From talking to Jimmy Crawford to Flo getting the call took about a week. If I'd gone through official channels who knows how long I would have been waiting.'

Not that it was all smooth sailing for Flo and the boys.

'I had a week to pack up a house and five boys and get to New Guinea,' she said. 'We weren't sure what we'd find over there so we left Greg, the second oldest, with my sister and brother-in-law at Aspley in Brisbane so as not to disrupt his schooling too much. As it happened the schooling in Wewak was excellent because there were a number of nashos over there who were schoolteachers and they were seconded to the local school, but we weren't to know that. So I had to get up from Victoria to Queensland and fly out from Brisbane to New Guinea. Well, everything was going fine until we got to Sydney Airport and there were no tickets. It was like one of those chains where everything has to fall into place or the whole thing collapses – and here we were at the first link and the tickets weren't there.'

As the boys stood at the gate calling out 'Come on Mummy, come on Mummy', Flo and the ticketing staff made frantic phone calls to Sydney's Victoria Barracks. At the last moment, with all the other passengers seated and the door almost closed, the tickets were approved and Flo and the boys clambered aboard.

'It was raining and they had this plastic carpet down the aisle,' she recalled. 'As we went down the back of the plane they were rolling it up behind us.'

Warrant Officer Payne ensured the family's arrival in Wewak was more auspicious. As Flo and the boys walked down the steps of the plane they were met by the Pacific Island Regiment pipeband.

'We all enjoyed Wewak,' Flo said. 'I enjoyed it, the boys enjoyed it. I got a job in the office at Jimmy Crawford's garage and I had a house boy to help with the boys. It was very similar to Malaya. The boys got on well with the native kids. They'd all knock about and go fishing together. One day they brought home one of those big glass buoys off a Japanese fishing boat. We've still got it. Greg used to come over during school holidays. It was really a great experience for all of them.'

The stay was not without incident. One day the boys were roaming around, climbing trees near the rifle range, and Derek slipped down into a stinging nettle. Flo heard his screams and came out to investigate.

'He took off up the street running so fast. I stood in front of him but he wouldn't stop, he went past me as if I wasn't there and headed straight to the Regimental Aid Post, just like a good soldier would. He was six years old at the time.'

And then there was the time Jimmy Crawford decided to install a new underground tank at his garage. Flo arrived at work to find the floor pulled up directly underneath the spot where she had sat for the past few months. Jimmy and the workmen were standing with concerned looks on their faces so Flo looked down to see what the fuss was about. There, half-buried, a few metres below the floorboards was an unexploded 250-pound World War II bomb.

'Flo got the day off that day,' said Keith.

As had happened in Malaya, six months before Keith's two-year posting in New Guinea was up he received a call forward from Australia. This time it was the posting he had been hoping for. WO Payne was going to Vietnam. Destiny beckoned.

9

The Team

IN THE SIX YEARS since the first thirty-man contingent of the Australian Army Training Team Vietnam (AATTV) had arrived in country led by Lieutenant Colonel Joe Mann – the officer who had led Operation Fauna in Korea – the role of the Team had changed considerably. At first their main job was to train soldiers of the Army of the Republic of South Vietnam (ARVN). It didn't take them long to realise they had their work cut out. Although the Vietnamese were brave and resilient soldiers who carried out their duties in often shocking conditions without complaint, they were poorly trained and equipped. At times discipline was next to non-existent. In his excellent book *The Team: Australian Army Advisers in Vietnam 1962–1972* (Australian War Memorial, 1984) army research officer Ian McNeill tells the story of a high-ranking Vietnamese general arriving by helicopter to witness a major demonstration of firepower by an ARVN battalion which had just finished its training cycle under Team supervision.

> The troops were positioned along the line of a ridge, their rifles and machineguns directed towards the plain falling away in front. To one side were the artillery and mortars. On a knoll stood the small group of Australian advisers and their Vietnamese counterparts.

As the general's helicopter approached, a single shot rang out, then another and another. The officers stood dumbfounded. No one had given the order to open fire, but by now the gunfire was intense. As the Australians looked down in disbelief, some of the soldiers began to break ranks and run down the hill, leaving their weapons behind as others continued firing at a mystery target. And then the Australians saw it: a scared rabbit, dodging through the spurts of dust made as bullets hit the ground. More soldiers joined the chase and finally one group of men surrounded their prey and grabbed it, returning to their position smiling and laughing, one holding it above his head in triumph as others cheered.

> The whole carnival episode had lasted only about 20 minutes, but it was enough to have the strike aircraft aborted and the plan for artillery and mortar fire thrown into chaos. The advisers could do little but look on dismayed. But no one else seemed to worry unduly and several lucky soldiers anticipated rabbit with their rice that night. This then was the army that the Australian jungle instructors had come to advise. (McNeill, *The Team*)

The first contingent of the Team was divided into four groups, three in the northern provinces of Vietnam and one on the central coast. Three of the groups were stationed at training centres that were set up and operated by the US Army. One centre was established to train ARVN recruits, another trained Civil Guard and Self-Defence volunteers and the third was based at the Range Training Centre at Duc My.

The fourth group, initially based at Danang, was given the job of training village defenders, border forces and trail-watchers recruited from the local indigenous population, the Montagnards.

In the two years he spent in Darlac Province from 1963, Payne's fellow North Queenslander Barry Petersen had turned his Montagnard Strike Force from a badly organised, disinterested group of a few hundred men into a well-trained force of around 1000. It was renamed the Truong Son Force after the area in which it operated and a special badge bearing a tiger insignia was struck. Supported initially by Warrant Officer Danny Neville and then Warrant Officer

Bevan Stokes, Captain Petersen organised his men into small units which patrolled the area, trained local militia, reported enemy movements and, if confronted, would engage in hit-and-run tactics against the larger North Vietnamese forces. By the end of his posting Petersen's rolling budget, funded by the CIA, had grown from US$350 to US$50,000. He had established hospitals, schools and even a performance group that presented traditional Montagnard songs and dances throughout the villages. All this was aimed at winning the trust of the Montagnards and keeping them from shifting their allegiance to the North Vietnamese. He was successful, but at a cost. Petersen's Truong Son Force was adopted as the blueprint for other mobile strike forces in neighbouring provinces but by the time Payne arrived in Vietnam Petersen himself was long gone. As far as the local Vietnamese authorities were concerned Petersen had become too close to the *moi*. When he was called in by the Montagnards as an intermediary to help put down their attempted revolt against South Vietnamese authorities, his standing with the local government suffered a blow. When it became known he had been approached by Montagnard leaders exiled in Cambodia, asking for US military aid supposedly to help fight the North Vietnamese, his luck ran out. The South Vietnamese considered the Montagnard problem an internal issue, of no interest to the Americans or Australians. Petersen was told by his superiors that the South Vietnamese government wanted him out of the area.

Petersen was farewelled from Darlac in November 1965 at a tribal ceremony in which buffaloes were sacrificed and he was proclaimed a chieftain. The Montagnards had lost their greatest advocate but their mobile attack teams, collectively known as Mike Force – or M-Force – would continue to serve under the umbrella of the US Special Forces, often led by Australian members of the Team – Keith Payne among them. Once he could finally get over there, that is.

When the Paynes arrived back in Brisbane from New Guinea, Keith went for an interview and medical to assess his suitability for joining the Team. It would have seemed a mere formality. After eighteen months in the New Guinea jungle, climbing up and down razorback mountains and leading border patrols for months at a time Payne was, at thirty-five, in the prime of physical health, wiry and strong. In his own words he was 'as fit as a mallee bull'. What he didn't know was that years of active service and training with various firearms from rifles to mortars had affected his hearing. Unable to register very high-pitched sounds, he failed the medical.

Flo was ironing when he arrived home.

'I took one look at his face and I thought, Uh oh. When he told me he might not be going I didn't know whether to be happy or sad. Of course I didn't want him to go but I wonder now what would have been worse, having him go or living with him if he couldn't. He wanted to go so badly. Even when we were out in New Guinea he was mentally preparing to go to Vietnam. That's the thing, he was a soldier through and through and if Australians were fighting somewhere, that's where he felt he belonged. It would have been very hard on all of us if he'd had to stay behind. I just don't how he could have settled. He already had post-traumatic stress disorder as far as I'm concerned. He'd had it since Korea. It's just that people didn't recognise it back then. Still, it never came to that. I remember him saying to me that day, "There's more than one way to skin a cat". The old mates system came into play. The director of infantry at the time was Lieutenant Colonel Dave Allen. He'd been Keith's company commander when he was serving with 3RAR in Brisbane in the early 1960s. Keith got on to him and it was all settled. Keith was going.'

It was now late 1968 and the Team's original thirty-man contingent had grown to around a hundred, made up of fifteen officers and eighty-five warrant officers. But the size of the training team was by no means the biggest change in Australia's involvement. Vietnam was no longer just an advisory role for the Australian Army. Things had escalated.

As Ian McNeill recounts in his book, when Colonel O.D. Jackson arrived in Vietnam in January 1965 to take over control of the AATTV program from original commanding officer, Colonel F.

Serong, he undertook a two-month familiarisation tour, visiting every area where Australians were deployed. In an interview in 1972 he told McNeill:

> The impression I gained, a very real impression, was the war was lost from a military point of view. I am talking February to March 1965. Wherever I went there were Vietnamese Army forces on hilltops, behind barbed wire. They very rarely went outside that wire. If they did go outside to relieve one post by another they were frequently ambushed in strength by the VC – and it was nothing for a whole battalion or more of South Vietnamese troops to be butchered.
>
> There was very little in the way of offensive action anywhere in the South Vietnamese Army; the Viet Cong were thoroughly on top from a military point of view. I would have said it was just a matter of weeks or months before the war was lost in South Vietnam. It was as bad as that in my opinion, and a lot of people agreed with me.
> (McNeill, *The Team*)

Just two months earlier the US Army had doubled the number of its advisers to 16,000, bringing the total of US uniformed personnel in Vietnam to 23,000. In February the Viet Cong launched a well-planned attack on the US advisers' compound at Pleiku and destroyed the US enlisted men's billet at Qui Nhon. The United States responded with airstrikes on North Vietnam. Finally, on 6 March 1965, US President Johnson gave the go-ahead for US combat troops to be deployed to Vietnam. Two days later US marines waded ashore at Danang, to be followed by more troops. On 29 April, prime minister Robert Menzies announced that Australian troops would also be sent to Vietnam. The days of the Australian observer were over. The Team was now in the front line, and Payne was itching to be in the action.

'Once I was accepted for the Team I had to wait around for the start of an advisers' course so I could do my training for Vietnam. While I was waiting I was posted to the Northern Command Training Cell at Wacol where we were putting CMF volunteers through an officers' course. When I'd been stuck in Japan waiting to go to Korea in 1951 I'd been trained on the Vickers machine gun so I was training people on that as well. The Vickers was used to supply overhead fire for troops in training. We had them with their tripods cemented into place so they supplied fire at the exact right height. I was at Wacol through October 1968, and then the advisers' course started at Canungra.'

The fourteen-day advisers' course brought Keith and his fellow warrant officers up to date on the tactical situation the length and breadth of Vietnam. They were briefed on the geographical and political lie of the land and lectured on enemy objectives and tactics. From there they were sent for another two weeks to a language course in South Australia.

'They were teaching us Vietnamese but as far as I was concerned it would have been a lot more helpful if I'd been taught French so I could converse with the Yards who spoke a bit of that. Either way, I wasn't much of a linguist. Just about the only thing I learned to say was *co*, which means 'girl'. At the end of the course we had to go around to all these tables where they pointed to different things and asked us to say what they were in Vietnamese. I just went around saying "*Co, co, co*" and they said, "Yeah okay, you pass". I think we were a lot more interested in the fact that we got weekends off and the Barossa Valley wineries weren't too far away.'

Things got more serious when the warrant officers returned to the Jungle Training Centre at Canungra. For three weeks without a day off they were up at six every morning to be put through a full day of field exercises covering navigation, ambush, harbouring, patrolling and shooting. Living in tents on a site known as Scale A Ridge, it was physically gruelling but hugely satisfying. For Payne, in particular, it was just like old times. After all, it was a shortened version of the six-month course he had given five times as an instructor at Scheyville. By the time he was ready to go to Vietnam he felt he couldn't have been better prepared. Only one hurdle remained: saying goodbye to his family.

'By now the boys were getting bigger and it was getting harder and harder to leave. I said to them: "This is the last time", but it wasn't. When I left I couldn't help but wonder if I'd ever see them again.'

According to Flo, saying goodbye to their father as he went off to war was just a regular part of the boys' lives.

'It had been happening for as long as they could remember. Keith was always going away for one thing or another. He'd go off on training courses for six to eight weeks at a time and when we were in Malaya and New Guinea he'd go off on patrol for a month. For their Dad to go away was nothing unusual. When he went to Vietnam they knew their father was going to be away for twelve months and they weren't happy but it was part and parcel of their lives. They accepted it. It didn't seem to scar them too much. Ron actually joined the navy when he was older and then had eleven years in the Army Reserves. The rest of them, if ever they were asked if they'd thought about going into the army used to say, "No, we got out the same day as Dad".'

10

In Country

ON 11 JANUARY 1969 Keith and Flo left the boys with her mother and flew to Sydney, staying with the parents of a friend at Brighton Le Sands for two nights before he left. Flo saw him off at Sydney Airport and watched from the observation deck as he boarded his Qantas flight, looking for all the world like a tourist heading off on holidays.

'We all went together, WOs, diggers, nursing sisters. There was some law that meant we couldn't wear uniform flying over Indonesia so we were all in civvies. Well, almost in civvies. We had on our uniform trousers with casual shirts hanging out. You didn't have to be Einstein to work out we were soldiers. We all had short hair and there were indents on our faces from our chin-straps. We got changed during a refuelling stop in Singapore and when we landed in Saigon we were ready for anything. The first thing that hit me when we landed was the smell. South-East Asia always smells like South-East Asia.'

The second thing Payne noticed as he walked down the stairs of the plane was the poor shape of the airport. There were bomb craters on disused tarmacs and damage to hangars and administrative buildings. Evidence of the Tet Offensive, the massive Viet Cong attack that began on New Year's Eve 1968 and was not fully extinguished for almost six months, was everywhere. As Payne put it in classic understatement, 'The country was in bad shape'. Despite the damage to the airfield it was still operating at full capacity. General aviation and military aircraft were taking off and landing every thirty seconds.

'The noise was incredible. The heat, the smell, it was all happening. You felt pretty safe at the airport though. There were flak batteries all over the place and everyone was heavily armed. We were loaded on buses that had mesh over the door and windows in case someone tried to throw a grenade in and the driver was surrounded by sandbags to protect him from mines. It all gave you the impression that this was one place the enemy couldn't get you, but after the war they found out that the Viet Cong had tunnelled their way right underneath.'

Payne and other warrant officers headed for the Team were taken to the Rex Hotel in downtown Saigon where they dumped their bags before going straight to army headquarters to be issued with gear and briefed by John Grey, who had been chief instructor at Canungra. Sitting in the corner, listening in but not saying a word, was the newly arrived Lieutenant Colonel R.D.F. Lloyd MC who would take over command of the Team in a matter of days.

'Before I'd left Australia I'd been told that I was going to be serving with US Special Forces but I didn't know how or where,' Payne recalled. 'It was at that briefing that I found out I was joining Mike Force at a place called Pleiku.'

The US Special Forces were formed in World War II when a unit of US and Canadian soldiers was trained to operate in snow-covered terrain, especially in German-occupied Norway. Made up of three regiments of two battalions each, the 1st Special Service Force became a separate branch of the service, with the crossed arrows of the Indian scouts as its insignia. The men were trained in demolition, rock-climbing, amphibious assault, and ski techniques and given basic airborne instruction. They fought in the Aleutians, North Africa, Southern France and Italy, where they earned the nickname 'The Devil's Brigade' from a passage found in the diary of a dead German officer.

US Special Forces troops began working in Vietnam in 1957, with a team from the 1st Special Forces Group training fifty-eight Vietnamese Army soldiers at Nha Trang, the coastal town in the Central Highlands where Special Forces would eventually make its headquarters. These trainees would later become the nucleus, as instructors and NCOs, for the first Vietnamese Special Forces units.

As American involvement in Vietnam grew, US President John F. Kennedy took a particular interest in the Special Forces program, believing it had great potential as a counter-insurgency force ideal for the situation in South-East Asia. President Kennedy made a personal visit to Special Forces headquarters at Fort Bragg, North Carolina, to review the program. It was by his authorisation that troops were allowed to wear the distinctive headgear that became the symbol of the Special Forces, the green beret.

The recruitment of the Montagnard tribesmen by the CIA from October 1961 was the first step in a broad-based initiative that utilised the paramilitary potential of some of the country's minority ethnic groups. Special Forces detachments provided training and advisory assistance to these programs, which eventually came to be known collectively as the Civilian Irregular Defense Group (CIDG) program.

In November 1961 the first medical specialist troops of the Special Forces were employed to provide assistance to the Montagnard tribes in the high-plateau country around Pleiku, about 300 kilometres north of Nha Trang. Out of this modest beginning grew one of the most successful programs for using civilian forces ever devised by a military force. Eventually the organisation, development, and operation of the CIDG proved to be the chief work of the US Special Forces in the Vietnam War and the Montagnards' mobile strike units – Mike Force – its crowning glory. By 1965 the camp that Barry Petersen had built at Ban Me Thuot was just one of around fifty in the Central Highlands.

After being informed of his posting to Mike Force in Saigon, Payne and three other members of the Team, Mick Gill – one of the warrant officers who had built the antenna so Keith could get Flo to New Guinea – Jock Kelly and Don Cameron, were flown to Nha Trang where they received a briefing from a Special Forces officer. They were educated on the history of the Montagnards and of the role they now played as mercenaries operating as mobile strike force units under the command of US and Australian officers. They were also updated on the current situation in the Central Highlands, with Special Forces teams charged with stopping the advance of communist forces from the north and infiltration from over the Laos and Cambodian borders. Camps were set up close to the border, with Mike Force units providing support. The Mike Force companies operated out of headquarters in Ban Me Thuot, Dau Tien and, the largest, at Pleiku. The Montagnard soldiers lived in their villages and came into camp when required for training or in preparation for operations.

Before they could join their units Payne and the other three Australians were sent for a week's training and orientation on Hon Tre Island in Nha Trang Bay.

'It was where we were taught the American way of doing things. We were professional soldiers but we had to learn how to fit in with the US system. There were little things like the way they talked on the radio. We used the same phonetic alphabet but there were different words to sign off and acknowledge a message, that sort of thing. We also had to get up to speed on the American weapons. We'd been trained on the AK47 at Canungra but when we arrived in Vietnam we were issued with an M16 Armalite rifle. We had to learn about the enemy's weapons as well. You can talk about what to expect back home in Australia all you like, but it's not until you are on the ground in country that you really find out what's what. Another thing they wanted to teach us was how to be picked up by a helicopter in a McGuire Rig, which was basically a long rope with a loop on the end. We never got to do that. The training program was supposed to last a week but we were called up after two days because reinforcements were so urgently needed. I suppose we were pretty cocky bastards back then. We were young and fit and looking forward to getting into it. The adrenaline was flowing and we were joking with the instructors. I remember when we left early the guy in charge of the McGuire Rig training looked genuinely disappointed. He said, "Man, that's a pity. I was looking forward to dragging your ass through the dirt". I guess he made up for it by going hard on the next blokes who came through.'

The course prematurely over, the Aussies headed to Pleiku to join their battalions. Of those four men Keith Payne would win the Victoria Cross, Don Cameron the Distinguished Conduct Medal, Mick Gill the Military Medal and Jock Kelly would be Mentioned in Dispatches. Sadly, not all would return home. Mick Gill was killed on 11 May in the action in which his company commander Ray Simpson won the Victoria Cross.

'When we got to Pleiku we were met by the training company commander who took us over to Mike Force headquarters. Mike Force was located at the northern end of Pleiku Airstrip and it was our responsibility to protect that sector. Jock introduced me to the Mike Force commander, US Special Forces Captain Green, who gave me my assignment. He told me I would be company commander of 212 Company, one of three companies in the Mobile Strike Force 1st Battalion. That was when I realised. I remember thinking to myself, Hey brother, you've got yourself a company. The battalion commander was Captain Art Austin, an American. I met him and he told me I'd better get ready quick because I was going out on operation in a few hours.

'The first member of my company I met was Kev Latham, my forward platoon commander and executive officer. Kev was an acting warrant officer who had served with the SAS. He hadn't seen any action with them but I was bloody happy to have an ex-SAS man as my XO. He was carrying a little 60 millimetre mortar along with his rifle and other gear and looked like he could handle himself.'

Payne was right with his first impression. Latham could handle himself. He got through Vietnam unscathed, before dying in Australia in 2005 at the age of sixty-four.

'With the operation coming up I headed straight over to the Q Store to start organising my equipment. That was when I was issued with my Special Forces tiger camouflage fatigues, some sets of American greens and a green beret. I had three of them at one stage but I only know where one of them is now. It's in the Australian War Memorial museum in Canberra. They've got it insured for only $500.

'When I was in the Q Store I bumped into this bloke who took one look at me and said "Dammit, you've got my company". I thought he was an American. I introduced myself and he told me his name was Barry Tolley. Turned out he was actually an Australian temporary warrant officer who had been a platoon commander and XO to Captain David Savage, the previous commander of 212 Company. Savage had already left when I got there but I found out later that he and Tolley hadn't gotten along. There had been a bit of a conflict of command. I suppose Tolley felt he would get the command when Savage left and he wasn't all that happy when I arrived and took over his men. He moved over to command 211 Company. My first impression of him at that moment wasn't great, but he turned out to be a good soldier and a good commander – and he saved my arse twice.'

With the changes in the three companies – Tolley taking over the 211th, Payne the 212th and US Special Forces Sergeant First Class Anastacio Montez, a 39-year-old Mexican American, commanding the 213st – battalion headquarters had ordered a 'shakedown' exercise to allow the Montagnards to get used to their new commanders and the officers to find out the capabilities of their men.

For Payne this was even more important than for the others. A few months before he arrived, the 212 Company he now commanded had been badly shot up on an operation to relieve a Special Forces camp close to the Cambodian border. Manned by around 200 Montagnard soldiers, a South Vietnamese Special Forces detachment and US advisers, the camp at Duc Lap was about 200 kilometres south of Pleiku. In mid-August 1968 the North Vietnamese Army had begun an offensive to wipe out the Special Forces outposts along the border and the camp at Duc Lap came under attack from superior NVA forces. The 212th, 213th and 221st companies of Mike Force were dispatched from Pleiku to rescue the camp.

By the time the Mike Force reinforcements arrived the camp was already partially occupied by NVA forces. The original plan was for the 212th to provide support for the 213th and 221st as they attacked under air cover but the first two companies received heavy casualties as they approached the camp perimeter across open ground and were forced to withdraw. Believing the camp could not hold out much longer, Captain Savage decided to continue the mission alone. Having seen what happened to the earlier attempt to reach the camp many of Savage's Montagnards were unwilling to leave their position. With the support of Tolley and his fellow platoon leaders Geoff Smith and Laurie Jackson, plus the Montagnard leader R'Com Toget, Savage managed to rally about a third of his troops and make a dash for the camp fence. When they reached the large barbed-wire gate it was found to be chained and padlocked. Exposed to heavy enemy fire, the Montagnards were attempting to dismantle the wire when one of their countrymen inside the camp jumped from cover and ran over, unlocking the gate, allowing Savage and his troops to rush inside. Seeing the gate open the rest of the 212th charged across the open ground and took their place in the trenches. Throughout the day, strengthened by some of the 221st who had joined them, the 212th spearheaded the defence of the camp. Twice the next morning the North Vietnamese attacked in force but were driven back. Around midday, almost twenty-four hours since Savage had led the charge to the fence, reinforcements arrived from Pleiku and Nha Trang and the camp was saved.

The ferocious action at Duc Lap had two consequences for Payne when he took over command of the 212th. First, it had brought Tolley and his men close together, as only the experience of facing death together can, and second it had made the Montagnards wary of entering such dangerous territory again. The first sign of the closeness between Tolley and the indigenous soldiers was evidenced when Payne met him the day he arrived at Pleiku. The Australian warrant officer was understandably peeved that it was a newcomer, and not he who was taking command of the company he knew so well but those feelings were soon forgotten as both men got on with the job.

The second part of the exercise would be Payne earning the respect of his men by convincing them that this new Australian was an officer worth following into battle.

The first step in that process began just hours after Payne arrived in camp. He had been told he was taking his company out on operations the next day, but he still hadn't met any of them. In fact, he had yet to lay eyes on a Montagnard soldier.

'I told Kev Latham to form the company up first thing the next morning. They all stayed in villages in the country outside the camp, living with their families and carrying on their traditional lives. We had 126 of them on our books but you were never sure how many would actually show up. It depended on what the operation was and how much they wanted the money. We paid them around $30 a month, which was good money, and they would get paid more depending on what happened on the operation. If they saw action they'd get a bit more, if they captured weapons or there were enemy casualties, a bit more again. We never told them where we were headed. Especially after Duc Lap, if we told them we were going somewhere hot like Ben Het we wouldn't get anyone turning up. That's why when they did arrive we locked the compound gate.'

The first Montagnard Payne met was the 212th's indigenous company commander and interpreter R'Com Toget, who had acted so admirably at Duc Lap.

'Toget's main role was to translate between me and Kev and the other Special Forces officers and the Yards. He was a good man, very brave, very smart, with excellent English, but to start with his idea of his position in the scheme of things and mine were different. He thought he was running the show. We sorted that out pretty quick.'

Latham put out the word and sixty-five Yards arrived in camp at 9 a.m. to prepare for the operation. Payne looked at his first command and liked what he saw.

'They looked pretty young but I knew what they'd been through at Duc Lap and I knew they had handled themselves well. They were physically small and very different in appearance to the Vietnamese, with darker skin and coarser features. For a long time they'd been pushed around. They couldn't have a say in how the country was run and the Vietnamese would push them off their land if they wanted it. It was like they were non-people as far as the Vietnamese were concerned, especially the North Vietnamese who had virtually banished them to the south. That was their big motivation for fighting with us. They liked the money, but there was a lot more to it than that. They saw the war as their big opportunity to improve their lot. They wanted some political influence and because of what had happened in North Vietnam they hated the NVA – or Viet Minh as they called them from the old French days. Not that they were fussed on the South Vietnamese either. They weren't backward in shooting up any stray ARVN if the opportunity presented itself.'

Throughout the day Payne watched on as the Yards were issued with their equipment and rations and test fired their weapons. Along with Tolley and Montez he attended a briefing at the Intelligence Office in which they received the orders of operation, radio codes and details of artillery support. They then went to Mike Force Club, a virtual clubhouse reserved for AATTV members and US Special Forces, to make up their maps and sort out the finer details of the operation. Wherever the Team was stationed a Team House would be set up where the Aussies could congregate between operations, receive mail and drink Australian beer. Team House in Pleiku also told the story of how the campaign was faring – and the reason why Payne and his fellow Team members had been called away from their training course early and rushed into the operation area.

'When a member of the Team was seconded to Special Forces he was given a wooden plaque with the arrowhead insignia and details of his name and unit. If he was killed that plaque was put on the wall of Team House. That wall at Pleiku was covered in those shields and as 1969 went on more and more went up there. We never found out what happened to them after the war. It is something which has upset a lot of people over the years.'

The mission might have been viewed as a 'shakedown' but was still a very serious operation. The three companies would be dropped by helicopter and embark on a five-day sweep through tough and mountainous terrain before being airlifted out. Tolley's company would be dropped first and establish a base. The other two companies would be taken further in country and push back, the aim being to herd any enemy forces towards Tolley's blocking force.

At first light Payne's company was loaded into three helicopters for the ride to the landing zone (LZ) in a convoy of nine choppers. Kev Latham was in the first, Payne and his headquarters group in the third. All went well – right up until the time Payne was about to land.

'The plan was that Kev would go in first and pop a yellow smoke canister if the area was clear, or cold. If it was hot and the enemy was around, he'd pop red smoke. The first chopper went in, Kev and his platoon jumped off and headed for cover and up came the yellow smoke, no problems. Number two went in and my 'copter was just coming in when up came red smoke. It was crack, crack, crack, bullets flying around everywhere. It was bloody on.'

Payne had just learned his first lesson about Vietnam. As in, there are no secrets. His Yards might not have known where they were going – or so he assumed – but that didn't mean the enemy didn't. The Viet Cong had eyes and ears everywhere. In weeks to come Payne would learn that a small welcoming committee was part and parcel of just about every helicopter insertion in Vietnam. Invariably when the choppers landed, a party of three or four enemy snipers was waiting, firing off a few rounds before disappearing into the undergrowth.

It became a pattern of the Vietnam War, as the US pioneered a new form of warfare, known as 'air mobility'. American H-21 helicopters had been used to ferry ARVN troops into battle as early as 1962 and at first the enemy had pulled back when the troop-carrying choppers landed. The enemy soon learned, however, that the helicopters were extremely vulnerable to ground fire. Despite this the Americans intensified their use of helicopters, with some operations involving over 100 aircraft. Large troop transport helicopters like the CH-47 Chinook were developed especially for this purpose but it was the workhorse UH-1 'Huey' which became synonymous with the Vietnam War. Also used in Vietnam was the AH-1 Cobra gunship which could be equipped with gatling guns, grenade launchers, rockets, or even guided missiles to provide air support to troops on the ground. The benefits of 'air mobility' were obvious: troops could be dropped into enemy territory and removed after the objective was won. They could be resupplied, casualties could be evacuated and ground troops could be supported by gunships – but it came at a great cost. Between 1962 and 1973 the US lost 4869 helicopters, with 1000 lost in 1969 alone. Of these 53 per cent were lost to enemy fire, the rest from operational accidents caused by mechanical breakdown and the difficulty of landing and taking off in jungle areas – especially if that jungle hid enemy snipers – as Payne soon found. Not even yet on firm ground in his first operation, he was under fire.

'Kev and the Yards were returning fire and we landed in one piece. I went over to the perimeter to try to work out how big the enemy force was. There was a hell of a lot of firing, but most of it going out from our side. From what I could work out there was only about three or four of the enemy and they withdrew after a couple of minutes without any casualties. It was all pretty worrying for me because there was a lot of ammo going out but no one was hitting anything. That meant one of two things. Either my men weren't marksmen, or they were hitting the panic button. Maybe a bit of both. They were certainly still on a high after Duc Lap and everything was happening at a million miles an hour. No one had settled down and tried to pick out a target; they'd just pulled the trigger and kept pulling it until we got them to stop. It was the first part of a pretty steep learning curve for all of us. I had to find out what their efficiencies were and they had to learn to trust me.'

The learning curve got even steeper over the next few days. After the early excitement of the hot landing, Payne and Latham calmed the men and headed off towards the area of operation, a mountainous region of steep hills and deep gullies. The company fell easily into the familiar four-diamond formation which Payne had learned as a recruit training for Korea and which could easily be changed to different formations to suit the terrain. Latham and Toget led the way with the forward platoon, the signals team went with the platoon on the left, heavy weapons on the right and the medic with his platoon at the rear. The Headquarters, led by Payne and his radio man, a Yard whose unusual height of around 5'11" had earned him the nickname 'Big John', were in the centre. It was just one of many Australian jungle warfare tactics which the Americans adopted in Vietnam, earning the Aussies the nickname 'The Professionals'.

On day three of the operation Payne's company came to a clearing on a ridge and uncovered a track leading down another spur-line. Payne called the platoon commanders in.

'We'll go down there and clear the spur-line,' he said.

Toget stood and shook his head.

'No,' he said. 'We don't go down there.'

Payne cocked his head.

'Oh really?' he said, and gestured to Toget to follow him out of earshot of the others.

'I took him to one side and told him I was commanding this company and I wanted him to cooperate fully. I said he could give advice if he felt it was needed, but I wanted him to act on my orders. He thought about it for a second or two but then he nodded and we went back to the others and from that moment on we got on famously.'

The company headed down the spur-line and found nothing but an abandoned hut. Payne ordered a cordon and search operation, then had the men comb the area looking for booby traps and any caches of weapons or food that may have been hidden in the area. Nothing was found but with every task he set them Payne was assessing the Yards' competency and they were assessing his. From the village they headed back up the hill and kept following the ridge. After some time they found another track that had obviously been used recently. Payne ordered the men to set up a linear ambush, with electronically triggered claymore mines positioned across the path. Eventually a small patrol of NVA soldiers walked along the track and the ambush worked perfectly – except for one thing. Nothing was hit. Again there was plenty of shooting by the Yards, but no casualties.

'There was probably three of them but there was some noise and they jumped off the track and disappeared – not that it stopped our blokes. Bullets were flying everywhere, everyone was yelling and running around but nobody was hitting a thing except trees. We stayed there overnight and the next morning I went around and had a look at the trees and there were very few bullets that would have hit the enemy unless they were about 10 foot tall. From there we moved on and met up with the other two companies at the base camp Tolley had set up. We had two and a half days there and it was probably the most beneficial part of the whole exercise. We had plenty of ammo left so we took the men out to a clear area, set up some targets and found out what they could do. We had M62 mortars and M79 rockets. Kev took the mortar men and put them through their paces. The results were pretty average. I wanted a strike rate of 75 per cent. What we had was around 25 to 30 per cent. The machine-gun competency was a bit better. We had four machine guns to a platoon, with three men operating them – one to shoot, one to feed the ammunition belts and the third to provide the ammo and protect the others. From what we saw over those two and a half days, the level was acceptable, apart from weapon handling when clearing stoppages. We didn't have a chance to test the riflemen but from what I'd seen on the operation maybe it was better not to know.'

The company was airlifted back to Pleiku and Payne reported to Captain Art Austin, passing on his concerns about the poor level of weapon competency. Austin immediately pulled the 212th out of the line and gave them a week's training in the Pleiku Airstrip area. Payne concentrated on weapons handling and the accuracy of the riflemen. They worked on staying calm in action and picking targets rather than spraying bullets in the general vicinity of the enemy.

'At the end of the week the machine-gun groups and mortarmen were up to scratch but the riflemen were still terrible. I had the armourer come in and check the weapons because the accuracy was so poor I thought there must be something wrong with the firearms. Unfortunately there wasn't. It was the men. First off I had them shoot at human-shape targets from a lying position. The rounds that did hit the targets were scattered, there was no pattern at all. There were probably only two in each squad who you would class as competent. From the sitting position it was even worse. The strike rate was atrocious. By the end of the week, after plenty of work, I'd worked out the pattern. We'd got to the stage where maybe three out of eight could achieve a strike rate of 75 per cent and no amount of work was going to help the others.'

Payne decided to elevate the competent riflemen, rather than try to bring the lesser marksmen up in standard.

'I picked out the best two or three in each squad and called them Snipers. We trained so that in case of an attack they would lie on the ground, aim and shoot. The others would put down suppressing and neutralising fire. The idea was that most of the men would just do what they had always done – fire away in the hope of hitting something – while the snipers would concentrate on picking out the enemy and getting a clear shot off. During training we used to say to the snipers "One shot–one kill". It became like their motto. There was a lot of pride involved. They were the ones who had been picked out and it made them feel special. They used to walk past us and hold up one finger and say "One shot–one kill". They felt like the elite.'

At the end of the training week Payne felt his company was competent enough in movement, formation and weapon handling to meet the enemy. They moved back to Pleiku compound for a refit of clothing and issue of new weapons. Payne went to see Captain Austin again. His report was short and clear.

'212 Company ready for operational duty, sir.'

11
Operational

WHILE THE TIME SPENT training was vital to the competent operation of the company, ultimately more important was the bond of trust and respect that was slowly growing between Payne and the Montagnards. The small clash of wills between Payne and Toget on the first operation had been handled quietly and resolved quickly, but it had been witnessed by the Yards who had seen their leader back down to the 'round eye'. By agreeing to follow Payne's commands Toget could have suffered some loss of face among his fellow tribesmen. As soon as the company returned to Pleiku, Payne gave Toget a chance to restore his reputation in the eyes of the Montagnards.

'The Yards used to get paid once a month but we liked to do it as soon as they got back from an operation. It was good that the act of receiving money was linked to them going out and actually doing the work. It was also easier to keep track of what everyone was owed when the operation was clear in the memory. The money came from the CIA and was sitting in the bank and I'd go along and collect it in a beer carton when it was due. The only problem was that the bank used to pay us for whatever number of Yards Kev had on his books. If it was ninety-seven, we'd get pay for ninety-seven even if only sixty-five had gone on the operation. The first time they did it I tried to give them some back but they didn't want to know about it, so we just put the extra into the company funds box and after it had built up a bit we'd buy some pigs or rice for the men's village.'

On their return from that first operation Payne arrived back from the bank with the pay. He handed it to Toget and told him to distribute it.

'No Penn,' he said, 'you pay'.

Payne pushed the box back firmly.

'No Toget. You pay.'

The argument ended, the beer box stayed in Toget's hands, and his face was very much restored. Not only had Payne shown the Yards that he trusted Toget, he had also given him enormous power over the men because as well as paying the wages, Toget could also instigate fines on those who had not fulfilled their duties to his satisfaction.

'There were little things. Someone might show up late or even head for home before the operation was over. Toget would keep an eye on them. He knew if they had done what they claimed to have done in battle, whether they had really shot one of the enemy or found some weapons. It worked both ways. Toget would pay them and reward them but he'd also fine them. When that happened he'd take it straight out of the pay and put it in the company fund.'

The deepening relationship between the two and the growing respect felt by the Montagnards for Payne and the other round eyes were illustrated in many ways over the months. One of the first was when Payne and Latham were invited by Toget to visit the village longhouse and partake of some rice wine. For the two Australians the prospect of sharing a few drinks with their new comrades was hardly daunting. Members of the Team considered themselves experts in everything they did. Being accomplished drinkers was every bit as much a part of the legend as their feats on the battlefield, but rice wine at a Montagnard longhouse was a very different story to beers in the sergeants' mess.

In his book *Tiger Men: An Australian Soldier's Secret War in Vietnam* (Craftsman Press, Bangkok, 1998), originally published twenty-three years after he had farewelled his troops in Ban Me Thuot, Barry Petersen gave an eyewitness report of a night drinking rice wine at a Montagnard longhouse.

Rice wine is made by boiling rice, adding yeast and other substances and allowing the mixture to ferment in large earthenware jars, covered with rice husks and banana leaves. Fermentation of the glutinous mess occurs after one or two months but can continue for up to 18 months. Water is added to the base about 20 minutes before drinking.

In the matriarchal Montagnard society, the senior lady in the longhouse is, by protocol, the first to drink. She uses a bamboo straw, drinks a little then hands it to the honoured guest. It has to be passed from right hand to right hand, with a hand always on the straw.

Then the male head of the longhouse tells the guest how many containers of rice wine he is to drink. A figure between five and nine is not unusual but generally impossible to achieve. A young lad generally keeps count of the corresponding number of containers he needs to use to keep the jar brim-full. The number of containers nominated by the host is a sort of hospitable challenge to the guest.

The rice wine is a little like cider in taste, whether it be sweet, sour or bitter cider. It is very filling and after drinking four or five glasses through a straw in one go I usually felt as though it was running out of my ears. There are few ways to escape drinking the nominated number of containers and the uninitiated generally returns bloated with rice wine to the sleeping mat, the hand-woven blanket and the cushion provided for his comfort.

My first heavy rice wine-drinking session was a disaster. It was late afternoon when we arrived at a village a short distance from Ban Me Thuot. By the time the rice wine jars were ready it was already dark. My hosts seemed to be honoured by my visit, and I wanted to do the right thing by them. On being invited to the jar I was told by my host that I must drink seven or eight glasses of rice wine before I could hand the jar over. Now that's a lot of liquid in anybody's language.

I struggled through as much as I could physically hold, then I pleaded to be allowed to hand the jar over. My request was granted and I uncomfortably made my way back to my mat, my insides totally awash. As other drinkers took over the rice wine jars, to my horror they began to send me glasses of wine from their jars. At that stage, food was being served and I received a bowl of rice with portions of meat and raw offal, and some fresh blood. As diplomatically as I could I ate some of the food and drank a little more wine until I felt I was about to explode. One of my Montagnard offsiders then nudged me to indicate I was about to be invited to partake of another jar. Suddenly I began to have difficulty in holding down the vast amount of liquid and food I had already consumed. All I wanted to do was get rid of it. The fight between my mind and my gullet to hold it down was causing me to perspire heavily. I knew I had to get out of the heavy, smoke-laden atmosphere – and quickly. I mumbled an excuse and, getting to my feet, made a rush for the door.

Longhouses are built on stilts and ascent or descent is by means of a pole with stepped notches cut into it. As I lunged across the veranda my paramount thought was to get down to the ground below as quickly as possible. I did just that as I cartwheeled over the high veranda edge. And as I sailed into space my mind finally lost that fight with my gullet.

Payne's introduction to rice wine was less dramatic but equally memorable – and just as symbolic. While at the village Toget presented Payne with a brass bangle to be worn on the wrist.

'For long life,' he explained.

For Payne the invitation to visit the longhouse was a show of hospitality, the locals inviting the round eyes for a night out. To the Montagnards it meant far more than that. It meant Payne had been accepted; he had shown himself to be a leader and worthy of their respect. When the company was next sent out on operations two Yards positioned themselves on either side of Payne. He hadn't ordered them into that position but nothing he could say would make them return to their platoons. It had been decided among the men; they were his bodyguards.

It didn't take long for them to come in handy. Three days after Payne declared 212 Company operational, they were ordered out to the area known as Ben Het. In time Ben Het would become synonymous with the Keith Payne story but on 2 March 1969 when he was being briefed on his first operation in the area, it was just another spot on the map. About 200 kilometres north-west of Pleiku, Ben Het was the site of a Special Forces camp close to the Laos–Cambodia border. Its position made it vulnerable to attack from North Vietnamese forces infiltrating into South Vietnam through Laos and as such the camp was regularly under siege. When that happened, Special Forces reinforcements would be airlifted into the area from Pleiku under gunship support, relieve the camp and, when the situation was under control, be airlifted out again. That was how the system had worked in the past anyway. Keith Payne's arrival in Vietnam in January 1969 coincided with a major turning point in the history of the war – the election of Richard M. Nixon as US president.

Nixon was elected to office at the height of the American public's opposition to the Vietnam War. While stopping short of ordering a full-scale withdrawal of US troops, Nixon announced that the United States would scale down its front-line involvement in Vietnam. Declaring the United States would 'only help those nations prepared to help themselves', he detailed a policy of handing control of the war back to the South Vietnamese. In June the president announced the gradual pull-out of US forces from Vietnam in what became known as the 'Nixon Doctrine'. More immediate was relinquishing control of key elements of the campaign such as artillery and helicopter air support to the South Vietnamese under a policy known as 'Vietnamization'. While the policy was a good public relations exercise to appease the opponents of the war back in America and Australia, for those on the front line like Payne, it was to prove a nightmare.

'Once the South Vietnamese generals got their hands on the artillery and the helicopters that was the beginning of the end for us. The artillery was used to support South Vietnamese troops, the same with the choppers. We were US and Australian soldiers – foreigners – fighting alongside Montagnards who they thought of as savages. They didn't want to know about us.'

The first experience Payne had of the effects of Vietnamization came during his first operation to Ben Het. All planning had been

Operational

done on the basis that helicopters would be available. At the last moment they were pulled away for what the South Vietnamese saw as a more important mission somewhere else. What should have been a straightforward trip in choppers from Pleiku Airstrip to a landing zone close to the area of operation became a seemingly endless ride in the back of dusty, bumping trucks the 100 kilometres to the city of Dak To and another 50 kilometres in armoured personnel carriers to Ben Het.

Experiencing the ride alongside Payne was a newcomer to Vietnam who sat in the hot, uncomfortable transport wondering what he had got himself into, and whether he would be able to step up when the time came. In many ways US Special Forces Sergeant Gerard 'Gerry' Dellwo was a mirror of the young Keith Payne who had endured a similar baptism of fire in Korea just over sixteen years earlier.

Aged twenty-one and a native of Spokane, Washington, Gerry was a promising high diver studying at junior college in Arizona so he could train with the country's best diving coach when he was drafted, at the age of eighteen. While waiting to be called up he made the momentous decision to enlist.

'I didn't want to spend two years spinning my wheels. If I was going to be in the army I wanted to make something of it. I wanted to be a good infantry soldier, and make a difference.'

At the recruitment station where he signed up Dellwo saw a brochure about the Special Forces and decided that was for him.

'You can't enlist in the Special Forces, you have to join the army, then go airborne and apply. I was real lucky to get in. I joined the infantry, did my basic training and volunteered for jump school. Then while I was waiting to get into Special Forces I did my medic training. When I finally got into Special Forces it was as a medic.'

Dellwo underwent two years Special Forces training at Fort Bragg and then, as Payne had done back in Australia, started knocking on doors in the hope of getting to Vietnam.

'I wanted to go there. I believed in us being there, but I didn't get the orders. I had to call the Pentagon several times before finally my orders came through.'

In February 1969 Dellwo landed in country and was sent to Hon Tre Island for the same orientation course that Payne had been forced to leave prematurely. It was there he first came in contact with members of the Team.

'There were two Aussies doing the course and I was intrigued by them. They told me about M-Force – it was the first time I had heard about it and I thought to myself that it was the sort of thing I wanted to do – and these were the types of people I wanted to do it with. There was something about those Aussies – and it came through in all the Australians I worked with over there. I was an idealistic kind of kid. I used to watch John Wayne movies. I had an image of what I thought a soldier should be and these guys represented that image. They were professionals, career soldiers who knew exactly what they had to do and how to do it, not some dumb kids running through the jungle shooting a gun. They were enthusiastic without being gung-ho. They gave the impression that if they were given an assignment they'd do it right. Based on that, I asked to go to Mike Force. I don't know what happened to those two guys. I ended up at Pleiku, they headed off somewhere else.'

Dellwo was sent to 212 Company as company medic and platoon leader of the 1st Platoon. He arrived straight out of training with no battle experience. He was keen to do a good job but had no idea of what was ahead and was apprehensive about how he would perform under fire. His first meeting with his company commander was a daunting experience.

'When I introduced myself to Keith he was a little short with me, a little terse. I always thought he was a good kind of guy but I found out later he couldn't believe someone with so little experience could have been given as much responsibility. He thought I was green, and he was 100 per cent right. It was a pretty intense time. Everyone was very busy and I was new in country. I still hadn't done what I'd been trained to do and I was trying to get all my equipment together and trying to communicate with the Yards. Keith was like the Aussies I'd met during my training. He was a professional and he was trying to kick the company into shape, so I suppose getting some green kid from the States wasn't exactly what he wanted right then.

'I always thought I would be a pretty good medic but I wasn't sure how I would be as a platoon leader. As it turned out Keith wasn't interested in that. I had a Yard platoon leader under me and he pretty well led the platoon. Keith was more interested in me doing my job as a medic. He didn't want me getting shot so he always demanded that I stay in the centre with the Headquarters instead of on the perimeter with my platoon. I felt straightaway that Keith was the kind of guy you wanted on your side. He commanded respect and that was important because I found myself in the action pretty much immediately.'

Another newcomer to the company was communications man Don Taylor. A 'thirty-year-man' career soldier from Clinton, Indiana, his experience could not have been more different from young Dellwo's. A Korean War veteran with the rank of Warrant Officer Grade 4, he had volunteered for Special Forces in 1955. By the time he joined 212 Company he had already been on operations with Barry Tolley's unit.

'The four of us – Payne, Latham, Dellwo and me – made a pretty good little team,' he recalled. 'We all got along pretty well. We'd work together and have a drink together when we were off duty. I guess we formed a clique straightaway. You had to in that situation. We depended on each other so we had to be close. We had our little arguments – mainly over map reading – but that's going to happen. Later on I thought I detected a little bit of tension between Payne and Latham. They seemed like they were in competition but again that's understandable in that situation. Everyone is really aggressive. If you're in Special Forces you're not a meek person.

'As far as Keith was concerned, I'd say he was a good, competent soldier who knew what he was doing. The decisions he made always seemed to be right. He was a good man to follow. You could tell that from that first operation up around Ben Het. We went up into that area two or three times. By the end we knew it like the back of our hands.'

As was so often the case at Ben Het, as Keith and his men approached the area for the first time it was the centre of furious activity on the part of the North Vietnamese. In time it emerged that the 27th Battalion of the North Vietnamese Army had engaged from the north and the 24th Battalion from the north-west. There was also another regiment, the 66th, getting into position to link up with the others in an attempt to take Dak To. The Mobile Strike Force had not been established to take on major enemy forces. Its role was reconnaissance, disruption of enemy supply lines and relief of Special Forces camps under siege through patrolling and specific tactical assignments. In regards to the enemy battalions massing around Ben Het, any large confrontation would be left to ARVN forces. Payne's company, along with those of Tolley and Montez, was given the assignment of clearing Fire Support Base 29, a strategic hilltop within mortar distance of Ben Het.

Payne recalled: 'The base had been set up by the US Special Forces. They'd blown the top off the hill, flattened it and put guns up there so they could control the area. After it had been overrun by NVA forces they'd abandoned it but it was still of tactical importance and with action hotting up in the area we were sent in to make sure there was no enemy up there.'

The armoured personnel carriers dropped the three companies at Ben Het and they moved straight onto the ridge they had been ordered to secure. Each took a different route to the top of the hill under cover of supporting artillery and mortar fire from Ben Het. They found it clear of enemy, but that didn't mean they were free from attack, Don Taylor recalled.

'I remember when we got up there getting shelled by enemy artillery from Cambodia. We were only about 10 clicks from the border and they were blasting away. I counted sixteen rounds.'

Over the next two days Payne's company followed the feature down to the west, patrolling along a ridgeline until they descended and hit a river, the Song Dak Kal. They crossed that successfully and were continuing the patrol when there was a short burst of gunfire. The men found cover but when there was no more shooting Kev Latham came back with a distressing report. The two forward scouts had gone different ways around a block of bamboo. When they came

Operational

back to the track they were facing each other. They opened fire and one was killed.

Payne nodded at Latham's report, angered that a man had been lost in such a senseless accident, but worse was to come.

'They were brothers,' Latham said.

With one man killed and another in no state to continue on the operation, Don Taylor called in an airlift for extraction and this time the chopper was available.

'When we were asking the South Vietnamese for a medevac chopper we never said who it was for,' Payne said. 'If they knew it was for a wounded Montagnard they'd never send it.'

Payne's men used C4 explosive to clear a landing zone and waited overnight until the sound of the Huey could be heard at first light next morning. It swooped down and hovered just long enough for the body of one soldier to be loaded on board and his brother to climb on alongside. Then they headed home.

Next morning Payne gave the signal and his company continued to head south-west, all the while alert to the possibility of running into enemy patrols. The chopper evacuation meant Payne's company had fallen well behind those of Tolley and Montez. The last thing he wanted now was to encounter the enemy in numbers, but even he couldn't have predicted what he did find.

The signal came from the forward scout. Enemy. Payne halted the company and Latham came back with his report. Bunkers, but no sign of activity.

'It was a large defensive area set up by the enemy but there was no sign of them. What we did find was tank positions, a whole line of bays where the tanks could be refuelled and rearmed. There was even all the ammunition piled up ready to be used. We brought in some choppers to take the ammo away and then called in a B52 bombing raid to destroy the enemy positions. They took down the coordinates and told us to get back down below the blue line, which was back near the river. It didn't sound too hard when we got the orders but there had been a lot of rain and the ground was all slippery. We were backtracking, wondering if anyone had been following us, hoping not to get ambushed and aware that in a very short time there was going to be a B52 bomber going over the top of us blowing the whole area to hell. We'd gone probably 3 kilometres from the site when time was up. I gave the order and we tucked ourselves into a re-entrant between two spur-lines as well as we could. It seemed a long way away but when those bombs came down it was still like being in an earthquake. The ground was shaking, the trees were rocking and bending. The destructive power was amazing.'

The mission was completed without further incident. The three companies met up and headed back to Pleiku. It had seemed an action-packed operation but in comparison to what lay in store, it was a walk in the park. As Payne said, 'Over the next three months every time I turned around someone was shooting at me'.

Sometimes Payne would head into the jungle to find trouble. Sometimes it found him. Vietnam wasn't a conventional war in terms of battlefields and major engagements. It was fought in villages, classrooms and streets. It was a battle for the minds as well as the hearts of the South Vietnamese. A war of idealism and politics. A war Payne fought on his own terms.

'Before we left Australia we were told just to fight the battles and keep out of politics. I was a professional soldier trained to fight the enemy head to head. I wasn't interested in all the backroom stuff. We used to see the CIA blokes creeping around the place making trouble. We called them 'Sneaky Petes'. One time one of them tried to get me involved. He wanted to start a unit to go around knocking off the leading collaborators, along with the tribal chiefs. He wanted me to train them. I told him to get lost.'

Sometimes a few well-chosen words weren't enough to keep Payne out of trouble. Part of the role of the Special Forces was to protect the area around Pleiku township. Throughout the conflict the Viet Cong continued a campaign of intimidation and disruption among the general population, murdering community leaders and US supporters. After the operation during which his men found the tank bays, Payne's company was placed on standby at Pleiku. He was in the Special Forces compound when word came through that the Viet

Operational

Cong were creating chaos in town, shooting up the streets and screaming political slogans.

'Kev and I grabbed a couple of platoons, jumped into trucks and headed into town. We got out and set up a cordon across the road as the Viet Cong came down the street, about six of them, blasting away and stirring up trouble.'

The Yards returned fire but one of the Viet Cong kept coming straight at Payne, a grenade in his hand.

'He cocked his arm, ready to throw it. I brought up my M16 and dropped him, simple as that. One shot, dead. The others shot a couple more and it was all over. I went and had a look at the one I'd shot. He was just a kid. I didn't feel good about it. I felt for the poor little shit, he looked so young, but when they've got a grenade in their hands they're all the same age. The police came and took statements, put the boot into the bodies to show they were on our side and took them away. We jumped back on the truck and went back to camp. The township was in the ARVN area of control so they gave me the Vietnamese Cross of Gallantry. The whole thing would have taken less than an hour.'

It was not the first time Payne had killed a man, but the first time he had stood over the body and seen the effects of his actions.

'In Korea I never got to shoot my weapon at anyone but there were plenty of times when I could have killed someone. Like when I put those grenades down the holes in that trench during Operation Fauna. And there were times when you would be leap-frogging from hole to hole, shooting and throwing grenades. Fire and movement, fire and movement. You didn't know for sure, but there was a very good chance you had hit someone. When I got to Vietnam, that was the first time I really saw someone through the sights of my rifle and pulled the trigger. You'd see them go down, and you'd just keep going. It was on those early operations in Vietnam when I first knew for sure that I'd taken someone out. You don't even think about it until later. It's when things calm down and you might be lying down for the night or back at base and you think, Jesus, I got that poor bugger. When you pull the trigger you don't think of him as a man, you think of him as the enemy. He'll shoot you, you shoot him first. It's about survival. Then later you think about him having a mother and father, a wife, girlfriend, kids. You wonder what type of life he had. That kid with the grenade was different. I actually got to walk up and look at him, and that really brought it home to me. I just stood there and thought, You poor little bugger. I wasn't a baby-killer, he wasn't a baby, but he was pretty young. He had an American grenade in his hand. We'd waited for it to blow, but it never did. He hadn't pulled the pin.'

Payne's next confrontation with the enemy wasn't over so quickly. Nor was it resolved with just a short burst of gunfire.

12

Anzac Day

ANZAC DAY (25 APRIL) is a holiday of remembrance for Australians, a day to commemorate the sacrifices made by servicemen and women in all conflicts. The Anzac Day motto of 'Lest we forget' has added significance for Keith Payne. He can never forget Anzac Day 1969. Nor can those who were with him.

The operation that Payne and the others would always refer to as 'Anzac Day' started on 19 April. After three days on standby the company, along with Tolley's 211th and Montez's 213th, received orders to fly south to the Special Forces camp at Nhon Co in Quang Duc Province, close to the Thai border. From there they would take part in a thirty-day, 30 kilometre wide by 30 kilometre deep sweep, Tolley and Montez moving off first on either side and Payne following 500 metres behind to create a 'funnel' into which any enemy forces would be pushed. Things started badly.

'It wasn't what you'd call a well-planned operation,' recalled Don Taylor. 'I remember it was a Sunday. I was having a beer in the club and Kev Latham came in and said, "Quick, grab your gear, we're going out to Nhon Co". We went straight out and jumped onto the C-130 transports. We were doing our maps on the plane.'

Taylor still has his situation reports (or 'sitreps') – hastily written on a small notepad during the operation. The reports record the call signs, map coordinates and brief resumes of action over the period during which Payne, codenamed Rivet 19, took his men into some of the 'hottest' territory in South Vietnam.

The three companies spent the night at Nhon Co, with Payne receiving news he wasn't happy to hear.

'I spoke to the Special Forces camp commander and he said, "Goddamn, you guys got here in a hurry". I didn't know what he was talking about. He said, "There's bad guys out there". Apparently his patrols had reported enemy activity but no one had told us. We thought we were just going on a routine operation; he thought we'd been sent because of his report. We didn't know the area was hot.'

Confirmation of that fact wasn't long in coming. The other two companies went in first, Payne's men reaching the landing zone later in the afternoon.

'We flew into a whole heap of trouble. We were in two Hueys and three Chinooks. Kev went in to secure the area and there were gunships buzzing around. Kev popped a smoke grenade that indicated a cold landing zone but that was the way Charlie worked. He'd have a couple of men at the landing zone who waited until the main force came in, then open fire. I was in the first Chinook going in. The landing zone was next to what looked like a duck pond, fed by a stream. We were nearly on the ground when the firing started. It was crack, crack, crack. The bullets were going through the fuselage of the chopper and rattling around. It was a miracle no one was shot before we even landed.'

It soon became obvious that Payne's company had landed on the edge of an enemy camp, boobytrapped with *punjis* – hidden bamboo stakes with poisoned tips – to protect it from surprise attack. From the wet clothes lying around on drying racks it appeared the enemy had been swimming or washing when the choppers approached. They had quickly grabbed their weapons and headed up the ridge, leaving a few men behind as a welcoming committee.

'We only had one casualty early on and that was from one of my men standing on a *punji* and getting it through his foot. The *punjis* were hidden by elephant ear lilies that were growing around this old garden area. They could be deadly – they were nasty people.'

The enemy wasn't the only danger. As the men leapt from the choppers and fanned out, heading for cover, the US gunships swooped down and started strafing the area.

'They came in too close. The shell cases were falling on us. I grabbed the radio from Big John and was telling them in no uncertain terms to pull back. They got the picture and moved up the ridge where Charlie was shooting up at them. The gunships blasted them.'

With the gunships clearing the way, Latham's platoon was able to move up and take the ridge while Payne stayed at the landing zone for the night.

'We had to care for the wounded. We had one killed, two shot and wounded, and the one who'd stood on the *punji*. Dellwo in his cool, efficient way looked after them and we had them airlifted out the next morning. We also got a resupply of ammunition and food. When the firing started the Yards had thrown their food supply away to lighten the load as they headed up the ridge.'

With the medevac chopper safely away, Payne joined Latham and the company headed off to make up the distance to Tolley and Montez who were now a kilometre in front. At the end of the day they had covered 8 kilometres. First thing next morning they set out again and came to a small, fast-running stream that quickly went from ankle- to knee-deep.

'The scouts went across, Kev went across with the forward platoon, and I was halfway across when Charlie started firing on Kev. I got across to the other side and brought another platoon over to cover our right flank. I started moving forward to support Kev when bang, everything went black.'

Payne had been hit by a bullet that struck him as it moved across his face. He was knocked unconscious but not badly injured. After twenty seconds he came to, just in time to hear Don Taylor on the radio back to Pleiku.

'We've got a bit of a problem going on down here.'

'I thought he was dead,' Taylor recalled. 'I was running past and as I was coming up behind him, he just went down. The bullet had kind of skidded past his face but I thought he'd been shot in the head. I wanted to stop and help him but I was trying to get up to where the shooting was. The way he was knocked over I just thought, He's gone. When I came back I saw him coming to and called it in as wounded.'

Taylor's situation report listed the incident simply as 'Rivet 19 WIA. Not serious.'

It might not have been a shot heard round the world, but it was certainly one that reverberated all the way to Brisbane, Queensland. As Payne cleared his head and got back into the battle, the unstoppable wheels of army bureaucracy were rolling. Before Payne could stop it, the report of his injury was in the system. A Wounded in Action notification went from Pleiku to Saigon to Canberra and finally on to Stafford, the western suburb of Brisbane where Flo and the boys had moved into an army house.

Flo was making the bed in one of the boys' bedrooms when fifteen-year-old Ronald looked out the window.

'Mum,' he said, 'there's an army car out the front'.

Flo kept her voice steady.

'I said, "Oh, is there?" I didn't let the boys know I went cold from head to toe. I took a deep breath and said, "How many people are in it?" I knew if they were coming to tell me that Keith had been killed there would be two of them, the officer and the padre. Ronald told me there was only one so I knew Keith was still alive. I gave a sigh of relief and said a good prayer.'

The scene that greeted Keith as he recovered his senses was not encouraging. Under heavy fire, Latham had tried unsuccessfully to organise his men into a 'fire and movement' counterattack, pushing forward under cover of gunfire.

'It was a hopeless mess because there were too many Charlie and the scrub was so thick. In the end Kev just picked up an M60 machine gun and went in alone. He just went straight in. It was boom, boom, boom and he cleared the place up. The end result was one of our blokes shot in the knee, three enemy killed and a strong blood trail. I put Kev in for a medal for that. He got Mentioned in

Dispatches which I wasn't too pleased about. I thought he deserved a Military Medal. The postal clerk at Pleiku got a Mentioned in Dispatches in the same orders.'

Gerry Dellwo dressed Payne's wound and wrapped a bandage around his head before he took the company up onto higher ground. They pushed through heavy jungle until the undergrowth cleared slightly. Using explosives they cleared a tree to make a landing zone and evacuated the wounded. Then they continued on into the area known as Bui Gia Map, trying to get back on schedule.

'We used to rotate the platoons,' Don Taylor recalled. 'It was late afternoon, starting to get dark. Kev Latham was leading and somehow he got us onto the ridge where we were supposed to be. He was really good at reading maps, Latham. I don't know how he managed to find that ridge. I know I wouldn't have been able to do it.'

Payne told Latham they would stay on the ridge for the night and the company automatically went into its evening routine.

'The three of us – Kev, me and Dellwo – used to carry these inflatable mattresses. The idea was we'd use them for putting our radios and gear on when crossing rivers, to make casualties comfortable while waiting for evacuation and, wherever possible, to sleep on. When I said we'd be stopping for the night one of the Yards blew up my mattress and leaned it against a tree. At the same time Kev had sent out a clearing patrol to secure the area and set up a perimeter. They only got halfway around when the shooting started. It didn't stop for four days.'

Payne's company had gone out with less than 100 men. He estimates they were under attack by a full battalion – up to 1500 enemy. At least five times their position was attacked and somehow, undermanned and with ammunition running low, they managed to hold on. They lost eleven men killed and many more were injured and only the bravery and ultimate sacrifice of two US chopper crews saved them from almost-certain annihilation.

'The first attack came when the clearing patrol was fanning out down the south-east ridgeline. They walked straight into the enemy, hundreds of them. One of Kev's men was killed with the first shot. We didn't get his body back for three days.'

Latham's men pulled back to the main force on the knoll, the company's machine guns returning fire as the enemy attacked. The area was a cacophony of sound, as North Vietnamese mortars and rockets began landing with deadly accuracy.

'They had us. We were outnumbered and out-gunned but for some reason they never finished us off. There were five attacks against us over those days, and our casualties were mounting all the time. After that first attack they didn't come at us again until the next morning, and then they just came straight up the same ridgeline that they had the night before. I couldn't understand it. Why didn't they come up the other way, try to outflank us? Plus, they only hit us with about twenty rockets and not a lot of mortars. After the third attack they left us alone for almost a day. In the meantime Barry Tolley had come in to reinforce us. It didn't make a lot of sense when I thought back on it later, but at the time I wasn't worried about any of that. All I was worried about was trying to keep the men and myself alive.'

For a while it seemed that might be easier said than done. As Latham's men pulled back up the knoll, returning fire with the advancing enemy, Payne ordered his men to dig in. They frantically scraped holes in the hard dirt and set up their mortars and machine guns. As Payne crouched behind a tree, firing at the shadowy figures making their way across the open ground, Big John thrust the radio handset at him. The words he heard were like manna from heaven. A US Air Force AC-119 'Shadow' – a reconfigured transport plane equipped with gatling guns – was on its way from Danang.

'I got Kev to put a strobe light in a shell casing so the Shadow pilot could see it but the enemy couldn't and we brought him right in over the top of us. He blasted away and as he finished his sweep an enemy gunner took a shot at him. I can still hear the pilot's voice over the radio. He said, "Well I'll be damned. That guy hasn't got my calling card." Then he swung around came back over the enemy again and really let him have it. It was boom, boom, boom. All over.'

All over for one night anyway.

Written in the anxious calm of the evening Taylor's sitrep summed up the attack:

Received ground assault from NVA approx 6.15. Had 1 KIA, 3 WIA Mobile Strike Force. Attacking unit appears to be in company strength. Casualties of enemy unknown. At least five enemy bodies seen outside perimeter. Enemy is still outside our perimeter. Enemy using AK-47, RP69 and hand grenades. Enemy attacked from two sides.

Early the next morning Payne sent out clearing patrols, arranged blasting of a landing zone for chopper evacuations and resupply and ordered the Yards to lay two lines of claymore mines around the perimeter of the area. Even as the work was being completed, the second attack was underway.

'That was the attack that really had me stumped. They'd had a whole night to prepare and if they'd come up on either side of the spur they would have got real close under good cover, but they didn't. Our forward platoon had been strengthened with men from the rear platoons and ammunition had been distributed but I didn't take anything from the right platoon because I thought that's where the next attack would come from. Instead they came straight at us, exactly as they had the night before. Their problem. Our good luck.'

With Payne's men having had the entire night to dig in, the North Vietnamese had lost their early advantage. Payne counted seven dead before the enemy pulled back, but the Yards were also copping a pounding.

'I saw Gerry going forward and pulling back the wounded, dressing their wounds and fighting, all at the same time. Geez he was a gutsy little bugger. There wasn't much to him, but it was all heart.'

After several hours the North Vietnamese pulled back, dragging their dead and wounded with them. Payne did a headcount. His casualties were mounting. Just as worrying after the second attack were the dwindling supplies of ammunition and water. Don Taylor was constantly on the radio, with Keith calling for air support and resupply of ammo and medical supplies, but the enemy strength made it impossible.

'I told them not to bring in choppers without tactical support, it was that hot, but thanks to Vietnamization, the South Vietnamese had control of the gunships and they weren't letting them go for us. There was always something they felt was more important, which left us in the lurch. Without support the supply choppers were sitting ducks so the Special Forces couldn't send us anything. You wouldn't believe it, only one plane got through on the second morning and it dropped leaflets telling the North Vietnamese they were surrounded and should surrender. Bloody surrounded? I'll tell you who was surrounded, and it wasn't them. Things were looking pretty grim. The wounded were stacking up, we had them lying in shell scrapes around the headquarters pits. It was getting so that we had more wounded than fit men. We lost a lot of them over those couple of days. If we'd been able to get them out on medevac choppers they might have made it, but they died right there where they lay.

'Headquarters at Pleiku ordered Montez and Tolley to come and reinforce us. It looked like Tolley would get there first and he had to cross the same stream where I'd been hit so I asked him to bring all the water he could get his hands on, even filling up bamboo cylinders if he had to. We were dead-set dry and almost out of ammo.'

It was on Anzac Day that the worst attack began. Once again the North Vietnamese came up from the same direction, but this time the Yards in the forward positions broke and started pulling back towards the headquarters pits.

'It looked like we'd be overrun. I really thought that was it. Me, Kev, Gerry and Don jumped up and started moving forward, firing as we went, and yelling at the Yards to come with us. You could see them waver. They didn't know whether to turn around or just keep running all the way home. Then Toget came with us and starting yelling at them and they stopped and came back. We refilled the hole they'd left at the front, but that was the closest we came. That was almost it. To see what those other blokes did ... I had some extraordinarily brave men with me then.'

Some respite came with the arrival of an armed reconnaissance chopper which hovered over an enemy machine gun and blew it away. As Payne put it, 'It just pushed away the undergrowth and said "Cop that"'. Again the enemy was repelled, but with little

Anzac Day

ammunition and mounting casualties it seemed to be just a matter of time. Payne, Latham, Dellwo and Taylor took up their positions and waited for the inevitable, knowing only a miracle could save them.

It came in the shape of two helicopters and Barry Tolley. Even as the North Vietnamese were mounting their fourth attack, Tolley's men came up the hill from the rear of Payne's position.

'They'd been about 2 kilometres away when we first made contact with the NVA,' Taylor recalled. 'They couldn't move at night of course but they left first thing the next morning. They came as fast as they could but they had to be careful of ambush themselves and you can't run through the jungle anyway. I just know I was very happy when they got there. That was when I first thought we'd be okay. I thought, We've got the numbers now. We can get out of this.'

As he approached the battle, Tolley contacted Payne and asked the best way to come in. Payne made sure there were no mistakes.

'I went back to get him so that our men wouldn't mistake each other for the enemy and start shooting. When I saw him I could have kissed the long-legged bugger. He asked where I wanted him to put his men and I said, "Mate, don't worry about positions. Just fill the empty bloody holes. There's plenty of them."'

One thing about Anzac Day that Payne will always remember is Dellwo in the midst of the enemy attack, doing his pill round.

'Gerry was an amazing bloke. He had his routine and he was going to stick to it, he was that determined to do the best job he possibly could. He had this system where every Monday or Tuesday or whatever day it was, he'd go around and give us an anti-malaria pill. There we were, under attack, all hell breaking loose around us, and up pops Gerry handing me a bloody tablet. There's a thousand North Vietnamese shooting at us, bullets flying everywhere, and Gerry is worried we're going to catch malaria.'

Payne laughs as he tells the story, but Dellwo has a different memory of the incident – one which has given him sleepless nights ever since.

'I did do that,' he recalls. 'It was my job and I was very conscious of my responsibility. There was enormous intensity at the time; I'd almost ignore bullets in trying to remember all the details of my job. I remember that day there was a lull in the fighting and I went around and passed out the tablets, but in thinking back on it now, I wish I hadn't. That was when the first supply helicopter finally got through to us. The pilot must have seen me moving around handing out pills and thought it was safe. He came in close and Pilkington, the operations sergeant from Ban Me Thuot, was in the doorway getting ready to push out the ammo and medical supplies to us. He was hit by machine-gun fire and killed. I knew that man. It has always played on my mind.'

Taylor said Pilkington wasn't supposed to be on the chopper in the first place.

'He just happened to be at the east field at Ban Me Thuot when the chopper was being loaded and said he'd go along. He was in the doorway looking down at us when he was shot in the face by a 12.7 millimetre machine gun. We heard later they got him back to base but he died fourteen hours later.'

Dellwo wasn't the only one who carried out his routine oblivious to the enemy. Taylor managed to scratch out a situation report, even in the height of battle. His report for Anzac Day reads:

> Today had four assaults by enemy unit using B-40 and AK-47 and RPG, grenades and SKS. (8400 Hours) Still in contact with enemy unit. Estimate unit 2 companies and weapons platoon. STILL IN CONTACT AT TIME OF THIS REPORT. Assault by enemy overran forward platoon. Situation became critical. Counter attack regained forward position and re-established company perimeter.

A second supply chopper also got through, but despite Payne's warnings it also came in alone, with no gunship support. Heavy machine-gun fire ripped through the fuselage. Black smoke billowed from the engine, leaving a trail as the aircraft spluttered away from the battle scene and disappeared to the south. Then there was a loud explosion as it crashed to ground. Payne and his men could only spare a moment to reflect on the bravery of the American Special Forces who came to help them and gave their lives in the process, before ripping open the few ammunition boxes that had made it through the jungle canopy.

'I kept telling them not to come without support, but they could hear the situation we were in and they took the chance. What can you say? They were heroes.'

When Tolley arrived his men shared their ammunition and water with the remains of Payne's company. The water was desperately needed to keep up the fluids of the wounded as they waited to be airlifted out. By now the Special Forces had prevailed on the US Air Force to provide aircraft and, while Tolley took over ground operations, Payne called in tactical air support. Taylor's sitrep records the last contact with the enemy was late on the 25th when a resupply chopper was fired upon. The 26th was spent receiving supplies and flying out wounded. 'Body of MSF evac on resupply bird,' he wrote. 'Brother of KIA on same bird for compassionate reason.' By the morning of the 27th the situation had eased enough for Payne and Tolley to consider a counter-assault down the hill to clear out the area.

'I said, "Barry, you've got to get down the ridgeline and clear it out", so he lined up his company and gave the order to move out and they just put the stoppers on. They wouldn't move. I said, "Bloody hell, Barry, just get them moving". I would have kicked them down there myself if I'd had the energy. I was getting pretty pissed off. I'd hardly been asleep for four days.'

Tolley's Yards finally agreed to head off into enemy territory, but refused to go in standard patrol formation as they felt they were vulnerable to ambush. They insisted on using the US procedure known as 'Recon by Fire' or, as the Australians knew it, 'shooting the shit out of everything'. They charged down the hill in full-blooded attack mode, machine-gunners in front, riflemen fanned out beside them, all guns blazing. They reached the enemy camp without one round being shot back at them. The North Vietnamese had vanished, taking their dead and wounded with them. Tolley called Payne down to join him.

'Have a look at this,' he said, leading Payne into what must have been an enemy training camp.

'I've never seen anything like it. It was so clean. There were no shell casings lying around, no bandages, nothing. There was a fully equipped hospital and an irrigation system that brought water up from the stream in all these bamboo pipes. Barry found mud maps and charts and training aids. We'd walked right into it. No wonder they had so much ammo.'

The next day Montez arrived and the US Air Force sent in jets with daisy-cutter bombs to blow trees off the top of a neighbouring hill so choppers could bring in artillery pieces.

'We finally had artillery support, a little too late. Once the main fighting was over the choppers started arriving with supplies and reinforcements at our landing zone. When the word got around that there had been a successful operation all these Yards were showing up trying to get involved. We were sending out our dead and badly wounded but there were some who weren't too bad who just wanted to get out of there. Kev, who'd been given command of the landing zone, was actually going out and grabbing them off the choppers.'

Before leaving the site of the battle, there was one moment of levity. As they packed up their gear and prepared to move on, Payne called to Tolley with a 'Hey Barry, look at this'.

There, still leaning against the tree where it had been placed four days earlier, was Payne's inflatable mattress. While hundreds of bullets and pieces of shrapnel had been shot around the area over the period, the mattress remained unscathed.

'Next time there's a firefight on I know where I'll be heading,' Tolley joked. 'Right behind that thing.'

'From there we re-formed and carried on with our operation which had now been reduced to an area of 1 square kilometre. Tolley took his men out first, then Monty, then us. Barry followed the trail of the blokes we'd been fighting for a while. He came across a hastily made grave with about ten bodies in it. They were obviously the wounded that had died on the trek out. A bit further down the track Barry had a slight action with one guy armed with an SKS rifle, but he took care of him. Then we went into a big harbour position, all three companies together.

'On 1 May we got our orders to go to the landing zone and fly out. We got picked up by Chinooks and taken back to Nhon Co. We slept beside the airfield that night and the C-130s arrived from Pleiku the next morning.'

The US Army awarded Payne the Silver Star, its third highest decoration, for his action during the Anzac Day battle. Latham was Mentioned in Dispatches for clearing out the enemy nest near the stream after Payne was shot. Both Dellwo and Taylor were recommended for medals after the operation.

'I never got anything but that happens,' Taylor said. 'A lot of the time paperwork would get lost over there. I think I put Dellwo in for a Silver Star and Keith put me in for one. He gave me a copy of what he wrote and I've got it lying around somewhere. No one really cared too much about medals at the time. We weren't really into that.'

Writing up his reports, Taylor calculated that over the course of the operation 212 Company had eleven contacts with the enemy in sixteen days.

Payne could have been forgiven for thinking that the odds were about to change in his favour. He was wrong.

'I thought things might get a bit quieter, and so did the others. We had no idea of what was to come.'

13

'Simmo'

PAYNE'S COMPANY WAS NOT alone in the lack of support it received at Bui Gia Map. Other members of the Team working in Mike Force at that time had reported similar experiences. It was a situation of particular concern to then AATTV commanding officer Lieutenant Colonel R.D.F. Lloyd. So much so, that he changed his schedule and went early to see the situation first-hand. What he witnessed on 11 and 12 May 1969 inspired and infuriated him in equal measure.

Four Victoria Crosses were awarded to Australians during the Vietnam War – all to members of the Team. The first, in November 1965, was awarded posthumously to Warrant Officer Kevin 'Dasher' Wheatley. Already something of a legend among his fellow Australians back home, Wheatley earned a reputation with American and ARVN soldiers within weeks of being posted to the Vietnamese Special Forces A Team at Tra Bong. Sheltering with his fellow advisers and ARVN forces during an artillery barrage, Wheatley spotted a three-year-old girl break away from her mother and run into the open. Disregarding his own safety, Wheatley broke from cover, scooped the girl up in his arms and returned to safety.

On 13 November 1965 Wheatley and fellow Australian Warrant Officer R.J. 'Butch' Swanton were on a search and clear patrol with members of the CIDG – the South Vietnamese version of the Montagnard forces – near Binh Hoa when they came under attack from a large force of Viet Cong.

Swanton was shot through the chest while attempting to carry a fatally wounded South Vietnamese soldier across a paddy field. Wheatley went to his mate's aid. As most of the CIDG soldiers fled, he continued to fire on the advancing enemy, while dragging Swanton to cover. Out of ammunition, he ignored pleas from the fleeing CIDG soldiers to join them and, with a hand grenade in each hand, stayed with Swanton as they were overrun by the Viet Cong.

The second Victoria Cross was also awarded posthumously to Major Peter Badcoe for three acts of heroism between February and April 1967. Operations adviser for Thua Tjien Province, Badcoe was an inspirational leader who defied his bookish appearance to lead from the front, time and again turning the tide of battle. On 23 February, in order to rescue two wounded US officers, he charged and destroyed an enemy machine-gun nest, carrying both men to cover. Less than two weeks later, on 7 March, he led a company to relieve the district headquarters of Quang Dien, charging across open ground despite heavy fire to outflank the enemy and send them into confusion, earning himself the nickname, 'the Galloping Major', in the process.

On 7 April he and his radio operator US Sergeant Alberto Alvarado joined South Vietnamese troops trying to dislodge a Viet Cong force in a heavily fortified hamlet north of Hue. Trying to rally his men as they encountered heavy fire, Major Badcoe was shot and killed as he rose from his position to throw a grenade at an enemy machine-gun post.

The first two VCs were earned almost two years apart. The next two, to Ray Simpson and Keith Payne, were less than two weeks apart and Lieutenant Colonel R.D.F. Lloyd, then commander of AATTV, didn't have to rely totally on eyewitness reports in writing the citation for the first. He saw part of the action with his own eyes.

Russ Lloyd, who had received a Military Cross in Korea, was very much a hands-on commanding officer. He spent much of his time visiting members of the Team wherever they served, and operating with them in the field. For three out of almost every four weeks he was away from his Saigon headquarters, experiencing for himself the difficulties his men were facing. It hadn't taken him long to realise that, in particular, members of the Team serving with the Special Forces in the Central Highlands were caught up in something beyond their control.

'Soon after I took command in January 1969 I could see from the look on the fellas' faces at Mike Force when I visited Pleiku that they were under excessive stress and strain,' he said. 'I tried to get to the bottom of it at the time but it wasn't until just before Simpson's performance in May that I became pretty convinced what the problem was.'

The lack of artillery and air support received by Mike Force, plus the shortfalls in planning, reconnaissance and intelligence, had led many Australians to feel that the Montagnard units were seen as less important, even expendable, by some American commanders and also the South Vietnamese. As Australians were actually leading Montagnard units, they were being put into situations of greatly increased danger as a result. R.D.F. Lloyd was determined to see the situation first-hand despite advice from Team members not to do so.

'I had served with the Americans in Korea. I was only a 23-year-old platoon commander at the time but it was obvious to me even then that they didn't have the same standards and systems as us, so what was happening in the Highlands of Vietnam didn't come as a great surprise. By the time I went out to have a look at what was happening with Simpson, I had been alerted to the fact that the situation was getting worse. The deployment of Mike Force elements was being done with insufficient preparation and inadequate use of available intelligence. It was all done with far too much of a rush by our standards.'

Lloyd had scheduled a visit to Mike Force in late May as part of his regular routine but circumstances saw him bring the visit forward.

'Going out into the field on operations with ARVN units wasn't unusual for me,' he said. 'I don't know if others did it on such a regular basis but I found it the best way to do my job. It wasn't necessarily a popular thing to do. I think most members of the Team understood that I had to see how they were being used, or misused, and try to rectify any problems, and I couldn't really do that unless I did it my way. Some were uncomfortable. They felt responsible for looking after the boss in potentially dangerous situations, and the Vietnamese were even more concerned. If anything happened to me, it was probably their head on the chopping block. The senior American advisers were un-approving – especially so when I ended up knowing more about the real situation than they did. Still, that was the way I worked and over time it proved valuable to see my men operate in location and in the field. I had been out to Pleiku before, but the exercise with Simpson in May was the first time I'd actually been out with a Mike Force unit into an operation.'

Simpson was then in command of 232nd Company of Mobile Strike Force 3rd Battalion. A career soldier who had served in World War II, Korea and Malaya, he was on his third tour of duty in Vietnam after being part of the first contingent of the Team in August 1962. His platoon commanders included Warrant Officer Mick Gill, who had arranged the radio aerial for Keith in New Guinea and had done the orientation course with him on Hon Tre Island, and US specialist sergeant Peter Holmberg.

In early May, the 3rd Battalion had been ordered from Pleiku into the Ben Het area. One of their assignments was to carry out a BDA – Bomb Damage Assessment – on the bomb drop Payne had ordered on the tank bays back in March, eight weeks earlier.

'It was another example of bad planning,' Payne said. 'If someone had been sent in straightaway to check it out they would have been okay. After all that time Charlie was back in the area. It was hot. After it was all over Simmo said to me, "Next time, do your own bloody BDA".'

Around 2.30 p.m. on 6 May, Simpson's company was approaching a small clearing when it came under heavy fire from well-hidden and protected NVA positions in front of them. The forward platoon returned fire as Simpson brought up the rest of the company. Placing himself at the front of his men, Simpson led an assault on the enemy. As they moved forward a second enemy position, which had remained concealed on the side of the clearing, opened fire, badly wounding

Mick Gill. As the Montagnards began to fall back, Simpson ran across the open ground under heavy fire, lifted Gill and carried him to cover. He then returned to the head of his men and attempted to get them to move forward again. With all but a few of the Montagnards having retreated or refusing to re-enter the fight, Simpson crawled to within 10 metres of the enemy. He threw grenades at their positions until he finally had to give the order to fall back.

Moving to a position 250 metres to the north of the attack, Simpson called in a medevac helicopter to evacuate Gill and the other wounded, but with his Montagnards refusing to form a perimeter, the chopper was forced off by enemy ground fire. Despite best efforts, Gill died during the night.

Simpson was scathing about the Montagnards' performance in his report. 'The performance of the company was a damned disgrace both during the contact and subsequently at the LZ,' he wrote. 'Men refused to manoeuvre or shoot and many in fact moved out of the position to the rear. At the LZ they refused to form a perimeter and laid along the trail.'

After rejoining the battalion and being resupplied, Simpson's company moved forward and again came in contact with the enemy. Without air support, they were again forced to pull back. On 11 May the battalion moved forward once more and occupied the position formerly held by the enemy. It was there they were joined by Lieutenant Colonel Lloyd.

Having been informed of the death of Warrant Officer Gill, Lloyd had immediately rearranged his schedule and made plans to join Simpson. Captain Peter Rothwell, a former Mike Force company commander at Pleiku and then based at Special Forces headquarters at Nha Trang, insisted on accompanying him. Rothwell only had about a week to go before he was scheduled to go home and Lloyd was very reluctant to approve it. In the end he did and has since said he probably would not have lived to tell the tale if he had refused Rothwell's insistence.

Lloyd and Rothwell called in to Mike Force headquarters at Pleiku to get final directions and Lloyd spoke briefly to Captain Peter Harris.

A khaki wedding. Corporal Keith Payne and Corporal Florence Plaw on 4 December 1954. 'We were pretty smart dudes, us.'

On training prior to secondment to US Special Forces, Hon Tre Island, January 1969. From left, Mick Gill, Keith Payne, Jock Kelly and Don Cameron. Only three made it home.

US Special Forces Warrant Officer Grade 4 Don Taylor, 30-year man and radio expert. 'If you're in Special Forces you're not a meek person.'

Relations with WO2 Barry Tolley didn't start well, but 'he saved my arse twice'.

Sergeant Gerry Dellwo, medic and platoon leader, with a CIDG Montagnard officer after receiving the Silver Star. 'There wasn't much to him, but it was all heart.'

Enjoying a beer with his XO, Warrant Officer Kev Latham, left. WO Ray Simpson VC is in the background.

With a US adviser supervising Montagnards' training at Pleiku.

Sharing a meal with Yards in the field.

The remains of Special Forces HQ, Pleiku, in 1995.

Third from the left in the distance is the hill near Ben Het where the action leading to the Victoria Cross took place.

With US Special Forces Sergeant Anastacio Montez at Pleiku. Medic Paul Auriemma, bare-chested, is in the background.

The emotional trip back to Vietnam's Highlands with son Derek and Ray Martin in 1995.

Flo congratulates Keith in Vietnam after the announcement of the Victoria Cross.

Striding across Brisbane's Kelvin Grove Barracks to greet his little 'cobbers'.

'Show us your medals Dad.' Derek points to his dad's 'fruit salad'.

Flo and the boys welcome home 'Queensland's new VC'. From left, Colin, Greg (in the cap), Ian, Derek and Ronald.

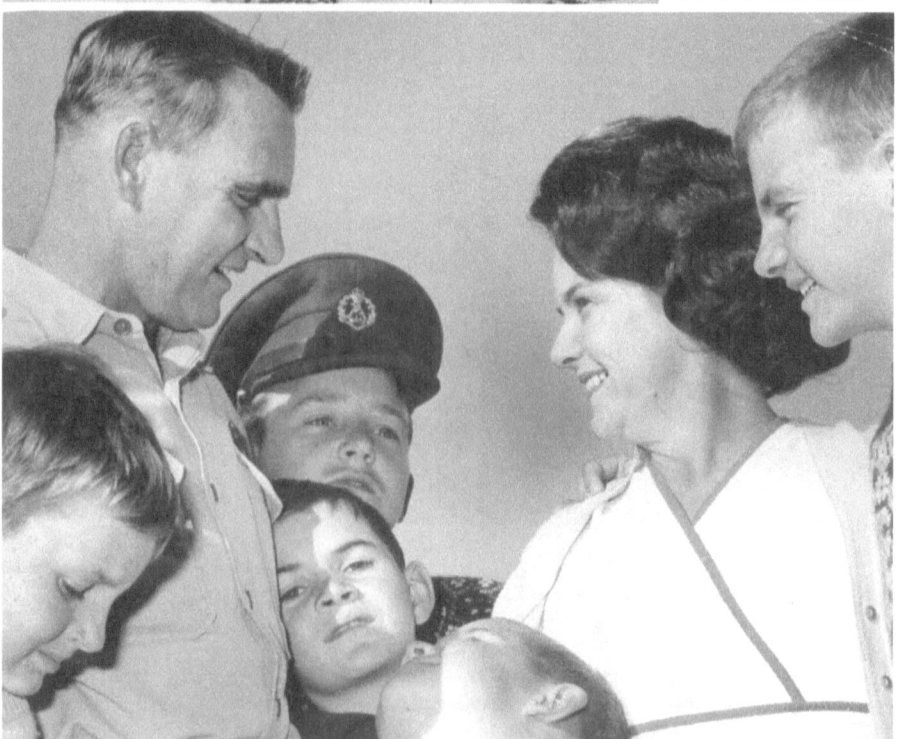

Not really dressed for fishing, the Paynes provide the first of many 'photo ops', this one on Queensland's Tangalooma Island.

Heading off for a day's fishing with Ronald, their bags filled with 'enough explosives to get me locked away for a long time'.

Brisbane's Lord Mayor Clem Jones hands over the keys to the city. Hundreds of well-wishers lined up to shake hands.

13 April 1970, and the Victoria Cross is pinned on by Her Majesty the Queen aboard the royal yacht *Britannia*. 'You don't really believe what's happening to you.'

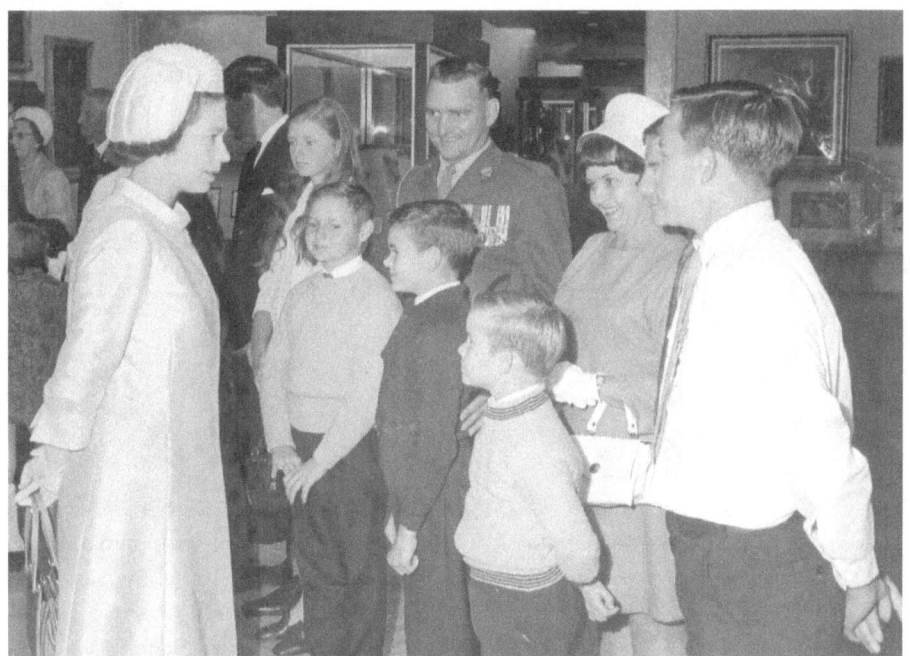

Flo and the boys meet the Queen. 'I thought it was only right they should be there,' she said.

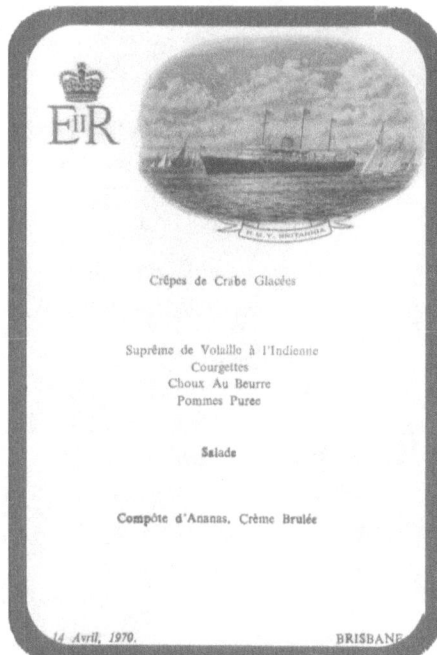

Lunch aboard the royal yacht. The menu is safely stored away in Flo's photo album.

A previous meeting with the Queen. In March 1963 Sergeant Payne opened the royal door.

Two old soldiers, Keith Payne VC with Ted Kenna VC.

Receiving life membership from RSL president Sir Arthur Lee. The mood was not as congenial when Gough Whitlam later joined them.

The opening of Keith Payne Park, Stafford, Brisbane, in 1971. The Paynes lived in Stafford during the Vietnam years. Later all four Vietnam Victoria Cross winners were honoured there.

Pulling the first beer at the Keith Payne Recreational Club, Lavarack Barracks, Townsville, in 1974.

During 'the dark years' professional fishing provided some solace.

Grassy Crisp would be proud of this one, a record-breaking snapper caught off Tangalooma Island.

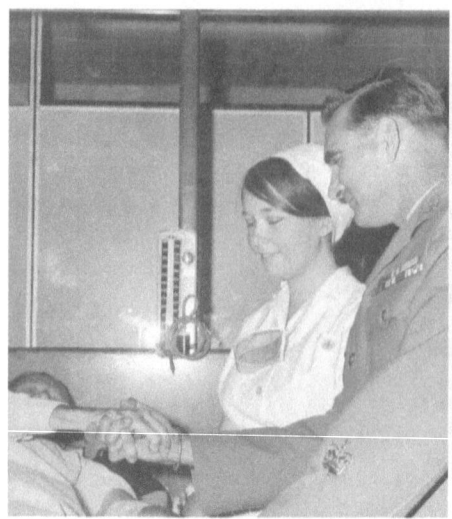 

Flying the flag at a Brisbane hospital soon after returning from Vietnam.

'Righto Mum, bye.' Just 18 years old and looking for adventure, a posed studio shot prior to departure for Korea, 1952.

Cold as hell. With comrades outside their bunker in Korea.

Sergeant Payne raises the flag at dawn, Terendak base, Malaya, 1963.

On patrol in Malaya, 1964.

'Where's Oman?' Facing the media at Brisbane Airport before jetting out to join the army of the Sultan, April 1975.

Receiving the Cross of Gallantry with Bronze Star in Canberra from the South Vietnamese government, 1971.

The American medal, the Distinguished Service Cross, was awarded by US Special Forces Colonel Lewis Millett (Ret'd) at Lord Howe Island, 1995.

As an elder statesman, opening the Queensland Museum's The Courage of Ordinary Men, a tribute to three Victoria Cross recipients, April 2008.

'Simmo'

'He insisted I carry additional ammunition and an M16. This didn't settle my nerves much but we didn't have time to argue. I was given a rough idea of what had happened with Simpson earlier, but no details. I knew that there was a number of my people in that company with Simpson, apart from Gill, who had been killed, and I wanted to see for myself what was going on.'

The two officers arrived about midday in their chopper at a clearing that had been roughly prepared and were met by Jock Kelly, another warrant officer who had done his orientation with Payne and Gill at Hon Tre Island. Because of the proximity of the enemy, Warrant Officer Kelly quickly got them moving.

'We virtually galloped to the company's location where Simpson was being given instructions by the battalion's US commander Captain Green. I didn't get much time at that stage with Simpson and had barely introduced myself to Green when within half an hour all hell broke loose.'

What Lloyd saw over the next few hours confirmed his worst fears about the situation with Mike Force.

'It was thick jungle near the border, a very busy place from the enemy point of view. They didn't like anyone else being there and the Americans didn't like to go there. US commanders at that stage of the war preferred to keep their troops clear of these trouble spots and we never saw them deployed in that area in force. Basically they were using the Special Forces and Montagnards to do a job that they avoided where possible in order to strictly minimise US casualties as was their government's policy at that time. I had become increasingly worried about the situation and what happened that day just confirmed everything that I had been concerned about.'

Leading the battalion out was 231 Company, led by the Team's Warrant Officer Brian Walsh, assisted by Jock Kelly. Lloyd and Rothwell stayed at the rear of Simpson's company, which was second in line. As 231 Company struggled up a steep hill the battalion commander Captain Green – the US officer who had handed Payne his first company command at Pleiku five months earlier – went to the front to urge on his troops. As they reached a small clearing at the top of the hill enemy fire rang out and Jock Kelly fell to the ground, wounded. Captain Green went to his aid and was also shot. Initially it was unclear then whether Green was still alive, but it was subsequently clarified that in fact he had been killed.

Still conscious, Kelly radioed back that the left flank offered the best approach. As he spoke on the radio he was again hit by enemy fire. Brian Walsh brought a platoon up the hill, but hearing the shooting, the Montagnards refused to continue. Walsh went on alone. He was soon joined by Simpson, Holmberg and Rothwell. Reluctantly Lloyd remained in the firm base and accepted the role of liaison to obtain artillery and air support.

Simpson moved forward, making attempts to reach the fallen Captain Green, but these were prevented by enemy fire. As Walsh and Holmberg went to Kelly's aid, Simpson put himself between them and the enemy positions, laying down covering fire. Meanwhile Rothwell, deserted by the Montagnards, carved out a landing zone with his machete, all the while under threat of enemy fire.

Further back at the firm base, with the Montagnards there becoming increasingly agitated, Lloyd made radio contact with the Americans and called for artillery support.

'I was told they would spare some artillery when they got around to it. Others had priority.' Lloyd recalls expressing anger about this on the radio for all to hear and then breaking security rules by indicating who he was, but to no avail.

Without artillery support Simpson held off the enemy as Walsh and Holmberg dragged Kelly out of the line of fire. With the majority of the Montagnards retreating down the hill, it was only Simpson and his covering fire that stopped the North Vietnamese from rushing forward and overrunning all before them.

And still Lloyd's calls for back-up went unheeded.

'The Americans knew there was a battle going on and artillery support had been repeatedly requested. There had also been requests for gunships and medevac but they seemed choosy about who they took risks for, albeit sometimes the situation on the ground was just too dangerous for unsupported dust-offs.'

Lloyd managed to have a medevac helicopter despatched to the area but it was driven off by enemy ground fire before it could land. Singlehandedly Captain Rothwell held off the enemy with rifle fire and grenades. With the assistance of Walsh and Simpson the wounded were moved back from the landing zone to safety. After several hours another chopper was sent on request and this time – as Lloyd said, 'to the great credit of the US pilot and crew involved', the evacuation of wounded was successfully and skilfully completed in darkness. Air support finally came, but the artillery that Lloyd had repeatedly asked for never arrived.

The next morning, after ensuring that the battalion would be evacuated, Lloyd flew to Nha Trang where he demanded an audience with the commander of the 5th Special Forces Group, the senior US Special Forces commander in country. Regrettably he was absent, but his deputy took Lloyd's attack and there was no doubt it was passed on.

When he returned to Saigon Lloyd wrote the citation that led to Simpson being awarded the Victoria Cross. In conclusion he wrote: 'Warrant Officer Simpson's repeated acts of personal bravery in this operation were an inspiration to all Vietnamese, United States and Australian soldiers who served with him. His conspicuous gallantry was in the highest tradition of the Australian Army.' His words that reached the US commander as a result of the meeting at Nha Trang were not so glowing.

'I advised that I would take all Australians out of Mike Force unless the situation was improved. I shook them up, but not enough. The commander of the Australian Forces in Vietnam, General Hay, talked to them too at my request and in my presence but he was more diplomatic than I was. There were some resultant changes but anything they did do was too little, too late.'

Certainly too late for Payne, who in a matter of days was headed back to Ben Het and thrust into a situation every bit as dangerous and chaotic as that which Simpson had just survived.

14

Ben Het

THE SPECIAL FORCES BASE at Ben Het was of immense strategic importance to both sides in the war. Entrenched in a hill overlooking the road known as Route 512 that led to Dak To, it commanded views over the main North Vietnamese supply line to the Central Highlands. Just 11 kilometres from the Cambodian border and 14 kilometres from Laos, Ben Het was fortified with a 175 millimetre artillery battery and manned by 400 Montagnards under the command of Green Berets. On 3–4 March 1969 it had been the site of the only tank battle fought by Americans in Vietnam when an NVA armoured regiment was repulsed by a platoon of US Patton tanks supported by an AC-47 'Spooky' aircraft – one of the heavily armed former supply planes known to the troops as 'Magic Dragons'.

As Simpson, Payne and the other Special Forces officers found over the next few months, the failure of the NVA tanks did not in the least lessen the North Vietnamese desire to take the base and open up the road to Dak To. Within days of Simpson and R.D.F. Lloyd returning from their operation near Ben Het, Payne, Tolley and Montez were ordered back in.

The increased activity in the area from March to May had convinced Special Forces intelligence that the enemy was building up to a major objective. Late in May that objective became obvious when two crack NVA regiments, the 24th and 27th, laid siege to Ben Het. Reinforcements were sent in, including Don Taylor who was dropped in with 'a whole pile of radios' to take up the position of acting communications officer, meaning he was not with Payne when his unit was called into action. US Intelligence had revealed that a third elite NVA regiment, the 66th, was moving into the area. All three companies of the 1st Battalion from Pleiku, along with members of the 5th Battalion out of Dak To, were ordered in to find the enemy regiment, report its position and wait for the arrival of South Vietnamese forces.

The plan was that the two battalions would embark on a wide sweep in search of the enemy – the 5th in the south-west and Payne, Tolley and Montez to the west.

'We were told not to get into heavy conflict,' Payne said. 'That wasn't what we were designed to do. Our initial orders were to avoid any large-scale battles; just find the enemy and get the ARVN to come in.'

Before Payne could even leave on the operation he had to find enough men to make up the minimum company strength of seventy-five. With the number of casualties inflicted over the Anzac Day action, plus the reluctance of the survivors to venture back anywhere near Ben Het, he could muster only fifty-two men. Before leaving Pleiku he approached Warrant Officer Jock Stewart who was company commander in charge of training Montagnard recruits at the camp. Stewart called for volunteers and thirty-seven offered their services. They had received just twelve days training.

The battalion was flown in to Dak To on the evening of 18 May and set off on foot towards Ben Het. After four days without any sight of the enemy they were contacted by Pleiku. The 5th Battalion, on a ridgeline about 15 kilometres south of Ben Het, had encountered the enemy and suffered heavy casualties. Payne's company, at the time the closest, was flown in to provide support first thing next morning. Tolley and Montez were due later in the afternoon.

The sight that met Payne and his men as they were dropped into the area wasn't encouraging. Body bags were piled up at the side of the landing zone and wounded Yards scurried to the choppers as they touched down, trying to climb aboard. Making a rare cold landing,

Payne found the commanding officer and ascertained that the 5th Battalion had encountered an enemy force of company-strength, maybe slightly more. What he couldn't know was that as his company and the remnants of the 5th – including a medic friend of Dellwo's named Elder Dugger – waited throughout the afternoon for Tolley and Montez to arrive, the enemy was pouring into the area, a battalion-strong. Anywhere from 1200 to 5000 of the very best, battle-hardened troops the North Vietnamese Army had to offer were massing to go up against a handful of Australian and US Special Forces and 300 Montagnards.

'The choppers dropped us right into the middle of it,' Payne recalled.

That night new orders came through. The two battalions were to combine and move forward, searching for the main enemy force. It was a rare combined battalion operation that required on-the-spot command. With 2nd Battalion commander Art Austin on leave his executive officer, a young American lieutenant, was flown in to take command of the operation. It was an unusual situation and one that didn't fill Payne and the others with great confidence.

'Mike Force was a different type of operation. Because we worked as small units we weren't under the same command as other battalions. The position of battalion commander of Mike Force was usually an administrative command. The battalion commander oversaw an intelligence sergeant whose job it was to make sure all requests for ammunition resupply and artillery from the field were followed through. They were virtually never in the field with us, but on this occasion because we had all joined up to form battalion-strength the lieutenant was ordered up to the line.

'We didn't really need him. Tolley, Monty and I were used to working with each other, we'd worked out our own structure. I tell myself the lieutenant did what he thought was right, but he was way out of his element.'

Gerry Dellwo remembers the lieutenant was a newcomer to the battalion and had yet to earn the respect of his men.

'He was new to us; not well accepted. It was hard for him,' he said.

After a series of airstrikes first thing next morning, Barry Tolley led his company out of the defensive position and was immediately hit by heavy fire from the enemy.

'Barry never cleared the perimeter. He ran into claymores and a hell of a firefight. Charlie was hitting him with everything, mortars, rockets, the works. Barry brought his men back in and they were in a bad way. Then Montez tried to take his company out along the ridgeline. He got maybe 25 metres past where Tolley had been hit and ran into similar trouble. He didn't get the casualties that Barry had but they had to pull back as well.'

Dellwo's recollection is that Payne's company was also going to try to move forward but the Montagnards refused to budge.

'They thought they'd be killed,' he said. 'They were probably right.'

In Payne's memory it wasn't just the Montagnards who dug their heels in; it was also the South Vietnamese.

'While all this was going on the ARVN units we were supposed to be scouting on behalf of were about 5 kilometres to the north with gunship support. We invited them to the party but they were reluctant to come. We never saw them the whole time.

'That night I was ordered to take my company out the following morning, clear the ridgeline and get on to the next feature, another hill about a kilometre away. By now the enemy was monitoring us. They knew where we were and they were planning an attack. The idea was that we would move first and disrupt their plans. We requested artillery support for around 9.30 a.m. so we could move out at 10 a.m. It never came. I was screaming down the radio for the shelling to start and we finally got just two guns and too late. Instead of leaving at 10 a.m. we headed off about 2 p.m.'

Not wanting to lead his company into an ambush like Tolley and Montez had the previous day, Payne went out on reconnaissance with just two men.

'We went down the hill and back up the flank on to the next ridgeline. We went for about 200 metres and it seemed to be clear, then we moved along the slope for another 100 metres before it started to go up towards the crown of the hill. There was no sign of enemy so I went back and reported the situation. We decided to go forward, my company in front on the left and Monty's on the right, with Barry in reserve coming up behind.'

Dellwo remembers there was also another party involved – a B52 bomber returning from a mission.

'It was late in the afternoon and we had radio contact with this flight crew. They said they'd been listening to our radio calls and they had a couple of bombs left and did we have a target for them. They weren't supposed to do it, they needed permission from the Pentagon before dropping bombs but they did it anyway. We dug our bunkers deeper and took cover and they circled around and dropped two or three bombs on the next feature. Then we just walked up the hill.'

The three companies left the remnants of the 5th Battalion, headed down the slope, across the gully and up the next hill about 1000 metres from their defensive position without problem. Tolley stopped to place his dead from the day before in body bags for later extraction and to retrieve some abandoned weapons from the earlier battle, causing him to fall a little further behind the two lead companies.

'We got to the top of the hill no worries at about 4 p.m. and had started to set up a defensive harbour to secure the ground when we were hit about 4.10. The enemy hit us with machine guns from in front and rifle fire from both flanks. As we'd moved forward they had brought up a company behind us. The situation we were in was an annihilation ambush. Me and Montez were completely surrounded but luckily, because nothing had happened earlier, Barry hadn't closed up. If he had, all three companies could have been wiped out.'

The enemy now had the lead two companies encircled, with Tolley's men on the outside of the circle at the rear. Tolley, his company already weakened from the previous day, moved forward and engaged the enemy, taking some of the rear fire from Payne and Montez, whose men were being cut up by heavy machine-gun, mortar and rocket fire. A tree near Payne was blown apart by mortar and a large splinter embedded itself in his scalp. He continued to move ahead under cover from Montez's company, trying to get his forward platoons close to the machine guns.

'We had no cover, no foxholes, we were taking heavy fire,' Dellwo remembers. 'It was like forest, not jungle. I remember seeing Kev Latham courageously standing in the open ground with a couple of Yards setting up a 60 millimetre mortar. The fire was just so intense. There were machine guns going off in front of us and then they started ground assaults, charging at us. The Yards started to run. Keith and Kevin and I were grabbing them and trying to push them back. We needed to form a perimeter but they'd lost it. They were dropping their weapons and running.'

Payne was blown off his feet by another mortar. He was wounded in the arm and hand and a piece of shrapnel went through the magazine housing of his rifle rendering it useless. He threw it aside and picked up another that had been dropped by one of the Yards, and kept firing and throwing grenades. Inspired by Payne and the other officers, some of the Yards kept fighting, but as the casualties mounted, they pulled back. To the right-hand side of the clearing Montez and his men were receiving a similar pounding.

Payne gave the order to pull back off the hill. By now it was around 6 p.m.

Dellwo was preparing to pull back when he saw Montez's medic Paul Auriemma half-pulling, half-dragging, a badly wounded Montez.

'His jaw was shot off. He was terribly mutilated. Paul wanted me to look after him so he could go back to his position. I said, "Paul. We're losing the hill, we've got to get Montez off the hill." Together we took him down the hill to the east to where some of the men were setting up a defensive position. Then I went back up to where Kevin and Keith were. Keith told me to get my equipment and get off the hill. They were pulling back so we could get organised. I went back to where I'd left my equipment and found my first aid bag and two radio backpacks and threw them all on and started struggling down the hill. I had my pistol belt, my rifle, two radio backpacks and my aid bag and I was pushing my way through the undergrowth when I got caught up in this bracken. I turned around and there was the lieutenant running down the hill. He said, "What are you doing? You've got to get off this hill." I told him to take one of the radios so I could pull myself free and keep moving.'

As he ran down the hill, struggling with all his equipment, Dellwo tripped and fell.

'The strap on my aid bag caught on something, a tree branch maybe, and it pulled out of my hands as I started tumbling down the hill. I must have fallen 10 metres. I was a springboard diver, a gymnast, so I was able to roll and get my footing, but my aid bag was still back up on the slope and I had to get back up and get it. I climbed back up part of the way but I could hear shooting over the hill so I crouched down, hoping it would stop. Then I heard rustling and voices close by so I had to give up on the aid bag, which was tragic because I needed it for Montez and the others. I went back down the hill, away from the voices and I ran into Keith who was coming back up, looking for me. He was mad at me, saying "What were you doing? What took you so long?" We kept going down and that's when we saw Paul and Montez. I helped Paul to carry Montez but all I could think about was that aid bag and how I needed to get it. Montez was a big man, very heavy, and we were moving very slowly. We went for maybe about 200 metres around the bottom of the hill until we caught up with all the others.'

What was left of the two companies – around thirty men in all – had congregated at the foot of the hill, forming a firm base. Tolley, whose company had been cut off and received heavy casualties, had already pulled back to the 5th Battalion defensive position, a kilometre to the west. Others, including a wounded Toget, had been separated from the main withdrawal and wouldn't reappear until the next day. Sergeant Ronald Hogbin, the lieutenant's radio operator, had been killed and Tolley's radio man, Sergeant Doe, had been wounded and separated from his unit. He was rescued several days later, along with a small group of Montagnards, when spotted by a light aircraft from Pleiku. He was in a bomb crater 7 kilometres away from the scene of the action, waving his shirt at the plane.

As Keith arrived with Dellwo, Auriemma and Montez, the lieutenant was on the radio, calling in a napalm strike on the hilltop.

'Keith yelled at him,' Dellwo recalls. 'He was like, "Countermand that order. We've got wounded up there." He called off the strike but I'm pretty sure there were a couple of canisters dropped. We settled Montez down and Paul flopped down on the ground near him. There were a lot of wounded lying around and Montez was in a bad way. Keith and the lieutenant were talking and I was trying to work out how to tell Keith I needed to get back up the hill to get my aid bag. He'd already yelled at me once and I didn't want to get into trouble again, but I needed that bag so I went up to where they were and I heard him saying "I'm going back up there" and the lieutenant was like "*What?*" Keith said he had to go back because there were wounded up there and I thought this was my chance to get my bag so I said, "I'm going too". He just yelled at me, he was so intense, he said, "No, you're not going with me, you're staying with those wounded", so I went back to Montez and then Keith picked up a radio and headed back up the hill and I thought, Well, that's that. I didn't think I'd ever see him again.'

15
Officer Payne

IT WAS JUST ON dark as Payne headed back up the hill. His radio operator Big John tried to follow, but Payne sent him back.

'I knew I had more chance on my own. It was going to be hard enough just being by myself out there without having to worry about anyone else, especially the Yards who were hard to communicate with at the best of times. Besides, I was used to foraging around in the dark by myself. I'd been doing it since I was a kid.'

Slowly he made his way up the slope. Halfway up he sensed movement. Two or three Yards, wounded and disoriented, were staggering down in the darkness. He whispered to them, gathered them in around him, then led them back down to the foot of the hill. 'Stay here,' he said. 'I'll be back.'

At the firm base, Dellwo did the best he could to stem the blood flow from Montez's wound and attend to the other wounded.

'There were two forward observers there, Americans. One minute they were there, the next they'd gone. I didn't see them leave but they just vanished. I didn't like the feel of what was going on. There was just Kevin Latham and the lieutenant left and I didn't trust the lieutenant to make a decision. I remember thinking, If this guy is in charge our situation isn't good.'

At that time Dellwo's main consideration was for the wounded.

Montez and one of the Montagnards were in a very bad way. He believed they could not be moved.

Payne headed back up the slope, finding Yards as he went, pulling them in together, forming them into some semblance of order, then leading them back down to the temporary harbour. All the time, from up on the hilltop, he heard single gunshots – a sound which forty years later still causes him to shudder as if trying to expel a pain that never goes away.

'They were executing the wounded.'

Back down the slope it was obvious that the main group could not have been in a worse position. Most of the Yards had thrown away their weapons. Those that still had them were out of ammunition. The group had simply dropped where they stopped, a few hundred metres around the foot of the hill from where they had withdrawn. If the enemy had decided to follow, they were sitting ducks. The lieutenant and Latham ordered the men to their feet and helped Dellwo carry the wounded to a more secure position, about a hundred metres further into the gully where they would be hidden by thicker undergrowth. The two officers then moved away to decide their next move.

Without his aid bag Dellwo was limited in what he could do for the badly wounded who lay around him, moaning in the darkness. Still, he worked furiously with the few resources he had, all the while aware of the conference taking place between Latham and the lieutenant.

'They were deep in conversation and I remember thinking, This can't be good. Then I saw the lieutenant say something to Kev, like he'd made a decision, and they started picking up their gear. I turned to Auriemma and said, "Paul, they're leaving, they're getting ready to go", but Paul was just laying there, sort of groaning, saying "I can't go, I'm too tired, I can't move". That was when I realised he was delirious.'

The lieutenant turned to the two medics.

'Dellwo, Auriemma,' he said. 'Come on, let's go. We're moving out.'

Dellwo was a young soldier, a Special Forces sergeant trained to obey the orders of a superior officer, but he was also a medic, with a responsibility to the wounded.

'I'm staying,' he said. The lieutenant was incredulous.

'What do you mean you're staying?'

Dellwo turned his back and busied himself with one of the wounded. Almost as a bluff to diffuse the situation and to cover himself for disobeying the lieutenant's order, he started listing the medical supplies he required.

'Okay,' he said. 'When you get back I need you guys to send a litter and some bandages and some morphine …'

Furious, the lieutenant turned on his heel and left, followed by around a dozen Yards. Dellwo was left with five wounded men – two very seriously – a delirious Auriemma, Big John, who insisted on waiting for Payne to return, a radio he later found to be useless as it didn't have a handset, one rifle and next to no ammunition.

'I told Kev I didn't have any ammo. He had four clips left. He gave me two, said "Good luck, mate" and headed off. He must have thought getting back to Barry Tolley and the others at the other base and sending some help the next morning was our only chance.'

Payne led a second group of stragglers back to his temporary position, taking the total number to just under fifty, and headed back up the hill for a third time. As he moved around in the darkness he could hear the enemy close by, speaking to each other and talking on the radio. While he couldn't speak Vietnamese, there was one word he could make out clearly enough. 'Payne.'

'I could hear them talking about me. They knew I was up there and they were looking for me. It wasn't unheard of for some of the Yards to be working for both sides. The NVA intelligence was very good. A lot better than ours. There were plenty of double agents.'

The North Vietnamese were now well organised, moving slowly across the top of the feature in formation. As he moved from his crouch position, Payne came face to face with two NVA soldiers.

'Two dudes came my way. We all fired. They missed, I didn't.'

His position compromised, Payne slipped back down the hill. Halfway down he thought he was being followed and rather than lead the enemy to his men he took shelter behind a log. It was then he did something which has since become part of the Keith Payne legend. He lit up a smoke.

'People have said it was a foolish thing to do but you had to be there to see the circumstances. Because of all the rockets that had been fired off earlier in the battle there was plenty of smoke about and I put the thing under my jacket between drags. I'm not a complete idiot, but to tell the truth, by then I was pretty much past worrying. I'd lost a lot of blood and wasn't feeling too brilliant. I'd been up and down that hill three times, I'd been shot a couple of times and I didn't let myself even touch my head where that bit of wood had gone in. I didn't want to know what was happening there. I just felt like a smoke, and I had one. Really the break gave me time to think. I thought it would be foolish to go back up there again. My responsibility at that time was to get the wounded that I had found back to the main group and then on to the 5th Battalion firm base on the other feature. I went back to where I'd left my group and got them moving around the bottom of the hill towards the others.'

Payne's group moved slowly to avoid making noise. It was pitch black, but while the enemy couldn't see them from the hilltop, they could certainly hear them.

'Charlie was shooting down the hill to try to get my people to shoot back so they'd have a marker. If any of them had, I hate to think what I would have done to him.'

Finally, the more able-bodied helping the wounded, Payne's party made it back to the spot where he had left the lieutenant and the others several hours earlier – only to find it deserted. It was then the old bushman's tricks learned with his childhood mates at the side of Grassy Crisp came to the fore. Payne picked up the trail.

'When you crush grass it leaves a trail of phosphorus. Once I found the trail all I had to do was follow it.'

PAYNE VC

★ ★ ★

Some 200 metres away at the end of the trail Dellwo had organised his band of five injured men and the delirious Auriemma into a tight defensive circle. It was a well-intentioned but futile attempt to ward off the inevitable. Once found by the North Vietnamese they would have neither the firepower nor the physical strength to avoid a slaughter. Exhausted, Dellwo lay on his back, his rifle resting across his chest, and waited.

With so many wounded in his group Payne made slow progress and as he followed the phosphorous trail he started to have doubts.

'It was pretty hairy. I was thinking, Are these my people's tracks or the enemy's? For all I knew the enemy might have got to the others before I did. I could be leading my men straight to them.'

Payne decided to veer off the track, move in a wide arc and come back from the opposite direction. Dellwo heard him coming.

'I heard rustling and thought it was the enemy. What troops of ours could it possibly be? I knew the lieutenant wouldn't be sending out anyone before morning and I never thought Keith would still be alive. I remember just laying there on my back, staying perfectly quiet and hoping they would go past us, but the noise was getting closer. I was holding my rifle and thinking, Well, this is it. Then one of the Yards turned to me and said, "Tipod Payne" – Officer Payne. I was ecstatic. For the first time I thought we were going to be all right. I trusted Keith, I knew we were in good hands. All of us were so happy, we couldn't believe he had found us. I remember saying to him, "Keith. I don't know what the Australian equivalent of the Congressional Medal of Honor is but you deserve it". I asked him how he'd found us, but he wouldn't talk to me about it. He was so angry. He was asking, "What happened to the others? Why did you move? Why did they leave you here?" He was furious.'

Forty years on, Payne has mellowed, but he is still hurt and bewildered by what went on that night at Ben Het.

'I still don't get it. The lieutenant was the commander and he had a responsibility, but he left wounded men out there. I know he was inexperienced and I suppose he did what he thought was right, and Kev was such a good man, such a brave soldier. That time at the stream when he went in alone and cleaned out that enemy nest, you've never seen anything as brave in your life. To be fair to him, he wasn't in charge. It was the lieutenant's call and Kev followed his orders. I don't know how it went down exactly.'

Lieutenant Colonel R.D.F. Lloyd, who sifted through every minute detail of the operation in writing the citation for Payne's Victoria Cross, sees the actions of the lieutenant as symptomatic of America's involvement in Vietnam at that time.

'Latham was a well-trained soldier. His actions and personal bravery in operations the previous month had already been noted by me, from reports I had received. Payne himself had praised Latham's actions earlier in this current operation. Altogether he was a highly credible soldier and trustworthy Team member. As far as the moving back incident is concerned, from Latham's point of view he must have either felt convinced that to do so at that time was the best option for all or, more likely, he wasn't able to convince the American officer otherwise. Circumstances at the time did not enable me to investigate that aspect further. Nor, in my opinion, did I need to. I did, however, speak to Mike Force commander at the first opportunity about the young lieutenant – as well as about other associated operational matters. Why that officer thought leaving Payne and what was left of the others on their own was the right thing to do is by any standards, let alone Australian military values, beyond belief.

'The US military commitment to the war was enormous by comparison with ours. They had all but run out of younger officers with any experience and when compared with our warrant officers in the Team who had served in Malaya, Borneo and some in Korea, the difference in professional quality and leadership was enormous. Notwithstanding, the failure in this instance to take proper responsibility and leave one's men in all probability to die, is inexcusable.'

★ ★ ★

Payne had no time to dwell on the actions of those who had headed off earlier; his priority was getting the remaining men across the gully and up to the defensive position a kilometre away. It was pitch dark, the majority of the men were wounded and Montez was in a very bad way. Dellwo was against moving him.

'Keith said we had to go, that if he could find us then the enemy sure could too. I said we should stay, that we'd lose Montez if we moved him, but he said we'd lose him if we stayed. He said, "If they don't find us tonight, they'll find us tomorrow". That's when I told him that we had another problem, that Paul was delirious and unable to help us. Keith just spun around, went over to him and pulled him up to his feet. He never hit him or anything like that, but he shook him and told him to snap out of it. He said stuff like, "You listen to me Paul, we're in trouble here and I need you to help so pull yourself together and let's get going", and that's exactly what happened. Paul snapped out of it and from then on he was a rock, as always. That was what Keith was like. He was someone you could buddy up with but he wasn't a best friend, he was a commanding officer. You could have a beer and laugh with him when the time was right but when the moment called for it he could be very intense and commanding. I liked that, I needed it. I needed someone to call the shots so I could focus on being a good medic, and that's what Keith did.'

The motley band set off into the darkness not sure exactly of the location of the 5th Battalion camp, nor whether the North Vietnamese were on their trail. It was a tortuous journey, Dellwo recalled.

'It was very slow and Montez was a very heavy man. Keith was on the radio most of the time, trying to get through to someone but he'd help with Montez as well. Some of the time Paul and I were carrying Montez on our backs. The others were carrying the badly wounded Montagnard and at one stage I looked back and realised he had died and they'd had to leave him behind. I don't know how long we were going but it seemed like hours. We were going up hills and down knolls and valleys. It was dense forest, with thick underbrush and briars. The ground underfoot was slippery, damp clay and we were sliding around, but we just kept dragging ourselves through the jungle.'

At one stage, as they pulled themselves through the bush, exhausted and almost on autopilot, Dellwo felt something warm and sticky on his hand.

'I was dragging Montez along, with his head on my shoulder and I felt a tapping sensation on the tips of my fingers. I realised it was blood from his jaw and that he had been bleeding a long time and was getting much weaker. I called Keith over and told him we couldn't move Montez any more. I was taking charge because I was the medic and my job was to not lose the patient. Keith agreed to stop and, while I tried to look after Montez, he kept trying to make contact on the radio. Finally he made contact with a Spooky, a Magic Dragon, overhead and it relayed Keith back to headquarters at Dak To.'

The sound of the Spooky radio operator crackling through in the darkness was the answer to a prayer. The reply to Payne's request for the urgent despatch of a medevac helicopter was anything but. None available, he was told, but then a window of opportunity: the commanding officer at Dak To, Major Jaegles, was on his way in his own command and control chopper. If Montez could just hold on …

Jaegles ordered a medical team into his chopper and, equipped with a McGuire Rig to pull Montez from the ground, headed to the area. Payne quickly scouted the surrounding forest. Not far from their position he spotted an opening in the trees. It might just be enough. He called the others up and they waited, looking upwards into the darkened sky, their ears pricked for both the sound of chopper blades and the noise of approaching North Vietnamese.

'It was then Keith had to make one of the most difficult decisions of his life,' Dellwo recalled. 'We were stopped there, with Montez in a very bad state, not knowing how far behind us the enemy was, and knowing the chopper would bring them right to us. Keith had over fifty men to worry about, plus the chopper could be shot down and it was unlikely Montez was going to make it anyway. He just said, "No, this is crazy, we're not doing it. Come on, we're going up the hill", and he started leading the way. We hadn't gone 20 metres when

Montez sort of gasped and collapsed and stopped breathing. I called to Keith and tried to give Montez mouth to mouth but he'd been shot up so bad, there was no mouth. I said, "I've got to do a tracheotomy" and asked if anyone had anything sharp. Keith had a knife and it worked and I managed to get some air into his lungs but Paul said, "There's no pulse", and started external heart massage. But that was it, he was gone. Keith was right. Even if the chopper had gotten there it wouldn't have made any difference. He never would have survived the harness.'

It was then that Dellwo was overcome with emotion.

'I was crying and cradling his head in my arms. Through everything that had happened through that day and night we had all stayed so strong and focused but when Montez went, I guess I just let go. When we were carrying him and trying to get him out, we felt such love for that man. I was sobbing. Keith finally had to ask if I was alright and get me moving. Keith was always in control. He had to be strong for the rest of us.'

Payne got back on the radio, aborted the chopper and asked Major Jaegles for permission to leave Montez's body behind.

'I didn't like to do it but there was no choice. He was such a big man, we couldn't carry him any further. We covered his body and took note as best we could of where he was so we could come back later but we never found him. Patrols were sent out but the air force had gone over and B52s had saturated the whole area so nothing looked the same. It is something I've thought about a lot since, but I had other wounded to get back and there was no way around it. We just had to keep going.'

The group kept struggling on, physically lightened but emotionally burdened by the loss of Montez. The Magic Dragon stayed above them, relaying Payne's messages to Tolley on the far side of the next hill.

'Even though we were getting closer I couldn't get through to Tolley on the radio because I only had a battle antenna and he was on the other side of the ridge. Without radio contact we had no hope of finding him in the dark. The Spooky relayed my signal. I told Tolley

Officer Payne

where I thought I was. As it turned out I wasn't off by much, which was a miracle in itself. I asked Tolley to give us a beacon so we could head towards him. We still had no idea if Charlie was on our tail so Tolley took two men and headed down the valley about 150 metres from the position and started shooting off flares and mortars. It was a pretty hairy thing to do. The enemy could have picked up on it, zeroed in and blasted away. When I think of that first impression I had of Tolley when we met at Pleiku, and here he was putting his neck on the line for me again. We got to the top of the ridgeline and I could see the fire down in the valley and from that point of reference we could come in. We must have been a pretty rough-looking crew when we finally got there. I was that buggered I could hardly stand up.'

One of the first people Dellwo saw was his fellow medic from the 5th Battalion, Elder Dugger, who rushed to his side. He told Dellwo that when the lieutenant and the others had come in hours earlier he had started to put together a party of Montagnard volunteers to head out and find his friend. When they heard Payne's voice relayed through on the radio by the Magic Dragon, they had called off the search.

Payne and the others settled down for the rest of the night, waiting for the attack they thought would surely come in the morning.

'Fortunately Charlie didn't come straightaway. Maybe he was licking his wounds. The artillery finally arrived and that gave us a bit of breathing space. The choppers starting coming in to evacuate the wounded and resupply with ammo, food, medical supplies and water. I went out on the last bird to Dak To. By the time I got there I was pretty pissed off. I went straight up to Major Jaegles and told him if they didn't pull Mike Force off that hilltop immediately I would withdraw all Australians from the battalion, which given that Tolley and Latham were the only two up there, wasn't much of a threat. Still, they told me they had problems getting the choppers up there because of the wind or something and they'd get them out the next morning. It was the best they could do but I was still worried. I thought they mightn't be there the next morning if Charlie got there first.'

Having done all he could, Payne stayed at Dak To, receiving medical attention for his wounds. That night the North Vietnamese hit the defensive position near Ben Het with everything they had for several hours before the last of the two battalions could finally be airlifted off the hill.

Up until then Dellwo had been in Vietnam only two months but had seen an inordinate amount of action – and come through it all unscathed. That night his luck finally ran out.

'They hit us with 82 millimetre mortars,' he recalled. 'The troops were pretty spooked after all they had been through and I thought, Here we ago again. I was with Auriemma and we both stood up to see if there was a ground attack coming under the mortar attack. We both got hit with the first rounds. Paul had shrapnel in the skull and abdomen. I was hit in the head, back and abdomen. It felt like I'd been stabbed with a red hot poker. It hurt like a son of a bitch. I remember yelling, "I've got an abdomen" and Dugger ran over. I had a puncture wound in the back. Dugger had a look and told me it wasn't a big deal. What we didn't know was that it had punctured a lung.'

Dellwo would almost drown in his own blood as he bled into his lung. He would run a dangerously high fever and eventually be transferred from a US field hospital and sent to Tokyo for treatment as his condition worsened. When he finally pulled through he was told by a doctor he would be sent back to the States. To some it may have been welcome news. Not to Gerry Dellwo.

'I pleaded with him. I told him I had to go back to Vietnam. I talked him into speaking to a colonel and convincing him that it was important that I go back, and it was. I needed to go back to Ben Het and talk to people who had been there. I had to get it all straight in my mind so I could move forward.'

Dellwo got his wish. He was posted back to the camp at Ben Het but no one he needed to speak to was still there.

'Keith had gone, Kevin had gone, but I was sent back there with orders to rebuild the medical facility and that's what I did. It was very important to me. I know of soldiers who have been wounded in battle and never get to go back to the battlefield and it haunts them forever. I did get to go back and I was able to come to grips with it.'

Dellwo spent the rest of his tour of duty building and supervising the medical facilities at Ben Het, a job he did so well that he was awarded the Bronze Star for meritorious service. Ever the conscientious medic, it is recognition he savours even more than the Silver Star he won for his action during the battle and its aftermath.

Payne knew nothing of the pounding that Dellwo, Tolley and the others were suffering as he left the medical tent at Dak To, having had the splinter and shrapnel removed from his head and hand. He had gone only a few metres before he sank to the ground, leaned against a communications pole, and promptly fell asleep.

He awoke to gentle shaking and opened his eyes to see another member of the Team, Warrant Officer Marty McLachlan. Asking McLachlan what he was doing at Dak To, he was informed he been sent to take over Payne's company.

'Marty,' said Payne sadly, 'there's no company left to take over'.

16

'Oh Shit, Sir'

MARTY MCLACHLAN, WHO PAYNE knew from Australia, had just arrived in the Highlands to take over from Jock Stewart as training officer at Pleiku. When word came through that Payne had been wounded, he was sent straight to Dak To to assume command of 212 Company. When Payne told him the situation McLachlan agreed it was useless heading out into the field and waited instead for the remnants of the company to be flown out of the combat zone. In the meantime he asked Payne if there was anything he could do to help him.

'I hadn't eaten for thirty-six hours. I told him all I wanted was a feed. He had some C-rations, the US combat rations which had all the bloody goodies in the world in them. Marty cooked them up and I ate the lot, then I slept my bloody head off.'

The partnership between Payne and McLachlan wasn't to continue so smoothly. On return to Pleiku where he received medical treatment from the Americans at the 71st Evacuation Hospital, Payne was replaced as company commander by Warrant Officer Frank Moffitt and assigned the role of assisting McLachlan in recruitment and training. It proved to be an exercise in frustration.

'I'd done my time as company commander and had a pretty rough time of it so R.D.F. Lloyd pulled me out of the front line and said I wasn't to go back in until I was 100 per cent right. As far as I was concerned that was in about a week or so. I'd been shot up a bit but I wasn't that bad. I was patched up and back at work a day after I got back from Ben Het so I felt I was ready to be given another command. R.D.F. Lloyd thought different. Obviously there was something going on behind the scenes that I didn't know about.'

The 'something' was Lieutenant Colonel Lloyd sitting down at his desk in Saigon and writing a recommendation for a Victoria Cross for the second time in a month.

The process behind the awarding of a Victoria Cross is involved and exacting which, given the reverence with which the decoration is viewed within Commonwealth forces, is not surprising.

The Victoria Cross was first awarded in 1857 to veterans of the Crimean War with Russia. Prior to the striking of the Victoria Cross there was no official standardised system for recognition of gallantry within British Commonwealth forces. With British newspaper correspondents reporting numerous acts of bravery during the Crimean conflict, the need for official recognition became obvious. In late 1855 Queen Victoria instructed the War Office to strike a medal that would not recognise class or rank. The Queen decreed that the decoration should be simple and highly prized. To maintain simplicity she vetoed the original suggestion that the decoration be called the Military Order of Victoria, preferring the less ostentatious Victoria Cross. On 29 January 1856 Queen Victoria signed a Royal Warrant officially recognising the Victoria Cross, a plain cross 41 millimetres high and 36 millimetres wide, bearing a crown surmounted by a lion. The first sixty-two medals, presented by Queen Victoria in a ceremony at Hyde Park on 26 June 1857, were cast from the bronze of two cannons captured from the Russians at the siege of Sevastopol. The cross is suspended from a bar ornamented with laurel leaves, through which passes a crimson ribbon. The reverse of the suspension bar is engraved with the recipient's name, rank, number and unit. On the reverse of the medal is a circular panel on which the date of the act for which it was awarded is engraved.

Queen Victoria rejected the suggested inscription 'For Bravery', preferring 'For Valour', believing that while many soldiers in battle show bravery, the Victoria Cross should only be awarded under the most exceptional of circumstances. This is emphasised by the official warrant, which states the Victoria Cross should be awarded for 'most conspicuous bravery, or some daring or pre-eminent act of valour or self-sacrifice, or extreme devotion to duty in the presence of the enemy'.

When the first reports of Payne's actions at Ben Het reached Saigon, and Lieutenant Colonel Lloyd assessed that a Victoria Cross recommendation might be the outcome, he began what he terms the 'gruelling process' of producing an appropriate citation based on the facts, descriptions and eyewitness accounts culminating in a recommendation for that award.

'It is the ultimate recognition for special acts of bravery, for valour,' Lloyd said. 'To get it right is not an easy road. First you have to take into account the reports from witnesses, then substantiate them. They are often conflicting. One has to be cautious and make sure you are not being misled by unwitting exaggeration or by others wishing to become participants in potential glory.'

This was particularly so because Lloyd had only just submitted the recommendation for Simpson's Victoria Cross, a situation which caused a certain amount of astonishment in official circles. In unofficial circles the reaction was less astonishment and a degree of suspicion. Such as: why were members of the Team receiving so many awards? The answer to that, of course, was that members of the Team were operating in exceptional circumstances. In the case of Special Forces they were working with indigenous soldiers who were not given high priority support by US or South Vietnamese forces, and who were growing increasingly discontented about their lot. All too often, members of the Team were being placed in situations of excessive danger. The degree and frequency of acts of gallantry were in direct proportion to the number of times they found themselves in critical situations.

As R.D.F. Lloyd put it: 'Pro rata there was a greater proportion of recognised gallantry amongst the Team than in most other areas of our forces over there because they were placed in situations which by normal standards were very unusual and of higher risk. In action they

'Oh Shit, Sir'

had few they could rely on. This had a huge impact on the men involved.'

Not that this meant the Mike Force people were receiving more recognition than those serving with South Vietnamese forces. To many Australians in Vietnam the numbers of medals being awarded by the Americans and ARVN lessened their significance. In some cases they were seen as 'Mickey Mouse' decorations, awarded for propaganda and morale purposes as much as for genuine acts of gallantry. It was a perception that R.D.F. Lloyd was well aware of and one that made him determined to check and double-check all eyewitness reports that came across his desk – particularly as in most cases the eyewitnesses were not Australian.

'The American system could be pretty flamboyant,' he recalled. 'You had to be guarded when you got their reports. You used those reports as the starting point and checked their validity as best you could. It wasn't always easy. I couldn't go everywhere checking the American and Vietnamese versions of events in every case to 100 per cent certainty. Sometimes I would have liked the checking process to be better and in some cases I might have altered the views of those assessments, but I like to think that I got it pretty right given the difficulties.

'The actual wording of the citation had to be somewhat diplomatic. You couldn't really say that the performance of others was disgraceful and had put the lives of other people in jeopardy. I wasn't able to portray Payne's whole operation as some sort of disaster; rather I emphasised the fact that Keith's performance had been the high point, as it had been, and that he had repeatedly shown unselfishness and bravery in the extreme.'

When he was finally satisfied with the facts at his disposal, Lloyd's recommendation was sent to Canberra by the Australian Commander in Vietnam.

'The questions started almost at once,' Lloyd recalled. 'There was almost a toilet roll of questions. They came from Canberra and some originated from London. They asked for information in detail: How dark was it? How many trees were there? Why did this fellow do this or do that? And I had everything checked again. There was obviously a very close hold on the quality of VCs, and rightly so.'

The veracity of the eyewitness reports was checked, rechecked and checked again to the satisfaction of the relevant authorities and finally the recommendation for the Victoria Cross was accepted by the Queen. As written by Lieutenant Colonel R.D.F. Lloyd, it reads:

> On 24th May 1969, in Kon Tum Province Warrant Officer Payne was Commanding 212th Company of 1st Mobile Strike Force Battalion when the battalion was attacked by a North Vietnamese force of superior strength. The enemy isolated the two leading companies, one of which was Warrant Officer Payne's, and with heavy mortar and rocket support assaulted their position from three directions simultaneously. Under this heavy attack the Indigenous soldiers began to fall back. Directly exposing himself to the enemy's fire, Warrant Officer Payne, through his own efforts, temporarily held off the assaults by alternately firing his weapon and running from position to position collecting grenades and throwing them at the assaulting enemy. While doing this he was wounded in the hands and arms. Despite his outstanding efforts the indigenous soldiers gave way under the enemy's increased pressure and the Battalion Commander, together with several advisers and a few soldiers, withdrew. Paying no attention to his wounds and under extremely heavy enemy fire Warrant Officer Payne covered his withdrawal by again throwing grenades and firing his own weapon at the enemy who were attempting to follow up. Still under fire, he then ran across exposed ground to head off his own troops who were withdrawing in disorder. He successfully stopped them and organised the remnants of his and the second company into a temporary defensive perimeter by nightfall. Having achieved this, Warrant Officer Payne of his own accord and at great personal risk, moved out of the perimeter into the darkness alone in an attempt to find the wounded and other indigenous soldiers. Some had been left on the position and others were scattered in the area. Although the enemy were still occupying the previous position, Warrant Officer Payne, with complete disregard

for his own life, crawled back to it and extricated several wounded soldiers. He then continued to search the area, in which the enemy were also moving and firing, for some three hours. He finally collected forty lost soldiers, some of whom had been wounded and returned with his group to the temporary defensive perimeter he had left, only to find that the remainder of the battalion had moved back. Undeterred by this set back and personally assisting the seriously wounded American adviser he led the group through the enemy to the safety of his battalion base. His sustained and heroic personal efforts in this action were outstanding and undoubtedly saved the lives of a large number of his indigenous soldiers and several of his fellow advisers. Warrant Officer Payne's repeated acts of exceptional personal bravery and unselfish conduct in this operation were an inspiration to all Vietnamese, United States and Australian soldiers who served with him. His conspicuous gallantry was in the highest tradition of the Australian Army. (courtesy Australian Department of Defence)

While all this was going on Payne continued to work alongside Marty McLachlan training Montagnard recruits at Pleiku in a state of anything but 'blissful' ignorance.

'I suppose they didn't want me going out and getting myself shot before the award came through but nobody told me that. All I knew was that they were keeping me out of the action and I was feeling pretty frustrated and under-utilised. All up, I wasn't the happiest bumblebee at that time. I felt my experience in the field wasn't being used.'

Payne would have been even more unhappy if he knew some of the suggestions for future employment and rules of safety that were being pressured on Lloyd. As the then AATTV commander recalled: 'I was destined to have two live VCs on my hands who I was required to protect from harm's way. It was impossible really.'

After two months in the training company Payne was given ten days leave and headed home to Flo and the boys – after a short delay so he could attend a very special function. The announcement of Ray

Simpson's Victoria Cross was held up as the military back in Australia tried to contact his relatives. With the army wanting all members of the Team to be in Vietnam to share the honour of the announcement, Payne was kept waiting for two days before he could fly to Brisbane and begin his 'R & R'. It was a strange experience for both Payne and his family. After a few hours on a Qantas flight he was transported from the jungles of Vietnam's Highlands, where danger and even death could lie waiting behind every tree, to suburban Brisbane and the steady routine of breakfast Weet-Bix, after-school pick-ups and the evening news on the telly.

'I followed the kids around, stood on the sideline for the weekend footy matches with the other dads but I was careful not to let myself get caught up in it all,' Payne recalled. 'I had this theory. I'd seen too many family men go back to Australia, switch off for a few days and then get hit as soon as they got back to Vietnam. I tried to keep myself distant. Keep myself on my toes.'

As Flo put it, 'He was there but he wasn't there'.

For the boys, excited to have their father back home, it proved an unusual time.

'I remember the first morning going in to wake Dad up and ending up on my tail,' recalled Ron. 'He might have been at home but he was still in combat mode. We learned pretty quick that you couldn't just go in and shake him or jump on the bed to wake him up. It would be like, "Dad, Dad, wake up" and next thing, bang, you'd be flat on your back. The only way to do it was crawl in, keep low and grab his big toe. The only one who could wake him up in safety was Mum.'

Payne returned to Vietnam still believing he would be given command of another Mike Force company for the remaining five months of his tour. When he arrived in Saigon, he was told this would not be the case.

'I had in my mind that I would be going straight back to the Highlands and all the time I'd been on leave and even on the flight back, I'd been thinking about how I'd go about things, how I'd use my experience to work things differently. When I arrived in Saigon I was

'Oh Shit, Sir'

told I'd actually been posted to an ARVN unit. That was fair enough, I was keen to get there and start work, but there were all these delays. I was left spinning my wheels in Saigon. What I didn't know was that they were waiting for the balloon to go up.'

With R.D.F. Lloyd away on leave himself, his job was being done by Major Frank Johnston. Finally it was Johnston who took Payne to see the Commander of Australian Forces Vietnam, Major General R.A. Hay.

'I was under the impression I was going to be briefed on the new unit and the new sector. It wasn't every day that you get to meet a general but I still had no idea what was happening. I didn't have a clue.'

Hay didn't keep Payne in the dark for long. As soon as he and Johnston walked into his office, the general rose from his desk and put out his hand.

'May I be the first to congratulate you,' he said. 'Her Majesty the Queen has awarded you the Victoria Cross.'

Payne's reply will not go down in the annals of British Commonwealth military history but it is a fair representation of the man, and the shock he felt.

'Oh shit, sir.'

After some brief pleasantries, Payne was taken straight down to the press room where a large media contingent, already informed of his award, was waiting.

'There were wall-to-wall reporters, and photographers climbing over each other to get pictures. Everyone was asking what I thought were pretty stupid questions and I was answering them as best I could. I was still in shock after being told of the award, let alone having been thrust into the middle of this. Even then I remember wishing that they'd brought R.D.F. Lloyd back from leave so he could be there. He was the one who'd written the citation, he was the one who was my commanding officer at the time of the action. I just thought he should be there.'

One person who was there, standing at the back of the media room, was Ray Simpson.

'Simmo was now a three-week veteran of all this VC business. He had this little smile on his face. When it was all over he just sidled up and grabbed me and said, "Let's go have a beer mate".'

By the time Simpson and Payne had sidled up to the bar in Saigon the word of Australia's ninety-sixth Victoria Cross had made its way to Brisbane. Flo was working on the switchboard for manufacturing company K.M. Cyclone and had just headed down to the canteen for lunch.

'I'd just got down there when it came over the intercom that I had a phone call, so I headed back up to the switch. The lass relieving me told me I actually had two calls and I remember saying to her, "Gee, I'm popular today aren't I?" I took the first call and it was my sister Margaret, who was a hairdresser. She ran a local salon. It was where I used to get my hair done and I knew everyone there. I could hardly hear what Margaret was saying, there was so much commotion in the background. She was shouting out, "Isn't it wonderful, isn't it marvellous", and I was saying, "What? What are you talking about?" She said, "Keith's been awarded the VC" and I just thought, Oh sure. I remembered how Keith had been held up for two days in Vietnam until the army could tell Simmo's relatives about his award so I knew that they always contacted the next of kin first. Besides, when something like that happens you think you'll hear it through the army, not through a hairdressing salon. Then I remembered the other call and I thought, Hang on, maybe that's the army. I told Margaret to hold on and took the other call. This time it was Daphne Stack whose husband Max was over in Vietnam with Keith. She was ringing to give her congratulations too, so I thought maybe there was something to it after all. I told Daphne and Margaret I'd better get off the line because Victoria Barracks might be trying to get through. A couple of minutes later I got another call.'

It still wasn't the army, but it was getting closer. The third call was from Flo's next-door neighbour in Falkirk Street. She was concerned because there had been an army officer walking around the house. 'Was anything wrong?'

At this point things started getting a little crazy. Army public relations officer Major Allan Hines – the man who had been walking around at Falkirk Street – arrived at Flo's office, right behind a reporter from a radio station. He gave Flo a quick briefing on the circumstances surrounding Keith's award, then stood by as she was hustled outside for a quick interview. Meanwhile the relief switchboard operator was fielding call after call – all for Mrs Payne. The management at K.M. Cyclone soon came to the conclusion that Flo wouldn't be good for much more work that afternoon and sent her home. She drove her car, with Major Hines following behind in his.

'When I came to make a right turn into our street there were so many people outside our house that I just couldn't believe it. There were TV cameras and reporters and people just standing around. If Major Hines hadn't been behind me I would have turned left and just kept on going.'

Flo drove underneath the house and had to push her way through the throng just to get to the front steps. Hines took charge of the situation. Telling her not to say a word, he put himself between Flo and the media scrum and announced, 'Mrs Payne is going upstairs to have a cup of tea and when she has done that she will answer your questions'. He then led the way in, asked for the location of Flo's kettle and tea, and made a cuppa. By now it was after 3 p.m. and the boys were heading home from school.

'Greg and Ron were walking up the street from the school and there were all these reporters parked outside and standing on our front lawn. Ron was thirteen, almost fourteen, I remember him walking in, dropping his schoolbag and saying, "What's going on Mum? What are these people here for?"'

Between when he had left for school in the morning and when he arrived home that afternoon, Ron's life had changed. The Paynes weren't just a family whose dad was in the army any more. For better or for worse, they were the family of Keith Payne VC. Within days they would be the best known family in Queensland. Ron remembers being called up at school assembly and presented to the students as 'the son of Australia's latest national hero'.

'All of a sudden it was like I was some sort of celebrity, and for me that felt very hypocritical. I hadn't done anything and here I was being put on this pedestal which I didn't feel I deserved.'

It was something the entire family had to get used to, and fast. Readers of local newspapers couldn't get enough of the suburban mum and five boys who waited stoically behind as their husband and father fought Australia's enemies overseas. The Brisbane afternoon newspaper *The Telegraph* was particularly interested in the family. The day after the announcement of Payne's medal it published a story that likened the family home to an army barracks. 'No. 28 Falkirk Street, Stafford Heights doesn't look much like an Army barracks but it represents everything that is traditional in Army life,' it said. Supported by a photograph of Flo on the top step of the home and the boys descending in order of age as they headed off to school, it spoke of 'reveille at 6.30am when an alarm rings in Mrs Payne's room'. After clearing the breakfast dishes, 'Inspection follows as Mum checks on hair and teeth'. Lights out was at 8.30 p.m. According to Ron that article might have taken some creative licence but it also contained a basis of truth.

'There were times when I felt we weren't really growing up in a family per se. It was like we were part of an army section, with a section commander. I remember one time Dad took us three older boys out through the backblocks near where we were living, down an old track to some mangrove swamps. He set up a little shooting gallery and taught us range shooting procedure with a .22 rifle. I would have been nine or ten years old at the time. To us it didn't seem anything strange. Our family life was pretty regimented. Everything was neatly racked, packed and stacked at all times. Dad was a good father, but he was still very much a soldier.'

When eleven-year-old Colin was admitted to hospital after burning his leg, it warranted a story and photo. The *Telegraph* even arranged an 'international trunk call' to allow Flo and Keith to speak – and published the photo of her speaking on the phone 'with glistening eyes as she smiled brightly and told her hero: "Darling, we are all so happy and very proud"'.

'Oh Shit, Sir'

The attention was something the whole family got used to and over the years dealt with in different ways. The press attention may have been overwhelming – and over-the-top – at first, but Flo soon showed she was no pushover. When *Australian Women's Weekly* journalist Jean Bruce wrote a colour piece on Flo in October 1969, she noted: 'Attractive, aged 34 (her husband is 36) with brown hair and grey eyes, Florence Payne thinks for a moment before speaking. When I asked, "Do you always consider what you are going to say?" she replied, smiling, "Yes, where Keith is concerned"'.

In the eyes of some the medal made Payne a hero, a celebrity. It opened doors around Australia and across the world. The son of the grocer from Ingham, North Queensland, would receive personally written Christmas cards from Buckingham Palace and Parliament House. It would be a source of both pride and depression; it thrust him into a spotlight that at times seemed like torture. It gave weight to his words and allowed him to become a spokesperson for men and women who had suffered as he had, and ultimately it offered financial security to his family. But back on 8 September 1969 as he shared a beer with Simmo, he couldn't contemplate any of that. Even if he had had the smallest inkling of what lay ahead he wouldn't let himself think about it. Victoria Cross recipient or not, he was still a soldier and, like all soldiers, he had just one thing on his mind: survival.

Payne stayed in Saigon for a week or so until R.D.F. Lloyd returned from leave, and went to see him in his living quarters. He'll always remember the words Lloyd uttered as he congratulated him on the Victoria Cross.

'Well,' he said as they shook hands. 'You and Simmo may not think well of me later on for writing you up this way. I'm afraid it's not going to be easy. You now have a cross to bear. Bear it well.'

Pleasantries over, they got down to business.

'What would you like to do now?' Lloyd asked.

'Get home in one piece,' came the reply.

They discussed the possibility of Payne working with the Vietnamese Regional and Popular Force – the locally recruited army that was the equivalent of the Australian CMF or US National Guard.

Payne himself preferred to go to an ARVN battalion and with Lloyd's approval that is where he was intended to be deployed. It was a posting he would never take up.

'I caught an aircraft up to Danang to await formal movement to an ARVN unit and when I was there I bumped into a bloke who I'd done my training with at Canungra. He asked me to go for a beer, as you do, and we went to the bar. They put the beer in front of me and I looked at it and couldn't drink it. He asked me what was wrong and I said, "Mate, you better get me to the hospital, I feel that crook".'

Months, maybe years, of stress had built up. The days of 'every time I turned around someone was shooting at me', the horrors of Ben Het, even the strain of spending time with his family for ten days R & R while staying distant, on his toes, had taken a toll. He was taken straight to the US base hospital. The diagnosis was instantaneous: duodenal ulcers.

For Keith Payne VC, physically at least, the Vietnam War was over.

17

Coming Home

WHEN HE HAD GONE to Vietnam some nine months earlier, it had been as Warrant Officer Keith Payne. When he returned it was as Warrant Officer Keith Payne VC. It didn't take long for Payne to realise what a difference those two letters behind his name meant.

Even before he touched down in Brisbane on the afternoon of 24 September 1969, the morning newspaper, the *Courier-Mail*, was leading the parade. Under the headline 'Welcome, W.O. Payne' the editorial read:

> Welcome, Warrant Officer Keith Payne, V.C., to your home city of Brisbane, when you arrive this afternoon!
>
> Queensland's new V.C. and the State's first since World War II is returning to a city which is full of admiration for his bravery. Most people will want to let him know of their pride. The Lord Mayor Ald. Jones has arranged to give a civic reception this afternoon and Brisbane's citizens tomorrow afternoon can take off their hats and cheer the Sergeant Major when he appears, necessarily briefly, outside the City Hall.
>
> Warrant Office Payne, V.C., can be assured that the city of Brisbane, and all the State of Queensland, are glad to have him back home safely and that the knowledge of the excitement that there will be at his home in Stafford Heights tonight brings a warm glow to Queenslanders' hearts.

There had been nothing quite as effusive about Payne's farewell from Vietnam. Quite the contrary. From the US base hospital in Danang he was transferred to the main Australian Field Hospital in Vung Tau. While there the unofficial Warrant Officers' Corps came into play once again. Quartermaster at the hospital was an old friend, Captain Dave Collier, a former warrant officer. 'He made sure I was well looked after,' Payne recalled, but there was no quick fix to his ailment.

'I was bloody ill, physically and mentally fatigued. I hadn't been eating … all I needed was a bloody good rest and fattening up.'

To a degree the army agreed, but Vietnam wasn't the best place for that treatment to be administered. Payne was ordered home – after he filled out some paperwork. As with Flo's towel and bedsheet in Malaya, the army was rather interested why the serial number of the weapon he handed back before flying out of Vietnam was different to the one he had been given when he arrived. He filled out the forms, reliving the action at Ben Het – the shrapnel through the magazine housing, the Montagnard's M16 lying on the ground – and the explanation was deemed satisfactory. Unlike the bedsheet, the cost of the original weapon wasn't taken out of Payne's pay.

Payne was flown from Saigon to Butterworth Air Force Base, Malaysia, in a C-130 Hercules, then on to Richmond in western New South Wales and finally to Amberley, outside Brisbane, where he transferred to a waiting helicopter. From there it was a quick trip to Kelvin Grove Barracks where he was met by Flo and the boys, the base commanding officer and a medical officer. His younger brother Frank and sister Janice were also there. But even before he could greet his family an army corporal snapped to attention, saluted and said, 'Your weekend leave pass, sir'.

'I thought, What's going on here? Warrant officers don't get weekend leave passes,' Payne recalled. Something even more bizarre was to come. Next in line was Chief of Staff of Northern Command Brigadier J.F. White – who also saluted the warrant officer.

'The brigadier started saluting me, I started saluting him. We both got about halfway up. It was all a bit of a mess, but by then the family had all run up and no one was worrying too much about protocol.'

The tarmac reunion with Flo and the boys was heartfelt, emotional – and captured in minute detail by photographers and reporters from the local media, including *Courier-Mail* photographer Eric Donnelly, the former POW who had been evacuated from Korea to Japan with Payne. The photos took up the next morning's front pages, and plenty more inside.

One reporter noted that Payne 'reminds you a bit of Rod Laver'. Another reported 'a little girl in a blue and white dress presented the Cong killer with a bouquet of deep red carnations … that matched the brand-new dark-red ribbon with its tiny cross, heading Payne's double bank of chestborne fruit salad'.

The media pressed Payne for his views on the war. 'I've got a great respect for the Viet Cong as fighters – never underestimate Charlie,' he was quoted as saying. 'Yes, when the time comes, I'd say the South Vietnamese will be quite capable of taking care of themselves against the North.

'Do I want to go back to Vietnam? Ask the wife.'

The press and public lapped it up. Payne was not only a home-grown hero, he was a family man whose laid-back, unassuming attitude to life and war seemed to epitomise the fantasy stereotype of the unaffected Aussie digger. His greeting to the boys as they ran to his side, 'Here's me old mates. G'day cobbers', made a headline. His brother Frank added to the legend when he told reporters of the time the teenage Payne had walked into the cinema in Ingham looking for his younger brothers and sisters, 'carrying a broken-down shotgun and with ducks hanging all over him'.

The youngest of Payne's 'cobbers' was Derek, born in 1962. He remembers very little of his father's days in active service, but does remember the homecoming.

'I do remember how we were all creating havoc at the base at Kelvin Grove and Dad hopping out of the helicopter. I was probably too young to feel proud, I was just excited that he was coming home.'

The next day, when Brisbane Lord Mayor Clem Jones presented Payne with a replica of the key to the city on the steps of Town Hall,

3000 people watched and workers on building sites shouted down congratulations.

There was more to come. After the weekend leave at home in Stafford, Payne was admitted to No. 1 Military Hospital, Yeronga, for six weeks treatment, at the end of which the family was treated to a week's holiday by the management of Tangalooma Resort on Moreton Island off Brisbane. The Paynes then headed to Ingham for what they thought would be a quiet few days with Keith's family. Hardly. Payne was now a national hero, and Ingham wasn't going to be left out of the party.

'It was the early days of passenger flights from Brisbane to Ingham and the local member of parliament came along so he could be seen getting off the plane with us. We landed at Ingham and they held this big civic reception in a park right across the road. The local member gave a speech, the mayor gave a speech, I gave a speech and they gave me the key to the shire. It was pretty amazing. Everyone in town was there: my family, old mates I knocked around with as a kid, my schoolteachers – all there to see old Keith Payne come home from the war.'

One person watching on with mixed feelings was Keith's father Henry. There had been no civic reception when he had come home from war, just a distant family and memories he had kept to himself for the best part of quarter of a century. When the speeches were over and they headed home for a cup of tea, Henry and Keith began to talk for the first time about war and soldiering and all the question marks in between.

'Father couldn't understand what Vietnam was all about. He couldn't get his head around battles where you took ground and then just left it for the enemy to take back. Most of all he couldn't understand how someone could win a Victoria Cross for shooting a few "raggedy-assed little guerrillas" as President Johnson had called them. That was one of the things with the World War II veterans. They didn't think Vietnam was a real war because not everyone was wearing uniforms. They thought we and the Americans should have been able to just go in there and take the place like they had. I'm not sure Father ever understood but that was the first time in my life we ever really sat down and talked as equals. We had been through something none of the others had. When he'd come back in 1945 he was sick of friggin' war and when I came back from Korea it was too soon to talk. This was different. We'd found common ground. As far as Mother was concerned, she was quite a reserved woman but I venture she was quite proud. By the same token there was very little understanding of what I had been through or what was happening in Vietnam. People were very nice, they all said "Well done, good job" and all that, but no one knew what was going on over there. I don't know if anyone really wanted to.'

Maybe not in Ingham, but elsewhere in Australia there were plenty of people who felt they knew what was happening in Vietnam, and they didn't like it. As Payne, Latham, Dellwo and the others had been pushing their way through the undergrowth in the Highlands, a groundswell of opposition to the war had started to take hold and spread like bushfire.

Opposition to America's involvement in the Vietnam War had begun as early as 1964 with small protests on the campuses of US colleges. The 1960s were the decade of radicalism, dissent and political awareness for a whole generation of young people no longer prepared to follow their parents' traditional views. The war in Vietnam became their rallying point, a central cause that could be used to encapsulate everything they felt was wrong with the status quo. Vietnam spawned an entire counter-culture. Singers and film-makers specialised in anti-war messages. A new genre, the 'protest song', was born. The anti-war views of the young radicals soon spread beyond the campuses to include Americans of all ages and walks of life. This was supported by uncensored reporting of the campaign in Vietnam and shocking images of war being beamed into lounge rooms across the country for the first time via television. In November 1965 TV news bulletins contained images of two young Americans setting themselves alight – one in front of the Pentagon, the other in front of the United Nations building – in protest against the war. In February 1968 the world was shocked by footage of a suspected Viet Cong officer being shot in the head by South Vietnamese National Police Chief Nguyen Ngoc Loan on a Saigon street.

On 15 October 1969, hundreds of thousands of people across the United States called in sick from work or skipped school to take part in an anti-war demonstration called a National Moratorium. A second, less well-attended round of moratorium demonstrations was held a month later.

Inevitably the anti-war movement began to gain strength in Australia too, mainly on the campuses of major universities in Melbourne and Sydney. While initially a popular movement with no real organisation, the anti-war message was given strength through the involvement of leading Australian Labor Party figures Gough Whitlam and Dr Jim Cairns. The ALP left-wing, together with members of the Communist Party of Australia, played a key role in formalising the anti-war movement, building it into what was later described by Whitlam's biographer and former speechwriter Graham Freudenberg as 'the most sophisticated and disciplined instrument of popular protest ever fashioned in Australia'. In August 1969, three months after the action that earned Payne his Victoria Cross, a Morgan gallup poll found that 55 per cent of Australians wanted their troops withdrawn from Vietnam. In May 1970, as chairman of the Victorian Vietnam Moratorium Committee, Cairns led a 100,000-strong demonstration that blocked the centre of Melbourne – at that time the largest protest march in the city's history.

By the time the moratorium marchers filled the main streets of Australia's largest cities, Payne was already home but he had been kept well informed about the anti-war movement during his time in Vietnam.

'Flo and I used to keep each other up to date about what was going on. Soon after I got to Vietnam I worked out this way to communicate. I was never much of a letter writer. It was hard to find the time to sit down and write, as much as anything, but one day I spotted this little tape recorder for sale in the American PX store. I bought two, exactly the same, one for me, one for Flo. That way we could send each other tapes instead of letters. I'd tell her what I was doing and ask about things back home and she'd do the same and put the boys on. That was the beauty of it. You could actually hear everyone's voice. It was like you were really there. I'd send all my messages to the boys and then go "Breaker, breaker, Flo only, Flo only", which meant the boys had to leave the room, and Flo would do the same with me, sending them out so she could tell me stuff she didn't want the boys to hear. She told me all about the protests and we'd get the Australian papers too, so it was all there. We knew what was going on but when you are over there doing your job you don't even think about that sort of thing. It's only when you get back and actually see it that it matters.'

After five days in Ingham, Payne returned to Brisbane to receive his orders. As the army's latest Victoria Cross recipient there was little chance he would be sent back for a second tour of Vietnam. His value in terms of army morale and public relations at home was too great to be risked on a South-East Asian battlefield. He was given two choices of assignment: instructor at Officer Cadet School, Portsea, in Victoria, or the same duty in Canberra at Royal Military College, Duntroon. He chose Duntroon, believing the climate would be more to his liking.

'I wish I'd gone to Portsea. At least I would have been able to go fishing. I thought it would be warmer in Canberra but I nearly froze to death there as well.'

The decision made, Flo was once again left with the packing up as Keith headed off to the Australian Capital Territory – but not before he first took care of some necessary business.

'When I left Vietnam the people in Saigon thought the people in Pleiku would take care of going through all my gear and the people in Pleiku thought the people in Saigon would. When I finally got out of hospital in Queensland and headed home to Stafford my stuff still hadn't shown up. I made a few calls and a message got through to Pleiku – "Send all Payne's gear", which is what happened, except they didn't go through it before they sent it on. Someone just went to my locker and grabbed everything that was there, stuck it all in a packing crate and sent it to Stafford. Well, I opened it up and nearly had a fit. When you are out in the field you tend to hoard things that you think you are going to need. There's no paperwork involved, no official channels, but when something is left over from an operation or you get your hands on something you think will come in handy, you just put it aside. So I opened up the crate and there were live grenades and flashette cartridges and morphine tablets – you name it. So I've thought, What the hell am I going to do with all this stuff? I decided to take a little fishing trip. The *Courier-Mail* newspaper in Brisbane had a nice photo of me and Ron heading off for a day's fishing. What they didn't know was that in the bag I was carrying were enough explosives to get me locked away for a long time. We went out a long way into very deep water where the trawlers wouldn't find it and, while Ron was dangling his line over one side of the boat, I was dumping everything over the other side.'

In Canberra there was another issue to be faced. For the first time the Paynes were confronted with the anti-war sentiment they had been largely insulated from in the suburbs of Brisbane.

'Up until I went to Duntroon I'd had no problem with it whatsoever. When I was home on leave and after I'd first got back, everyone was very supportive. Even young people in their teens and early twenties would come up and say "Well done", but when we got to Canberra it all changed. Obviously Canberra was a very political place. In 1970 and 1971 the moratorium was really taking off and the Labor Party was using the war as a way to win votes. For the first time the animosity hit me, and it hit the boys too. We sent them to the local schools and they came into contact with the children of public servants. They got called sons of a baby-killer and all that garbage.'

The shock of those early days in Canberra is one of Derek Payne's earliest memories.

'We'd been pretty protected up until then. We didn't know anything about the politics of Vietnam. We'd been very much guarded from all that because we were living on army bases or within the confines of army life. Then we went to Canberra and I vividly remember leaving Duntroon School and being taken over the hill to Campbell School. It was the first public school I had been to and it was an absolute shock to see how different it was. It took us a long time to find our feet. Some of the schoolkids there had parents who were part of the anti-Vietnam movement. There were lots of sons of politicians and bureaucrats. We got told "Your dad's a baby-killer".

We didn't know what they were talking about. We didn't know anything about the rights and wrongs of Vietnam. We ended up fighting with other kids a lot. I remember we were in the principal's office quite a lot in those first few weeks.'

While Derek remembers schooling in Canberra as an ordeal, Ron is less scarred. As the oldest son, he had been through it all before.

'I'd learned not to make too many friends amongst the civvies. You'd just get friendly with someone and then you'd have to pack up and leave. If we made friends it was with kids from military families. It was like we were on the same cycle. You'd get friendly and then you'd move or they'd move but chances were you'd meet up again at the next place or the next. I think Colin, Ian, Derek and I all adapted pretty well but Gregory didn't have the same ability to cope with constant changes. He suffered when we went to New Guinea and he had to stay behind. He didn't like being separated from the family. It hurt him educationally and emotionally. It was hard for him.'

It was becoming hard for Keith as well. Right from the start he felt uncomfortable in Canberra. It wasn't just the climate or even the fact that the proud Queenslander was a long way from Queensland. It was more the feeling that he had become something of a curiosity, as much a local landmark on the tourist circuit as Parliament House or the National Science Centre. Arriving in January 1970, his job title was Warrant Officer Instructor, Infantry Wing, but for the first few weeks he wondered if it shouldn't be reclassified as VC Winner, Photo Opportunity.

'When I first arrived they showed me the house they wanted me to take. It was a nice big two-storey house that looked great, except for one thing. It was part of the tour of Duntroon. Tourists used to get off the coach right outside the front door. I took one look and said "No bloody way".'

Perhaps Payne was being overly sensitive, but at the time he arrived in Canberra the military college at Duntroon was reeling from a 1969 public inquiry into allegations of 'bastardisation' or initiation rites among students. The inquiry, chaired by Supreme Court judge Russell Fox, resulted in the removal – many felt unfairly – of Duntroon commander Colonel Colin Townsend DSO, former commanding officer of 6RAR in Vietnam. Townsend was replaced by Vietnam Task Force commander Brigadier Sandy Pearson. It was to Pearson that Payne continually turned as he battled the downside of celebrity.

'I knew when I got there that the army had just gone through the bastardisation business and that it couldn't have come at a worse time. The anti-war people were looking for reasons to make the public hate us. The stories about incoming cadets at Duntroon getting tortured and bullied by older cadets fell right into their hands. The army was looking for something to pull them out of the mud. I don't know if it was the army's intention to use me, but that's what happened. There were some bloody fine instructors at Duntroon, a lot of old mates. I didn't want to be treated any different to any of them, I just wanted to get on with my job and be left alone, but it proved pretty hard at first. The first problem was the tours. One of the jobs of a warrant officer at Duntroon was to be duty officer and give visitors a tour of the college. Well, everyone wanted an autograph or to have their picture taken with me. I don't know if they tried to find out when I would be giving a tour or what, but it seemed to me that the groups I led around were a lot bigger than everyone else's. After a couple of times I had to go to Sandy and say, "I'm not a tour guide and I'm not a movie star". You can't refuse the public, and I never say "No", but the best way not to be put in that position was not to take the tours. Sandy took me off the roster. The other problem was the media. Everything I did they were trying to follow me around. Every lesson I did was like it was a photo shoot and it was pissing me off. They were getting in the road of the training program. I had to go up to Sandy again and tell him that the press people had to go or I couldn't do my job. Sandy called them off.'

There was one other matter that Payne needed help with, and once again Sandy Pearson came to the rescue. This one didn't concern tourists or press photographers and it certainly didn't become a cause of irritation. In fact, it was one of the greatest moments in his life. A message came through from the British Consulate. Her Majesty the Queen was coming to Australia, and she'd like to give him a medal.

18

'Yes, Ma'am'

THE QUEEN HAD BEEN in Australia seven years earlier in 1963. On 7 March of that year she had visited Coolangatta on the Gold Coast. The next day's newspaper had a front-page photo of Her Majesty being shown to her official car by local dignitaries, as a white-gloved army sergeant held open the door and saluted. The sergeant was Keith Payne.

A lot had happened in the ensuing seven years. Sergeant Payne was now a warrant officer and the fresh-faced 29-year-old of 1963 was now a war-weary veteran. One who was still just as prepared to follow orders and protocol, but who was also more than happy to stick up for himself within the constraints of the army bureaucracy.

When the invitation came from Buckingham Palace it was addressed, as was customary, to Warrant Officer and Mrs Payne. It also gave the choice of two venues for Payne's investiture: Canberra or Brisbane.

'I'm a Queenslander. I told them I wanted it to be in Queensland. I suppose that was the first problem for the bureaucrats. Then I told them I had to take my sons with me because we had nowhere to leave them. That was the second problem. They could have made it easy for me. They chose not to.'

Payne went to Sandy Pearson with his requests and Pearson made it all happen – but not without bending some rules and sidestepping regulations.

'First up the army said they would pay for Flo and me to fly to Brisbane for the investiture, but they wanted me straight back to work virtually the next day. The thing was, I'd been invited to take part in a whole heap of ceremonies and events, virtually from the time Her Majesty the Queen arrived in Brisbane until the time she left. There was a civic reception at City Hall, a function at Government House, the investiture, lunch on board *Britannia* the next day. The visit was a huge thing for Brisbane and for Queensland and the organisers wanted me to be part of it. I wanted to be part of it too.'

The next issue was Payne's insistence that his boys also travel to Brisbane as their father became Queensland's first recipient of the Victoria Cross since World War II. Payne now had to get another five people to Brisbane. The army would not back down. Two economy-class plane tickets were all they would supply – and they still wanted him back within forty-eight hours.

'It could have all been done so simply. They could have given me temporary duty in Brisbane for a couple of weeks and transferred my family as part of that, but they didn't. I didn't even have a second summer uniform to wear to all the different functions and the army wouldn't give me one. Finally, Sandy said to go down to the tailor at Duntroon, get a cadet uniform off the rack, then have it changed, and send the paperwork to him so he could write it off somewhere.

'In the end I took a couple of days standdown – overtime – two days off my annual leave and the weekend. I cashed in the two plane tickets and used the money for petrol. We folded down the seats and stuck a mattress in the back of the Ford stationwagon, laid the boys down on that and Flo and I took turns driving through the night to get to Brisbane. We stayed with Flo's sister Margaret. It was all pretty tight. The army wasn't helping with accommodation and money wasn't floating around the ridges. You could say we'd been pretty well stuffed around.'

But all that was forgotten when the Paynes arrived at Margaret's. Waiting for them was another invitation from Buckingham Palace, this time inviting Masters Ronald, Gregory, Colin, Ian and Derek Payne to the investiture aboard *Britannia*. To this day the Paynes do not know who made the request that led to the change in the 'one guest' protocol. It may have been Sandy Pearson or R.D.F. Lloyd, perhaps both. All Payne knows is that, during one of the proudest moments of his life, his wife and sons were watching on.

'I'm not sure which of them it was, but he told them I was a family man who wanted my family with me,' Payne recalled. 'I like to think it was Her Majesty the Queen who gave the okay. She's a mother herself, she understood.'

With the boys resting up for their big day, Keith and Flo stood on Newstead Wharf at 3 p.m. on Sunday 12 April 1970 as the royal yacht *Britannia* sailed up Brisbane River, surrounded by an enormous flotilla of private craft.

Some forty years later it is hard for those born after 1970 to appreciate the excitement and adulation stirred up by the first royal tours of Queen Elizabeth II. At the time of the first, in 1954, the prime minister of the day Robert Menzies tried to encapsulate in an article in the *Sydney Morning Herald* (24 January 1954) what the visit meant to Australians. 'It is a basic truth that for our Queen we have within us, sometimes unrealised until the moment of expression, the most profound and passionate feelings of loyalty and devotion,' he wrote. 'It does not require much imagination to realise that when eight million people spontaneously pour out this feeling they are engaging in a great act of common allegiance and common joy which brings them closer together and is one of the most powerful elements converting them from a mass of individuals to a great cohesive nation. In brief, the common devotion to the Throne is a part of the very cement of the whole social structure.'

They are words Keith believes to be true over fifty years later.

The second visit in 1963, and the third seven years later, were not as pompous or ceremonial as the first. By 1970 the Queen herself had asked that the tour be less formal as she brought not only her husband, but her eldest son Charles and daughter Anne with her. An official history of royal tours to Australia noted, 'The first thing that was noticeable was the royal knees – hemlines for the Queen and Princess Anne were up'. That may have been the case, but nothing could distract Payne from the significance of the occasion. The world may have been changing. 'Make love not war' might have superseded 'For Queen and country' as the catch-cry of a generation, but WO2 Payne remained a loyal subject and dedicated servant of Her Majesty. Monday 13 April 1970 was one of the proudest days of his life.

The royal party had flown to Australia and visited Sydney before joining the *Britannia* in Launceston and sailing to Melbourne and then up the east coast to Queensland. The royal yacht entered Moreton Bay at Caloundra around 9.30 a.m. on Sunday. At 11.45 a.m. the next morning the Payne family went aboard.

'We went up the gangplank and Flo and the boys went one way and I went the other. There was quite a few of us there being invested with one thing or another.'

Fifty to be exact, including John Deighton, John Keldie and Raymond Ryan who were receiving military medals for service in Vietnam and Sunshine Coast businessman Clarence Byrne and politician James Sparkes, both of whom were to be knighted.

'They called us out and explained what would be happening and how we should act. The guy in charge was telling the blokes who were going to be knighted how to kneel down and where the sword would be and all that and I was thinking, Beauty. All I have to do is watch what these blokes do and I'll be right. Then he turned to me and said, "Warrant Officer Payne, you'll be first", so that was the end of that.'

Payne was led out and stood at attention in front of his Queen.

'Normally they just read out part of the citation. It's like "For services to ..." and that's that, but I was standing there and the Queen's secretary went through the whole thing, read every word. It seemed to take forever.'

The Queen had said she wanted the 1970 tour to be less formal than in the past. Midway through the reading of Payne's citation, she proved it. As the reading went on, and Payne looked more and more uncomfortable, she looked up and broke the tension in the room.

'If he can do all this,' she said of the citation, 'surely he can stand here and listen'.

'It was all a bit bloody daunting,' Payne said. 'But it was great. I didn't know whether to be nervous or proud or what. I couldn't comprehend my feelings at that moment. I was certainly on a high, I know that, but it's hard to explain what I was feeling. You don't really believe what's happening to you. You go away and do a job and then there you are standing in front of the Queen, listening to her secretary reading all these things about you. It's quite unreal. The really good thing was that as I stood there I could see Flo and the boys in my peripheral vision. All the rest of the public were behind me but because there was so many of them, Flo and the boys had been put in their own little alcove away to the side. To know they were there and to be able to see them out of the corner of my eye, well, that made it even more special. From start to finish those boys were absolutely bloody marvellous. They were real little men, I couldn't have been prouder of them. They stood there having tea and bikkies on the royal yacht like they'd done it all their lives.

'I remember after the investiture the Queen and the Duke circulated around and she came up to me and said what a pleasure it was to be able to approve a VC on such a marvellous citation. She said, "Your wife and sons must be very proud of you" and all I could say was, "Yes, Ma'am". Then the Duke came up and wanted to talk about military things. He asked me about the parachute wings I was wearing. We've all met the royal family since then of course, even the boys when they grew up, but that first time was really something; something you never forget.'

The next morning's official function was a garden party at Parliament House. Before Keith and Flo left the house to attend the function Colin, then eleven, asked his mother, "Mummy, if you're talking to the Queen, will you please say thank you".'

When they were presented at the function Flo summoned up her courage. As the Queen was about to move on she said, 'Excuse me Your Majesty, but before we left home our number three son asked me to thank you for having them on the boat yesterday'.

The Queen smiled.

'How lovely,' she said. 'I thought it was only right they should be there.'

She began to move on, then turned back.

'And we will see you for lunch, won't we?'

'I thought that was wonderful,' Flo said. 'With all the things on her schedule, she remembered that we were invited for lunch. It said a lot about her.'

For Keith and Flo the few days in Brisbane were a whirlwind of formal functions and rubbing shoulders with the royal and famous.

Recalled Keith: 'We had lunch on the *Britannia*, then went to all the other things like dinner at the Governor's – then jumped back in the Ford and drove back to Canberra. It wasn't easy to get back into work after that.'

The ceremony and emotion surrounding the act of the Queen pinning the cross on Payne's tunic were a far cry from two other medal ceremonies he was part of.

After the Anzac Day action near Ben Het, Payne was informed he had been awarded the US Silver Star. His performance in the same area just weeks later would earn him more than the Victoria Cross. Before leaving Vietnam he was told he had also been awarded the US Distinguished Service Cross.

The second highest award in the US Armed Forces behind the Medal of Honor, the Distinguished Service Cross is the highest American award presented to a non-US serviceman. During the Vietnam War four were awarded to US allies: three to South Vietnamese soldiers and the other to Payne. It was an honour that would see his photograph and citation placed on display in the Hall of Heroes at Special Forces headquarters at Fort Bragg, North Carolina, but one which he accepted with mixed emotions.

'It was completely different to receiving the Victoria Cross. For starters as Australians we weren't even allowed to wear US medals at the time because they were considered "foreign awards". There were some pretty strange instructions going around over there at the time. Things like that "destroy the village to save the village". I think the instruction on US awards was something like, "You can receive them but not accept them". It wasn't until 1994 that the regulations changed and we could apply to have the awards officially recognised. I already had the medals. I remember getting the DSC in Pleiku. A general pinned it on me. That's the way the Yanks used to do it. If you were lying in hospital, wounded, a general would walk through and pin a Purple Heart on you. We did things differently, more formally, so I wasn't really bowled over by it at the time. I know it is a big honour for the Americans but it wasn't such a big thing for us because we couldn't do anything about it. As far as the Australian Army was concerned it didn't exist.'

That all changed when the Australian government passed legislation recognising the awards and calling on Vietnam veterans to apply to have them presented by the US government.

In 1995 Payne was contacted by the US Embassy in Canberra asking him to come to Canberra to be officially presented with his Distinguished Service Cross. As he had when invited to be invested by the Queen, Payne had some conditions.

'I asked them who would be presenting it. When they said it would be the ambassador I asked if he was a military man. When they said he wasn't I asked if they had any military personnel on station there. They told me they didn't and I said I wanted it to be presented by a military person, which they were happy to do, but it was matter of finding one.'

Payne knew that Colonel Lewis Millett, a retired Medal of Honor winner from Korea and Special Forces commander in Vietnam, was making a visit to Australia. The two men had met in the United States a few years earlier and kept in touch. Payne asked the US Embassy if they could arrange for Colonel Millett to make the presentation. They did, at what must have been the most unusual site ever for a US Distinguished Service Award – Norfolk Island. A tiny island situated between New Zealand and New Caledonia, the former penal colony of Norfolk represents Australia's eastern-most territory. With Millett holidaying there for a few days it was decided that Keith and Flo and the US Ambassador should join him for the investiture. Almost the entire population of around 2000 was on hand to witness the event.

The setting wasn't quite as exotic when Payne received his Silver Star two years later, but close. Once again he asked for the medal to be officially presented by a representative of the US military, and once again the US Embassy was happy to make it happen.

In May 1997 US forces were in North Queensland for a massive joint training exercise codenamed Tandem Thrust. A US naval warship, USS *Harpers Ferry*, would be visiting Payne's home town of Mackay, he was informed by the embassy's military attache. Would he agree to being presented with the award on board by the ship's captain? He certainly would. A few days later he received another call from the embassy.

'Mr Payne, there's something you should know. The captain of the USS *Harpers Ferry* is African-American.'

'Yeah? So what?'

'Well, we just wanted to make sure you are okay with that.'

'Mate, I have no problem with that and neither should you.'

There would be plenty of other honours. In 1971 the suburb of Stafford, where Payne had been living when serving in Vietnam, named a local recreation area Keith Payne VC Park in his honour. Three years later there was another honour, perhaps even closer to his heart, with the opening of the Keith Payne VC Club at Lavarack Barracks, Townsville. A recreation centre for rank and file soldiers and civilian employees, it included a games room, reading room, restaurant and bar. Keith pulled the first beer. His home town of Ingham also created a lasting memorial. When the school where Payne had learned to read and write was knocked down and turned into a national park, it was named the Keith Payne VC Botanical Gardens.

There were also plenty of public appearances. Less than two months after his return from Vietnam, Keith and Flo were met at Hervey Bay Airport by the pipeband of Hervey Bay High School, where Keith had agreed to present the sports medals at the annual speech night. It was one of the first of many hundreds of invitations that have not dropped off in intensity over forty years.

At one such function Payne was given a glimpse of the future – both his and Australia's. On 27 October 1969, just days after his discharge from hospital, Keith was invited to speak at the annual congress of the Returned Services League in Brisbane. After being presented with honorary life membership by national president Sir Arthur Lee he addressed the delegates.

'The world is getting smaller,' he said. 'In seven hours flying time you could be in Vietnam. In eight hours, to put it bluntly, you could be in a body bag.'

The words were well received by the delegates, but it was the next speaker who received the headlines.

Opposition leader Gough Whitlam had seen active service as a navigator and bomb-aimer with the RAAF during World War II and had been a member of the RSL since 1945, but he left no one at the meeting in any doubt about his views on Australia's involvement in Vietnam. The father of three sons said, 'My sons would not be prepared to fight in Vietnam and the RSL would be gravely out of touch with the young if it feels this attitude is rare amongst young people'.

After the official part of the function had ended, Payne and Whitlam continued the debate, on less than friendly terms. Payne was chatting to Sir Arthur Lee and secretary of the RSL Bill Keyes when the tall, imposing figure of Whitlam strode towards them and broke up the conversation.

'I didn't appreciate what you said earlier,' he snapped at Payne.

Angered by the interruption, Payne replied sharply, 'Well I can't help that – and don't speak down to me', before turning back to his conversation.

But it was Whitlam, and the Australian electorate, that had the final word. As Bob Dylan wrote, the times were 'a changin'. Within three years Whitlam would be prime minister with anti-war campaigner Jim Cairns as his deputy, all Australian troops would be withdrawn from Vietnam, and Keith Payne would be looking for a new job.

For Payne, the three years after he returned from Vietnam were a gradual downward slide out of what he calls 'the Green Machine'. Returning to Canberra after his investiture he went back to work training cadet officers at Duntroon but found himself part of an organisation that was fast moving away from the army he had joined twenty years earlier.

'It wasn't the teaching that was frustrating. I was used to instructing, it was what I did. No matter where I went in the army I would always come back to instructing so it wasn't the work itself that bothered me. For me it was the fact that I knew it wasn't leading anywhere. From a personal point of view I knew I wouldn't be going away anymore. My medical papers had been stamped "Home Only", which wouldn't have been so bad if I'd thought what I was doing was worthwhile but the army was changing. Public opinion was turning against us and that meant the politicians were worried. A lot of people believe that Whitlam pulled Australia out of Vietnam, but withdrawal was already on when he got voted in. What he did do was spoil my army for me and plenty of others. Budgets got cut; I'd be writing requisition forms for equipment needed to do my job properly and they never got filled, simple as that.

'At the same time I was still getting paraded around and invited to everything going. Flo was working at the Vietnamese Embassy and every night was a different function. Just the cost of dry cleaning and buying new dresses was sending me broke. You have to live in Canberra to know what it's like. I decided I'd had enough, I was getting out – and I wasn't the only one. Senior NCOs, warrant officers, captains, majors, colonels … all good men, all experts at what they did, couldn't cop it any more. The army lost an entire generation of experience. The pyramid broke in the middle.'

The army wasn't the only thing that had changed. According to Ronald, Payne's family detected changes in him as well.

'Dad was probably not a very emotive person before he went to Vietnam, but when he got back he was worse. He was really closed off. The smile was there, but there didn't seem to be any warmth behind it. He had changed a lot.'

After twenty-one years of letting the army map out his next move, Payne had to decide which direction to take. Automatically his mind went back to his youth, to Ingham and Grassy Crisp, the fisherman whose bush skills, passed on around the campfire outside his rough timber shack, might just have saved the life of Payne and his men at Ben Het. Payne had always loved fishing and he had a gift for it –

even on the family's week-long free trip to Tangalooma Island he had managed to land a record-breaking 19-pound snapper. He decided to become a professional fisherman, just like Grassy. But where? In his youth Payne had played rugby league for the Herbert River junior side. When the senior team went to Mackay to play a Foley Shield match, the juniors had played the curtain-raiser. The town made an impression. In 1959 he was back as part of Exercise Grand Slam, a large exercise involving the 1st Infantry Brigade Group. Again he was impressed.

'It was a nice friendly little town. It still is, and best of all, it was barramundi and mud crab country.'

So Mackay it was. Payne arranged a job exchange with a young warrant officer based at Mackay. He went to Duntroon, Payne headed back to Queensland. He and Flo bought a block of land and built a house in the beachside suburb of Bucasia, put the boys into local schools and Payne finally made the move he thought he never would. He 'posted his bill' and resigned from the army.

He applied for, and was issued with, a professional fishing licence and was working out his time in Mackay – making nets in the drill room – when he received a phone call in his office. It was an old army colleague, Rex Clarke.

'Payney,' he said. 'Do you want to go to Oman?'

'Where's Oman?'

19

In the Service of the Sultan

THE SULTANATE OF OMAN is a country on the south-east coast of the Arabian Peninsula, bordering the United Arab Emirates on the north-west, Saudi Arabia on the west, and Yemen, including the former British port of Aden, on the south-west. It is made up of four governates, the most southern of which is Dhofar. Some 800 kilometres south-west of the main population area of Oman, Dhofar is linked to the capital of Muscat by a single road, the Midway, which passes through a 250-kilometre long plateau called the Dhofar Jebel, home to around 100,000 nomadic herders known as Jebelis. For more than ten years to 1975 a fierce battle was fought for control of this plateau between various groups of disgruntled revolutionaries and the forces of the Sultan of Oman, strengthened by British troops and professional soldiers hired to bolster their numbers. One of these soldiers was Keith Payne.

Rex Clarke quickly explained the situation to Payne in basic soldierly terms. The Sultan of Oman was an ally of the British. The revolutionaries were being backed by the communists. It was Vietnam in the sand, a clear case of good versus evil. To Payne it was even simpler than that. Oman represented another opportunity to do what he had been trained to do. Go to war for something he believed in.

'Rex was a former member of the Team who I'd met when I was working in Canberra. He'd taken long service leave from the

Australian Army and gone to work for the Sultan. He said to me, "Here's the go. Oman is a British protectorate and we go in under British military control." I gave it some thought and told him that as long as I'd be working on the right side of the fence, I was in.'

The Dhofar Revolution had begun when dissatisfied tribal leader Mussalim bin Nafl formed the Dhofar Liberation Front with the support of Saudi Arabia. The Saudis had earlier clashed with Oman over the ownership of the Buraimi Oasis, an area housing nine villages on the border of Oman and the United Arab Emirates. The dispute bin Nafl had with Oman's Sultan Said bin Taimur was far more heartfelt. In the early 1960s Oman remained one of the most underdeveloped countries in the Middle East and, although he was married to a woman from Dhofar and lived in the area, the Sultan treated it particularly badly. Dhofar was subjected to severe economic exploitation and its people suffered even greater restrictions than other Omanis. As far as Oman's ruling class was concerned, the people of Dhofar, particularly the Jebelis, were a sub-class, much as the Montagnards had been considered by the Vietnamese. Bin Nafl and his followers sought to free Dhofar from the Sultan's rule and create an independent state. Significantly it was around this time that large oil reserves were discovered in Oman, making it an attractive target for overseas interests.

As early as December 1962, bin Nafl's guerrilla band had carried out sabotage operations on the British air base at the Dhofar capital of Salalah and ambushed oil industry vehicles. After undertaking training in Saudi Arabia, they began a campaign of hit-and-run attacks on oil company installations and government posts.

With the British pulling out of neighbouring Aden and the establishment of the communist-backed People's Democratic Republic of Yemen in 1967, communist activity in the region increased. The Dhofar Liberation Front immediately had an almost endless supply of arms, supplies and training facilities, ostensibly coming from Yemen, but in fact financed by Russia and China. By late 1968 the idealists who had started the Dhofar Liberation Front had been pushed aside and their organisation was renamed the

Popular Front for the Liberation of the Occupied Arabian Gulf. With Russian and Chinese backing, the rebel forces, known collectively as Adoo, made significant inroads against the Sultan's outnumbered and badly trained and equipped troops. Within a year the Sultan's British advisers were faced with an undeniable reality: either Oman received new leadership and increased military support, or it would fall to the insurgents.

On 23 July 1970, Sultan Said bin Taimur was deposed in a bloodless coup and replaced by his son, Qaboos bin Said, who immediately instigated major social, educational and military reforms. The army was reorganised and placed under British command. Health and education reforms for the Jebelis were undertaken to counter communist propaganda. Former rebels were given amnesties and re-formed into irregular units under the command of British advisers, much like the Montagnards under the US Special Forces in Vietnam. Other countries in the area with an interest in Oman remaining a sultanate offered assistance. The Shah of Iran sent a brigade; Jordan provided intelligence officers and engineers. Also, the Sultan opened the purse strings and employed experienced soldiers to fight under his flag. The British, with the Sultan providing an open chequebook, scoured far and wide in search of recruits for the Sultan's Armed Forces, or SAF. The net spread all the way to Mackay, Queensland.

When news broke in Australia that Keith Payne, the country's most recent Victoria Cross recipient, was signing up to fight for a foreign army, the word 'mercenary' wasn't far away.

First mention of Payne's involvement came on 18 April 1975 when the *Courier-Mail* under the headline: 'Payne VC Finds A War' announced that 'VC winner Keith Payne will join the army of the Persian Gulf oil sultanate of Oman as a captain – "because I want to help again, to fight the Communists"'.

With a sub-heading 'He'll Help in Oman', the story gave a supportive view of the local hero heading overseas to do his bit against the communist scourge. Three days later as Payne waited at Brisbane Airport for a connecting flight to Bombay en route to Oman, the mood had changed somewhat. Reporters who had been dispatched to Kelvin Grove six years earlier, and had covered in breathless prose his triumphant homecoming, now had another story on their minds.

The *Courier-Mail* (21 April 1975) began its report of the airport press conference with the word that still makes Payne see red forty years later.

'Mercenary?' it read.

> Don't even suggest it to Keith Payne VC who's going to fight for the oil sultanate of Oman.
>
> His fists clenched. Veins stood out. His voice choked. He controlled his emotions with difficulty when he heard the word 'mercenary' at a press conference at Brisbane Airport yesterday. Australia's great Vietnam hero, the man who led 40 Vietnamese to safety through enemy lines and fire replied coolly: 'A mercenary is a man who would fight without principle, for monetary gain. I don't have to go to Oman for monetary reasons. I could be sitting on the beach at Bucasia in top hat and tails and catch fish.' (He is on a $165-a-week pension.)

Payne refused repeated questions from reporters about how much he would be paid to serve in Oman. He maintains it was not an enormous amount, nor was it the motivating factor in him signing a three-year contract.

'The Sultan of Oman was paying the bills and when people heard that, they could hear poker machines going off in their heads. The truth was it was pretty much the same pay I was getting as a warrant officer in the Australian Army. I was promoted to captain but that didn't make all that much difference. The contract outlined all these amounts I'd get paid if I was wounded or incapacitated. Basically the Sultan would look after me or my family for life if anything happened, but luckily it never came to that. To me it was a job. It was what I'd been trained to do and also I felt strongly about the communist threat. We'd given South Vietnam to the communists and I could see them coming further south. Since I was nineteen years old

I'd been fighting them all over Asia. This was just a chance to fight them somewhere else as far as I was concerned. It turned out to be a great experience. I don't regret it for a moment.'

Payne headed to Oman, thinking he would be based in the capital Muscat, training the palace guard. Instead, on arrival he was told he would be leading a Frontier Force company in the field in Dhofar. All the better.

'When I got over there Rex Clarke was waiting to meet me at the Seeb International Airport. Only problem was I didn't have an entry visa. Rex had got hold of some official-looking paperwork and gone around the British Army headquarters with it. Every officer he could find who had a stamp, he got them to stamp it. When I got to customs Rex handed over this piece of paper with all these stamps on it and they just said "Yeah, okay, in you go".'

Payne spent the first night at Baital Folaj, the army headquarters just outside Muscat. He soon found that the British way was different to what he was used to.

'They told me they were going for a run the next morning and I was welcome to join them. I fronted up in all my gear, just how I would if we were going for a run in Australia. I had on all my equipment, my rifle, pack, everything I would wear in the field. The Poms were in shorts and running shoes – and I still beat half of them home.'

But if the early-morning run was an eye-opener, it was nothing in comparison to what awaited him when he joined Frontier Force in Dhofar.

Payne's company position was an outpost known as Oven, which was so far south that, as he put it, 'You couldn't go further into the desert if you tried'. Positioned high on the Jebel, Oven overlooked a series of wadis, or dried river beds, often used by the Adoo as a thoroughfare to the north. Payne's orders were to keep watch over the wadis. The men he was to command were from Baluchistan.

Baluchistan is a large region covering south-west Pakistan, south-west Afghanistan and south-east Iran. Noted for the fighting qualities of its tribesmen, it had a historical link with Oman, the Sultan owning the Baluchistan port of Gwadur. For centuries Baluchistan had provided armed forces to the Sultan, the palace guard being made up entirely of Baluch soldiers. As the hostilities in Dhofar escalated and the British reorganised the Sultan's army, recruits from Baluchistan made up the majority of two battalions permanently based at the most forward point of the action.

As he had been six years earlier, Payne was given a foreign uniform – this one including a striking turban headdress – and told to take charge of a company of soldiers with little to no grasp of his language. As he had in Pleiku, Payne assembled his troops and liked what he saw.

'They were natural soldiers. Very ferocious and loyal. They did have some customs and habits I had to avoid. When I arrived at the company position I met the Baluch officer who was my second-in-command and he said he would show me around. As we started walking he tried to hold my hand. I had to tell him in the nicest way that was against my religion. It was the same when he tried to pick someone to be my batman. They just thought it was natural that he should be the best-looking young boy in the company. I told them I wanted an experienced old soldier who could cook. They looked at me as if I was a bit strange, but we worked each other out. They were Muslim and they wanted to pray seven times a day and I had no objections to that. I don't interfere in people's beliefs, but we had to do it in such a way that we could all keep doing our job. Once we understood each other we got along fine.'

Especially since Payne soon showed that he had his men's best interests at heart. It didn't take him long to realise that the British looked on the Baluch in much the same way as the Americans and South Vietnamese viewed the Montagnards.

'Basically the Poms treated the Baluch soldiers in a way that they never would have found acceptable for their own men. My priority was my men. Geez, it caused some problems early on.'

The first problem was in regard to food. With Payne's men being Muslims, they needed to be supplied with meat that had been prepared in compliance with halal requirements. In Arabic *halal* simply means 'permissible' or 'allowed'. To be deemed halal the meat had to be prepared by a Muslim butcher under conditions set out in the Koran, and eaten on the same day. Under the terms of their employment, the Baluch were supplied with halal meat, but it was the method of delivery that concerned Payne.

'The meat was prepared at battalion headquarters at Salalah on the coast and then sent out to us in the desert in metal ammunition boxes. It would be killed in the morning and get out to me in the late afternoon. By then it was going off. I went out to Salalah and saw all these foam packing cases lying around. They'd been used to bring fresh produce out to the base. I told them, "Put my meat in those with some ice, thanks". They made pretty good eskies. It seemed an obvious solution to me but the British didn't seem too impressed. The other problem was the water. We were operating in the desert and water was always an issue. It would be brought in by helicopters in these 30 gallon plastic drums, six at a time, and my company was the last drop-off of the day. During the monsoon season the 'copters couldn't fly in and water rationing was always below what I would have liked. I'd never been one to suffer quietly. For me it was all about getting my men what they needed but it didn't make me too popular.'

While Payne never stopped asking the British to solve his problems, in time he came up with his own solutions. Both gained him notoriety and one even earned him a nickname – 'The Goat Man of Oven'.

'The Poms already thought I was a bit odd. When I got into the desert I asked one of the officers at headquarters about hygiene and latrine arrangements. He told me the men just went to the toilet over the rocks and the dung dried out and blew over the sand. I didn't like the idea of that for a couple of reasons. I didn't think it was hygienic and I didn't like the idea of the men going outside our secure position at night. When I got out to Oven and saw that the men organised gun pickets when they wanted to go, it eased my mind, but it still wasn't good enough for me. I built a dunny for myself out of an old wooden box up on a high spot. The RAF pilots used to laugh when they flew over and saw me sitting there.'

More was to come. A few months into his time in the desert Payne's lifelong skill as a water diviner came to the fore.

'We had a small outpost down from Oven about 50 metres higher than the floor of the wadi where I would have six men based on a rotating roster. Early one morning a small group of Adoo had come through and there was a bit of a firefight. At daybreak I went down to have a look and noticed some green foliage down in the wadi. Pretty early in the piece after I'd got over there I'd spotted a forked stick that looked a lot like the sticks I used for water divining back home and I'd picked it up and kept it. When I saw this foliage I went back up and got my stick and sure enough, I found water. I reported it to HQ and after a little while a civilian engineering company came out, drilled a bore and pumped the water back up to our position. The men started a garden, and we had all the water we needed. One day we got word that the CO was coming out to inspect us, so I cut the top off one of the 30 gallon plastic drums the water used to be delivered in, filled it with water from the bore and was standing in it, pouring water over my head with a mug when he arrived. I was like, "Hello skipper. Fancy a bath?" Water was never a problem again.'

Pretty soon neither was meat. Once again Payne's men spotted what appeared to be Adoo making their way through the wadi. This time it was only two, but they were shepherding a herd of around fifty goats.

'One of the problems over there was that everyone carried rifles and you never knew who the enemy was. When these two blokes came along the wadi we didn't know whether they were friendly or Adoo, so we picked them up and sent them to HQ at Salalah for interrogation. The word came back, "What about the goats?" I told them I wasn't sending any goats. Until the blokes who owned them were released and came back to claim them, they were mine. That's how I got the name 'The Goat Man of Oven'. We herded them up and fed them and every now and again one would be killed and eaten. I had a man in my company who was qualified to do the butchering so it was all according to halal and my men thought that was great. I was King Billy.'

The work was routine and, for the most part, enjoyable if lonely. Contacts with the enemy were rare and Payne felt the British did a good job. 'They knew what they were doing,' he said. But on one occasion there was a clash which, in retrospect, was a sign of problems to come.

'There were these large caves along the sides of the wadis and the Adoo would ride their camels in there and either wait until night so they could keep moving up the wadis, or use them as a way to ambush our patrols. Our problem was trying to get the buggers out of there. We worked out a way to fire a 2 inch mortar straight into the caves, like a rocket.

'One day we were down in the wadi engaging the enemy when all of a sudden artillery started dropping on us and my men were getting hit. I hadn't called for artillery and I got on the radio and shouted "Check fire, you're hitting our own bloody blokes". By the time it stopped, four or five of my men were wounded. It was a miracle no one was killed. I still don't know what had happened. Either someone just wanted to get in the fight for some reason or someone up on the Jebel had taken it upon himself to stop the enemy and had used the wrong coordinates. All I know is that I lost it.'

Back at headquarters Payne went straight to the battalion commander and let him know in no uncertain terms what had happened. The commander already knew. It was the fault of an inexperienced British captain, Payne was told. In shades of Payne threatening to withdraw all Australians from Special Forces jurisdiction if the remnants of his company were not airlifted from Ben Het, he demanded action be taken. When the commander told Payne that nothing would be done, he took his own action. As he left the commander's office, a furious Payne spotted the young captain walking through the base. He caught up with him, spun him around and … saw red. Words turned to a push, and another, resulting in the young Englishman sitting on the ground, with Payne shouting down at him. At the time Payne didn't think it was any more than a one-off burst of emotion. Now he knows otherwise.

'In retrospect that was one of the first signs of post-traumatic stress disorder. It was starting to get to me, I was very edgy at that time; anything could have set me off. It was a concerning factor to me – it is to every soldier – how will I perform in battle? Will I let my mates down? It just eats at you and eats at you until finally you crack. I'd seen it happen to some top soldiers and it's a bloody terrible thing to see. One day they just say "Enough is enough". I'd seen it happen to a damn fine Special Forces medic at Ben Het when I had to shake him out of it. Sometimes doing that works, sometimes it doesn't. Looking back on what I did to that little Pommy captain that day … well, it just makes you think.'

After seven months, Payne headed back to Australia on leave. While he was home the Sultan declared victory over the insurgents. The Dhofar Revolution was over and Oman has since gone on to become one of the most stable and progressive countries in the region. Although he had signed a three-year contract, Payne sent his resignation to the SAF headquarters and has never returned.

Soon he had enough battles of his own to fight without putting on a uniform again.

20
Collateral Damage

FOR THE FIRST TIME since he was eighteen, Keith Payne found himself without a job and without a mission. As he sat in front of reporters at Brisbane Airport before jetting off to Oman he had spoken confidently of not needing to work, of having the luxury of 'sitting on the beach at Bucasia in top hat and tails' and catching fish if he wanted to. To a degree that was true. The Paynes were in relatively good shape financially. After over twenty years of subsidised accommodation, they were able to live comfortably in the house they had built near Bucasia beach in Mackay. Keith received regular payments from the Defence Force Retirement Benefit Fund. But it wasn't so much money that was the problem. It was acclimatising to a world outside the military.

For twenty-three years Keith had been immune to the vagaries of civilian life. The army told him where to go and when to be there. When he travelled, the army took care of the arrangements and the accommodation. He was fed, clothed and housed, and he was surrounded by men and women who lived exactly the same way. They went through the same things he did, spoke the same language and harboured the same beliefs and fears. They understood.

Then suddenly, he was out. The trip to Oman had only delayed the inevitable. If anything, it made it worse.

'I'd left the Australian Army but I hadn't left the military. I'd gone straight to Oman and, instead of easing me out, it had fired up my desire for soldiering again. Before I'd put in my papers I'd been stuck in Canberra trying to do my job in an army that was having its budget cut. I was frustrated and bored, but when I went out to Oman I was in the field, doing what I loved. I came back from that all fired up, and thought, What the hell am I going to do now? It was something I'd never had to think about before, and I found myself in a world I couldn't understand. I'd go down the street and see people pushing their way on to a bus and think, How can you people function? They were so disorganised. I'd feel like going up to them and getting them into two straight lines.'

Even that, the obsession for order and discipline, was symptomatic of an illness that Payne didn't know he had. He found himself fixating on little things, and working himself into a rage if he couldn't control them. The boys had always seen their father as a proud, disciplined man in uniform. When he returned from his final posting, they found him a stranger, hanging around their house and losing his temper at the slightest provocation. On one occasion he and Ian came to blows over a roll of toilet paper placed the wrong way round on the holder.

'In the veteran community we call them "brainos". The brain explosions you get over nothing. Little problems become big problems. You work yourself into a state and then you just blow up. At that time everything was worrying me. I was worried about the way things were done around the house. Even today, if I go into a public toilet and the paper is in the roll the wrong way, I'll try to fix it. Most of all I was worried about our finances. I'd never had to worry about money before, the army took care of everything. Now here I was, forty-one years old, with no job and nowhere to go. I was fixated on my superannuation. I was getting a small payout every fortnight but I was lying awake at night thinking about what would happen if I started eating into the principal. I didn't know which way to turn.'

Finally Flo convinced Keith that he had to see someone about his problems.

'I was crook, there's no doubt about that, and deep down I knew I was crook but I wouldn't admit it. Flo was saying "Go to the doctor, go get checked out", and I was telling her not to be silly. There wasn't anything that a doctor could do for me. No one spoke about post-traumatic stress disorder back then. The government wasn't admitting to it; even us veterans weren't admitting to it. It wasn't something you spoke about. You thought you could handle anything that came your way. Finally I went along to the local doctor and told him about the brainos and he just pulled out his Department of Veterans' Affairs (DVA) prescription pad and started writing out scripts for Valium and Serepax and Mylanta. I can't blame him, he was just doing what he'd been told to do. I still didn't know what was wrong with me or what I was going to do. The only difference was I was walking around pretty well topped up with all these drugs.'

Not surprisingly, Payne turned back to the only thing he knew, the thing that in his mind represented order and security. The army.

'Basically I said to them, "I'm home, how about letting me back in?" I got a letter from the Minister of Defence saying thanks, but no thanks.'

The rejection, on medical grounds, was met with yet another braino but this time it was one fought out in very public view. Brisbane journalist Frank Robson was dispatched to Mackay to get the story for the *Sunday Sun*. With a bit of licence from the sub-editors, he got more than he'd hoped for.

'I'll Give Their Bloody Medal Back To 'Em' read the headline of 24 July 1977, above the sub-heading 'VC hero blasts the army that won't let him fight on'.

'One of Australia's foremost heroes of the Vietnam war has delivered a withering blast against the army he says prostituted and then deserted him', the article began.

Payne's actual statement at the time, 'Sometimes I seriously consider writing to Her Majesty and sending back my VC with a brief description', was somewhat less colourful than the headline, but there was nothing half-hearted about his 'withering blast against the army'. He told Robson:

> The army is full of men who have no idea what they're supposed to be doing. I am a victim of petty jealousies by men in high places who have never had the responsibilities of active service.
> I left the army in 1975 because I was sick of white-washing bricks, no action and because I couldn't cop the politics of Gough Whitlam. Now the army has reached the stage where if there was some action none of these twits would be able to command anything.

Asked why he would consider serving in such an army Payne replied:

> Because it is my calling ... it is in me. And because I can't do anything else.

To prove his fitness to Robson and his readers, Payne stripped to a pair of shorts and 'charged around on the sand dunes near his home'. The photo of Payne, still as physically lean and wiry as he had been when he'd signed up twenty-four years earlier, accompanied the story. But it wasn't his physique that was in question. It was his mental fitness.

'He'd had enough but he didn't know he had had enough,' says Flo. 'He was suffering stress, just like he was when he came back from Korea and when he'd come back from Vietnam. When he said he wanted to go back into the army, what was I going to do? He was adamant and if it was going to make him happy and easier to live with, I'd give it a try. It wasn't any fun living with him as he was. If going back in the army might help, I'd go along with it, but they had more idea than he did.'

The official reason the army gave in rejecting Payne was his hearing. The issue had come to a head when he had gone to the firing range in Duntroon and couldn't hear the weapons being fired.

'I went to the doctor, who sent me to the acoustics lab. The bloke who tested me said if I ever wanted to hear my grandchildren I should give the job away. Then he told the army. They downgraded my papers to H.O., for Home Only. It meant no promotion this side of the ocean, no go here, no go there. I stayed at Duntroon but I couldn't go near the firing range when weapons were being fired. I'd set things up for my cadets, make sure everything was in place, then have to leave before they started shooting. When I went to Oman they never asked anything about it so I never told them. I thought it wouldn't be a problem if I went back in. I thought if I watched myself and wore earplugs I could get away with it, but they never gave me the chance. Once I got out, they shut the door and locked it behind me.'

With the army no longer an option, Keith returned to another early love. He still had his professional fisherman's licence and decided to follow in the footsteps of Grassy Crisp. He bought a 4-metre boat and became a net fisherman. He even had two little huts, just like Grassy, where he would stay for two or three days at a time when fishing.

'I was dead determined that I wasn't going to spend my super and by gee I made it a living. I worked my butt off, went out in all sorts of weather. Anything you could sell, I caught. Barramundi in the wet weather, king salmon, you name it. Towards the end I went to crabbing, it was better money. I did it for maybe four years and it was a good life, but my health suffered, mainly my back. And my nerves were going too. I used to take this young bloke out with me, Dave Caracciolo. He was a good little fisherman – owns the big fishing co-op in Mackay these days – but back then he couldn't lift the heavy nets, so I had to do it myself. If I had a whole heap of fish in the net and the tide was going out and I knew I had to get them out, I'd start to get all shaky. Like with the brainos, everything got to me. In the end I had to give it up. I just couldn't cope. Things started to go to pieces pretty drastically after that.'

Which is not to say they had been good previously. The Paynes refer to that ten-year period as 'the bad times'. The brainos, the nightmares and the drugs, mixed with heavy drinking, all combined to create a scenario of almost constant tension, punctuated by rage and occasional violence. Keith was a lost soul, wracked by an illness he had never heard of. An unknown, unnamed illness that affected not just him, but the entire family.

The words 'post-traumatic stress disorder' roll off the tongue so easily now and the initials 'PTSD' register immediate recognition, but until 1980 the condition didn't officially exist and it was another ten years before the Australian government accepted its existence.

To the uninitiated whose knowledge of the Vietnam War is restricted to Hollywood movies or old newsreels, scenes of burning villages, screaming children and napalm strikes come easily to mind, as do headlines bellowing of atrocities such as My Lai. But Keith Payne wasn't involved in that kind of war. He was a professional soldier, better trained than just about anyone else in the field. The question must be asked: what was it that sparked his mental disintegration? How did he, of all people, find himself struck down by the same illness as the rawest recruit thrown into the unthinkable horror of battle?

'It was everything. The overall pressures of all the actions I was involved in. The whole bucket-load.'

It is a vague answer at first, but then comes the crux. As he speaks, Payne's mind goes back to Vietnam. Back to Ben Het, in fact. Yes, he was a soldier, a man willing to die in the service of his country. He was at ease with that. What he couldn't cope with was not being able to stop others from dying. Just as he was a father to his five sons, Payne felt a paternal responsibilty for his men. If there was one single moment when that responsibility became too much and he snapped, it was when he heard those single gunshots at Ben Het. The moment when he heard his men being executed, and couldn't do a damn thing about it.

'You're a commander,' he says, his voice shaking. 'And a commander is responsible for looking after his men. You have to keep as many of those buggers alive as you can. That was what did it to me. The pressure of command. The pressure of being on the radio and not being able to get fire support, the pressure of knowing your men are up there and some bastard is walking around shooting them as they lie there. It never leaves you. It's still with me now, but you have to learn how to handle it. You have to go on with life. You have to work out when things are going to blow up, and how to walk away.'

Payne has learned those things, but not without years of counselling. And not without years in the dark.

Dr David Forbes is associate professor in the Department of Psychiatry at Melbourne University and clinical director of the Australian Centre for Posttraumatic Mental Health. According to Dr Forbes, the lack of adequate medical care available to Keith would not have been unusual in the early 1980s:

'Sadly what Keith went through would not have been uncommon. It was only in the late 1970s that medical practitioners in the United States began to recognise a pattern amongst Vietnam veterans. They began to note symptoms that were common to people who had suffered extreme trauma such as sexual assault or severe motor vehicle accidents. Of course there had been an awareness of problems with returned servicemen in the past. After World War I they called it shell shock. After World War II it was combat neurosis or battle fatigue. In the United States they used the term 'Vietnam Syndrome' at first. It was only when post-traumatic stress disorder was classified in the US psychiatric system and included in the *Diagnostic and Statistical Manual of Mental Disorders* in 1980, that it received formal recognition. There was a lag of about ten years before Australia caught up.'

In 1999 the Department of Veterans' Affairs commissioned a study by the Australian Institute of Health and Welfare to look into the high rate of suicide among Vietnam veterans. What the study uncovered, almost by accident, was that it wasn't just returned soldiers who were committing suicide in abnormally high numbers, but their children as well. A second study found the rate of suicide among the children of Vietnam veterans was three times the national average. Further studies found equally high levels of drug and alcohol abuse and increased likelihood of being incarcerated or involved in domestic violence later in life. The US military has a term 'collateral damage' which the Department of Defense defines as 'unintentional or incidental injury or damage to persons or objects that would not be lawful in the circumstances ruling at the time. Such damage is not unlawful so long as it is not excessive in light of the overall military advantage anticipated from the attack.' While it was never intended to be applied to peace time, the term perfectly fits the circumstances the Paynes and other families found themselves enduring. The servicemen and women went to war but the wives, partners, children and parents also suffered. They were collateral damage.

Says youngest son Derek, now a psychologist working in a youth detention centre in western Sydney, 'You just can't underestimate the trauma PTSD has on families, particularly younger children and how they develop'.

Of course when the Paynes were going through their own trauma there was no comprehension of post-traumatic stress disorder, just the knowledge that things were bad and each day was a matter of survival.

For Keith most days started at the nearby Emieo Hotel.

'I bought enough booze at that place to own the bar. I'd sit in the same place every day, with the same old drunks, telling the same old stories. I wasn't an alcoholic, I'd go three or four days without a drink when I went away fishing, but I was still drinking very heavily. Drinking isn't really a part of the army culture. You might have a drink with your mates, but not like I was drinking then. That was more part of the veteran culture. Drinking to feel better, drinking to get to sleep. I was a cagey drinker. When I was fishing I'd set my nets early in the morning and walk up the hill to the bar, have a few beers, check my nets and go back to the bar. I'd drink early in the day and get back by three o'clock when the boys got home from school, but when I got there I'd be an angry bugger. The booze and the pills was a bad mix.

'There would always be trouble. The boys were growing up, they were in their teens. They weren't playing up, not really. They were just doing the things I would have done when I was their age but I couldn't tolerate things and it caused a rift between us. The boys didn't understand what was going on because I couldn't understand. It was just a bad, bad time.'

Again, not just for Keith, but for a lot of veterans and their families. Dr Forbes says before post-traumatic stress disorder became officially recognised the symptoms were easily misinterpreted.

'There is a whole range of symptoms,' he said. 'Excessive drinking is one of them, so the diagnosis could have been alcoholism or inadequate personality disorder. It is so much clearer now but back then everyone, including the medical practitioners, was in the dark.'

It is a fitting choice of words. The Paynes were very much in a dark place, with no idea of how to get out.

Recalls Derek: 'Every morning Dad would drive away in his truck. He'd flutter around saying, "I have to go, I have to go", and where he went was up to the hotel to drink and God knows what happened up there. A couple of times he'd come home and it was obvious he'd been in a biff or two. There was this sense when it was time for him to come home and the anxiety would build up. He'd come home and he'd be into Mum. How she got through it is beyond me. It was never physical but the psychological stress was unbelievable. He'd be nagging about this and that and just explode. The rest of us followed the same pattern. Something would trigger it and it was explosive.'

Ronald had left home when the family was still based at Duntroon, taking up an apprenticeship with the navy in Western Australia at the age of fifteen and a half.

'The navy had always interested me but it was more a way to get out of the environment at home. My interpretation now is that Dad was having trouble adjusting to the pressures coming on to him from the Victoria Cross. He'd started drinking, and things weren't what they should have been. I went to HMAS *Leeuwin* in Western Australia which was probably an easy out. It was an opportunity to get out, get a trade and it also offered me a way to go from one ordered, controlled environment to another.'

Ron went from Western Australia to the Naval Training Establishment at Nirimba in New South Wales, but the Victoria Cross followed.

'Wherever I went there was an awareness of who my father was and there was this feeling of expectation and of me having big boots to fill. I was young. I didn't adjust as well as I could have.'

Ron stayed in the navy for almost three years before returning to take up an apprenticeship in Mackay. He moved back into the family home – and walked straight into the firing line.

'My memories of that period are of Dad getting into his truck in the morning and pissing off up to the pub, then coming back pissed as a cricket and creating havoc. It was like, "Righto boys, Dad's home. Everyone run for cover."'

And always, in the background looking down on them all like some sort of all-seeing idol, was the medal. In April 1970 the Queen had pinned it to Payne's chest. Now, some fifteen years later, it seemed as though the roles had been reversed, and Keith had been pinned onto the Victoria Cross. According to Derek, Keith was 'obsessed with it'. It defined who he was, and in that way defined his family as well. He was Payne VC, his children the sons of a national hero. That being the case, why were things going so badly? Why was Payne spending his days in the bar of a hotel, and his sons dreading the sound of his truck turning into the driveway? The pain and frustration gnawed away at all of them, just a cross word or sideways glance away from exploding.

Keith says the role of the Victoria Cross in his life changed markedly over the years.

'At first it was just another medal. I knew the significance of it historically and all that, but we were soldiers doing our jobs. Awards just come along out of the blue. When I got out of the army I was just an ex-soldier with a whole bunch of medals. This was just one of them but then, when things went bad, it took on a new meaning. In a way the Cross meant I was different. People saw me as special but I didn't see myself as that. Knowing how other people saw me and knowing what I was going through seemed to make it all worse. You have to remember I was completely muddled. I was in a bad way. I didn't know what was happening. It was only later, when I came out of the fog, that I felt I had a responsibility to represent the medal in a certain way.'

Says Ron: 'It was not so much the medal, but the expectations Dad put on himself and others put on him because of it. Because of the medal he had extra obligations to fulfil. It seems to me his view on it was that now he had to be on this pedestal. He wasn't seen as an ordinary person any more.'

Derek remembers the day he confronted not just his father, but the medal itself, as one of three defining moments in their relationship.

'I think, of all the boys, for some reason Dad put up with me confronting him; I have no idea why. I remember this one incident very clearly. It was when I was sixteen and he was in the depths of PTSD. He'd hit rock bottom in a long, lingering process. I remember he was pissed and over-medicated and he was just sitting there in the lounge room looking at the framed copy of the citation that they'd given him after the investiture. I just said, "Bugger this, I'm sick of this, we have to move on", and I took it off the wall and put it in a cupboard, out of sight. We could all see that he was obsessed with it, but it wasn't just the VC that upset me, it was that he was missing us. He was there but he wasn't there. The amazing thing to me when I took the citation off the wall was that he allowed it to happen. I thought he was going to rip my head off, but he didn't. He left it in the cupboard for a year or two.'

Yet, for all the pain the medal could have represented, Derek bears no animosity.

'I never think of it as a curse, although I did at one stage. It didn't really impact on me until I was about eighteen, when I started to think, What does it mean? In some respects I think being awarded the VC was the thing that saved Dad. When he got out it gave him a connection and a presence. The other veterans haven't got that. They're just battle fodder. I read recently in a book about Vietnam how all these young men went off to learn to be soldiers and spent the rest of their lives trying to work out who they were. In a way the VC told Dad who he was. He had to work out a way to deal with it.'

It was a hard lesson to learn. With his fishing days over, Payne went through a number of jobs. He sold roof cladding. Once again his nerves let him down.

'I was up on a roof measuring a gable for a bloke and I started shaking and I couldn't stop. I had to get the bloke to write out the order form for me. It wasn't a height thing, I'm not afraid of heights. No one could ever work out what it was. I've still got it today. Sometimes I've got the shakes so bad I can't walk. That was the end of that job. After that I worked for a bakery for a while but that ended when they bought out their major competitor and didn't need me any more. Later on, when things got really bad, I went to the mayor of Mackay who was also state president of the RSL. I told him I needed something to do to keep me out of the pub, something where I'd be out of sight of people. I thought maybe something like a storeman in a depot. You wouldn't want to know. I got a job on the council all right – sweeping drains. There I was, on the side of the road with a broom in my hand, as the whole of Mackay drove by. That one didn't last too long either.'

Meanwhile things at home went from bad to worse: Keith getting verbally stuck into Flo and the boys, the boys getting stuck back into Keith. By now there was another member of the family, Keith and Flo's 'adopted' daughter Shelley. A friend of Ian's, who had walked away from her own troubled family life, she was taken in by the Paynes and stayed for years. When she married, Keith walked her down the aisle. One by one, the boys left home, staying away months, sometimes years, before returning and trying to connect with their father. Derek remembers his departure as defining moment number two.

'I came home and he was into Mum about some little thing and I thought, I can't cope with this any more. I had a fist full of change in my hand for some reason and I threw it at him and it buckled around him like shrapnel. Mum was upset because we were arguing and she shrank into the background. He came back at me with punches and I pushed him down a few little stairs and as he came back I slapped him hard across his face. The pain for me was horrible and the shock and shame for my father was unbelievable. He looked at me with these deathly eyes and went outside and when he came back in he said, "You've got two effing minutes to get out of here or we'll play my game and you won't win". That was my grand departure from the nest; the defining moment of me leaving home. I came back in six months or a year, but it was time to go.'

It was a painful time for both men, but indirectly it led to Derek's third defining moment, the one that shone a light of hope at the end of what had been a very long, dark tunnel.

When Derek left home he went into a world that he, like his brothers, wasn't fully equipped to handle. He had attended twelve schools as the family had followed Keith from one army base to another. Much of his life had been spent living within the confines of the army system and he was still coming to grips with what he calls 'the civilian world'. He was also, in his words, 'almost illiterate'. He spent several years working at odd jobs to earn enough money to travel, before going to TAFE to re-do the last two years of his schooling. From there he took up nursing, and found himself working in the psychiatric unit of Sydney's Royal North Shore Hospital, continuing to travel whenever he could.

'It would have been 1987 and I was travelling in South-East Asia and I had Dad in mind. I was walking through the jungle wearing this small backpack and sweating and I was thinking, I wonder what it must have been like for Dad? I was wondering what it must have been like, doing what I was doing but with so much more gear and getting shot at and crawling through the mud, with people trying to kill him, and it was so far from my life. Just thinking about that helped me to reconnect with Dad. It made me appreciate a little of what he'd gone through. When I got back I was working in the Cummings Unit at Royal North Shore Hospital and I started talking to a psychiatrist and mentioned to him a bit of what my family was going through and he pulled out a pamphlet on PTSD and said "Read this", and I read it and I just thought, My God. It was so obvious that Dad was a textbook case. We'd had no idea. I'd never heard of it before. Maybe Mum and Dad had heard of it, but Dad didn't want to listen. He didn't accept he had an illness. I photocopied the brochure and sent it up to him. When I talked to him on the phone a little while later we didn't go into details, but he said "Yeah, I can identify with that" and he told me he'd thrown out all his Valium. I have to say, of all the things he's done, that to me was an example of his courage. It wasn't just that one particular time when he won the Victoria Cross. He's shown lots of courage at different times and that was one of them. He didn't understand what was happening to him, but he identified that he had a problem and he took action. That's when things started changing.'

The arrival of the photocopied pamphlet came at a time when Keith was starting to come to a crossroads. Flo had taken just about all she could and told Keith he had to get some help or their marriage wouldn't survive. A new general practitioner had arrived in Mackay and had taken over supplying Keith with prescriptions.

'I would just walk in and walk straight out with all these scripts for Valium. Again, I don't think it was the doctor's fault. I'm sure it was the DVA telling them, "Look, these blokes think they've got a bit of a problem but it's all in their heads. Just keep 'em quiet, keep 'em calm". Well, I just couldn't go on like that. I told the medico I wanted to see a psychiatrist and he said "Why?" and I said, "Because, mate, there's something wrong".

'I went to the psychiatrist and he was pretty good. He'd give me these sessions and he'd say, "Well, you've got problems and you have to pull yourself together", but he still never mentioned PTSD. I don't think he knew about it. For years people had been denying it even existed. We weren't real popular, you know. There were a lot of people who thought to themselves, Well, these are the blokes who wanted to go to Vietnam. If they think they've got problems now, they asked for it. Let them work it out themselves. And some of those people were high up in the government, let me tell you.'

Finally, Keith did work it out himself. It might not have been the way prescribed in the more recent medical textbooks, but it was typical Keith Payne.

'We'd moved from the beach to a place closer to town. It was as much to get me away from the pub as anything. Soon after that I just said "Enough. I'm not doing this any more." I threw the pills down the toilet and that was that. No more scripts, no more bloody drugs. It was hard, bloody hard. I went through withdrawal, just like any addict. I was hurting physically and mentally but I just battled on without them.'

Getting off the booze came later, but it was even more dramatic.

'I was at the pub one afternoon, sitting in my usual seat, with the same blokes around me and I looked up at my reflection in the mirror and I thought, Jesus Keith, look at yourself. Would the blokes who died like to see you doing this to yourself?' There's a saying amongst the veterans: "Live for the dead". The only living I was doing was sitting in a bar and listening to the same drivel, day after day. I didn't finish the beer that was in my hand. I put it down and walked out and I haven't been back since. I'll still have a couple of light beers or a wine most nights, but never until after 5 p.m., and when I go to functions I have a bit of a trick. I'll just hold on to the same beer for as long as I can and when no one's looking I'll put it on the bar. You know how it is, someone will be offering me another one in a second or two, and I'll take it, but I'll nurse that one too. I'm not an abstainer, but I'll never be like *that* again.'

As he speaks Payne gestures to a photograph of himself that sits above the fridge in the back room of his Andergrove home. It is of Keith at the opening of the Vietnam and Associated Veterans Club at Albury-Wodonga in 1984, at the height of the 'bad times'. The sinewy physique of the professional soldier is long gone. His face is fleshy and his gaze watery. The photo sits there as a reminder of how far he sank, and how far back he has climbed.

'Look at the gut on that,' he says, shaking his head in disgust.

'We called all the boys together, had a family council. I told them what had been wrong with me and what I was going to do about it. They all rallied. Instead of fighting each other, we started supporting each other. I stopped worrying about getting out to work and began working around the home, tidying up, doing bits and pieces around the garden.

'I started to live again.'

21
Fighting Back

KEITH HAD TAKEN TWO giant steps in recognising he had a serious mental condition and turning his back on pills and booze. The third step would be even greater. Convincing the authorities.

His battle for compensation had begun in 1983, at the height of the bad days. The US government had classified post-traumatic stress disorder three years earlier, but it hadn't yet been officially recognised in Australia.

'I was going through the Department of Veterans' Affairs trying to get compensation for my injuries, and it was like I was back in a firefight in Vietnam. Physically they accepted that I had problems with my ears, but mentally they weren't admitting to anything. They were sending me off for tests for this and that and the time was dragging on and of course my PTSD was getting worse. This is a mental condition which is brought on by stress so you can imagine how battling with bureaucratic red tape affected it. Some of the tests they put you through were pretty intrusive. They were asking all sorts of personal questions. It was the last thing I needed.

'It was something so many veterans were going through at the time. The DVA was saying they were doing the right thing but they weren't, because they weren't admitting to PTSD. The medicos hadn't been informed about it and people like me thought we were beating our heads against a brick wall. At the same time everyone was talking about Agent Orange. There were those veterans who wanted compensation for Agent Orange and those who had PTSD who were saying "Hang on, what about us?" All it did was split the veteran community. The whole thing was a mess.'

Agent Orange was the nickname for a herbicide developed by the United States to defoliate trees and shrubbery so that the enemy could not use them for cover. Named because of the orange bands painted on the drums in which it was stored, an estimated 64 million litres of Agent Orange was used in Vietnam between 1961 and 1971. In the early 1980s US Vietnam veterans began instigating lawsuits against the manufacturers of Agent Orange, claiming contact with the herbicide caused various kinds of cancer and genetic defects. In 1984 they received a US$180 million settlement. The same year Australian, New Zealand and Canadian veterans who had come into contact with Agent Orange received an undisclosed pay-out. While veterans welcomed the outcome, many felt the high-profile case had been used as a wedge to divide the two major factions within the veteran community. Keith Payne was among them.

In 1979, as concerns over exposure to Agent Orange had spread from the United States, the Vietnam Veterans Association was formed in Australia to lobby for government attention. It became the main action group in the fight for compensation and was seen as the body that most had the interests of the Vietnam veterans at heart. This did not sit well with the RSL, the organisation that purported to represent all Australian returned servicemen and women since 1916. According to Payne the tension between the two organisations was used by the Fraser government.

'The veteran community was divided and the government was using that to stem payments to the vets. We had the Vietnam Veterans Association fighting Agent Orange and the RSL saying "That's bullshit, you're all bludgers". The government took advantage of that. There were issues that had to be addressed apart from Agent Orange and they weren't being addressed because the RSL was too busy fighting the Vietnam Veterans Association.'

Without a combined front, the veterans were forced to fight the bureaucracy on their own. It was a very frustrating and, at times, painful battle for the Paynes. Keith could not work, he was battling alcohol and drug dependency and his quality of life was severely compromised. The burden of proving he deserved compensation made a bad situation even worse. Keith had been wounded several times in Vietnam. He had been shot and hit with shrapnel. At Dak To following the action at Ben Het he'd had a huge splinter of wood dug out of his skull. Yet for all that, his deepest wounds were psychological and that is where his problems, and those of many other veterans, really began. With the Australian government and medical community not yet following their US counterparts and recognising post-traumatic stress disorder, the veterans had very little ground to stand on.

'I felt like I was being pushed from pillar to post. I was dealing with the DVA in Brisbane but it was the DVA in Canberra that had the final say. At one stage early in 1985 I got a letter back saying the army had no record of me ever being wounded. Never wounded? There was the time I was shot on the operation to Bui Gia Map, and again at Ben Het when I had to be patched up at Dak To and back at Pleiku. I couldn't believe it. I had them though. I wasn't supposed to, but I'd kept a copy of the AATTV's ROs – Routine Orders – from the Bui Gia Map operation. I sent them a copy and suddenly they found they did have details after all. Later that year the office in Brisbane put together the results of all the tests and all my details and sent them off to Canberra for final assessment. That was what it all came down to. Someone in Canberra was going to decide whether I was entitled to a service pension and, if I had a disability, whether I deserved compensation.'

Finally, after nearly two years of constant battling, countless medical and psychological tests and a bulging manila folder full of correspondence, Payne received his answer.

'They told me yes, we recognise your injuries when it comes to assessing you for a service pension, but we do not recognise those same injuries when it comes to assessing you for compensation.'

This piece of bureaucratic double-speak was the final straw as far as Payne was concerned. He called the Department of Veterans' Affairs

(DVA) in Brisbane and told a case officer: 'You've got twenty-four hours to sort this out or I'm going to the press'.

Payne asserts it was the first and only time he ever used his profile as a Victoria Cross recipient as a bargaining chip.

'They knew my name would make headlines, and they knew I'd been royally stuffed around. Within fifteen minutes I got a call from some bigwig in Canberra asking me to hang on. He said they'd reassess and get back to me, but twenty-four hours wasn't enough time for them. I said to him, "You blokes had no problems sending me into action on twenty-four hours notice. Why should I give you more than that?" The message came back: I'd been reassessed as TPI – Totally and Permanently Incapacitated. The first payment came through within a month. The official notification followed after that. They still didn't recognise PTSD, that wouldn't come until later.'

The official recognition of his disabilities was a tonic for Payne on a number of levels. It meant he was not a 'bludger' in the eyes of the authorities and, equally important, he no longer had to worry as much about finances. But there was still something that gnawed away.

'I couldn't help thinking, If this is what they did to me, what are they doing to the other veterans? I had a profile. I was able to get on the phone and because of my name, someone usually got on the other end. But what about some poor digger who hadn't had his picture in the paper? How was he going to get someone to listen to him?'

Payne didn't have to look far for the answer. During Keith's dark days Flo had joined the Vietnam Veterans Association. In one of the Association's regular newsletters she saw an advertisement for a counsellors' course being run by the Department of Veterans' Affairs. She signed up, both to understand more about what Keith was going through, and to help others. To her son Derek, the course was just another example of Flo trying to 'maintain her own level of independence'.

'Mum fought to work, and sometimes it wasn't easy. The hounding from Dad was endless. Through that really bad period she had got involved in the surf lifesaving movement and she stuck it out and stuck it out. No matter how hard it was for her at times, she just had to have something outside the house that didn't revolve around Dad.'

Whether it was paid employment in a variety of office jobs, or volunteer work linked to the boys' interests, Flo was always busy. She became involved in the Boy Scouts when the family was posted in Malaya. In 1973, when the boys joined the junior lifesaving division known as Nippers, she began a 25-year-plus association with the Surf Life Saving movement. At various times she was club secretary and president of Mackay Surf Life Saving Club before going on to branch level. In 2000 she received life membership from Mackay SLSC, North Barrier Branch, and Surf Life Saving Queensland.

As with all her outside interests, Flo threw herself into the role of counsellor to Vietnam veterans and their families. She was appointed an area representative. When Keith received his disability pension he decided that he too would do the counselling course and join Flo in offering advice and support to veterans trying to work their way through the system.

'Once the word got out, we were getting calls from all over the country. There is no better telephone tree in the world than the veterans' community. Flo would speak to the wives and I'd speak to the veterans. I suppose you'd call it welfare work. We'd listen to their problems and then try to help them as best we could. It might mean filling in their forms for them or getting on the phone and following things through. I'd already been through it all myself, so I knew how hard it could be and what some of the pitfalls were, so we had that experience to fall back on.'

The trouble was, Payne immersed himself in the process too well.

'Eventually Flo said I had to stop. I was living their problems as well as my own. It was as if I was going through it all again. The frustrations and anger kept coming back, so I had to withdraw from the program. It just wasn't doing anyone any good, but after a while I found a way that I could be of a lot more help. When I started to feel better and was able to travel to official functions more, I found myself sitting next to some pretty important people in the government. From the prime minister down I could get them away from the media and their advisers for a few minutes and have a bit of a whisper in their ear. I'd tell them that there was a problem in a certain area, or it might be that a specific veteran's case had been brought to my attention and I could ask if the Veterans' Affairs Minister could look into it. I suppose you'd say I became an unofficial advocate for the veterans. I stopped trying to climb over the hurdles and worked out I could be a lot more effective by going around them.'

By the early 1990s life had changed considerably for Keith and Flo. The Australian government and medical system had recognised post-traumatic stress disorder and the treatment of sufferers steadily improved.

'The US diagnosis in 1980 drew attention to PTSD,' said Dr Forbes. 'In 1984 the Australian government commissioned a report into the mortality rates of Vietnam veterans and that gave us more information to work with. It was all about accumulating enough data to confidently identify the problem.'

In 1989 the National Center for Post-Traumatic Stress Disorder was created within the US Department of Veterans Affairs to set the agenda for research and education on post-traumatic stress disorder. In 1995 the Australian Department of Veterans' Affairs established the Australian Centre for Posttraumatic Mental Health in collaboration with the University of Melbourne and the Austin and Repatriation Medical Centre.

'Our mission was to improve the recognition and treatment of PTSD and related conditions within the veteran population,' Dr Forbes said. 'Before 1995 the work being done in the US still hadn't permeated down through the ranks of practitioners here in Australia. That lag isn't uncommon, but since the establishment of our centre we are certainly more confident that the practitioners in the field can adequately diagnose and treat the condition. The treatment of veterans coming back from recent campaigns in places such as Afghanistan or Iraq is so much better than the experience of Keith Payne and others who came back from Vietnam. The Australian Defence Force screens people as soon as they return from active duty. There is triage to ensure they get help as soon as possible and the practitioners are educated so they are knowledgeable enough to provide the correct treatment. The system is still imperfect, but it is a lot better than it was even five years ago.'

When post-traumatic stress disorder was officially recognised in Australia, Payne was reassessed and correctly diagnosed and treated. Like many other veterans, he felt that a dark cloud had been lifted. His life changed immeasurably.

'Probably the main change was that I could now travel. I could accept more invitations to carry out various functions.'

Which is not to say that Payne hadn't been invited to attend functions in the past. Virtually from the day he returned from Vietnam he had been asked to speak and hand out awards at everything from school speech days to Anzac Day parades. Keith was a soldier, not trained for public speaking or appearing in public, but as one of only three Australian Victoria Cross recipients still alive in the late 1980s his letterbox was always full of invitations. With Ted Kenna and Roden Cutler getting on in years, Keith accepted as many as he could but, as Derek explained, it was not always easy. There were times, especially during the dark days of the early 1980s, when it would have been better if he had said 'No', but his pride and sense of duty was always too strong for that.

'Dad wasn't so much gullible as untrained for what he had to do. I mean what are the parameters of the Victoria Cross? There is no job description. One day you are a soldier doing your job, the next the Queen is pinning a medal on your chest and you are expected to play a role that no one ever explains to you. Dad wasn't like Roden Cutler who was the Governor of New South Wales and could be a Victoria Cross recipient in that context. Dad was a soldier who had to make up the context as he went along. That's how I think people used him at first, in the way that they expected him to be a certain thing but they couldn't see how sick he was, and there may have been times when he embarrassed himself. Even now I think there are times when the people who get him to do things don't provide enough support. They certainly don't always appreciate the influence that my mother has on making everything happen. For a long time people would invite Dad somewhere and just expect him to arrive. They wouldn't see how anxious he gets before an event, and when it comes time to leave home the anxiety levels go through the roof. That's when Mum steps in and makes things happen but there have been times when they have arrived somewhere and Dad has been whisked away and Mum has been pushed aside.'

The more effective Keith's medical treatment proved, and the more functions he attended, the more confident he became. Rather than a returned serviceman struggling to come to terms with the effects of his wartime experiences, he became an unofficial ambassador for the Cross and all it stood for. Flo gave up her outside interests to become what Keith terms 'transport officer', coordinating the seemingly endless trips, functions and appearances both in Australia and internationally. Whether it was attending as guest of honour at a major commemoration or opening a hospital children's ward with just a few sick kids and their parents in attendance, Keith would be there, a replica of the Victoria Cross and his twenty-two other medals gleaming proudly on his chest. As Derek so rightly points out, at first there was no blueprint for Keith to follow. He made it up as he went along. What had started as a few invitations to open RSL club function rooms or parks and rec rooms named in his honour, became weekly, sometime daily, appearances. The back room of the Paynes' Andergrove home became so cluttered with plaques of appreciation, along with memorabilia pertaining to Keith's days in the military, that eldest son Ronald jokingly suggested his parents should build a small flat above the house, and charge admission to the rest as a museum.

Payne never charged for his services – in the early days he even found himself out of pocket, but the government eventually came to the rescue.

'At first when people asked if I could do something I'd say, "If you can get me there, I'm available", but there were still plenty of expenses that Flo and I were picking up ourselves. With Ted Kenna getting on in years it got so that Roden Cutler and I were the only VC recipients available. Sir Roden was fine when he was Governor of New South Wales, he didn't need any help, but when he left office in

1981 he got to experience what I was going through and he went in to bat to get some assistance. The Fraser government gave us six flights a year, then it was upgraded and legislated when Labor came in in 1983. What happens now is that the government picks up our airfare and provides Commonwealth cars. If someone wants me I tell them we'll get there and they have to put us up. It works well and the more functions I've done over the years the more at home I am with it. I prepare a speech but the funny thing is half the time I'm sitting there being introduced and the bloke is saying all the things I've been planning to say, so I'll just go up and do my best. I've got a good judge waiting for me when I sit back down. I'll say, "How'd I go Flo?", and she'll give me a nod if I've done alright. We get through. People seem to like it because they always invite me back.'

Indeed they do. Rarely a week goes by without at least one official function, and special occasions such as Anzac Day need all the split-second planning of a military operation. April 2008 was a typical 'Anzac month' for the Paynes. It involved nine official functions and trips to Melbourne, Singleton in New South Wales, Toowoomba, Brisbane, the Gold Coast, Lismore, New South Wales, and a visit to the local school in Mackay. In between there were four trips home to recharge the batteries.

'Sometimes we just drop the bags, fall on the bed and sleep around the clock,' Keith says.

The hectic calendar of official functions did more than 'take the VC on the road'. The enormous amount of planning and travel brought Keith and Flo closer together than they had ever been before. Where once Keith had been the one away while Flo kept the home fires burning, they were now a team, rarely out of each other's sight. When Flo fought, and beat breast cancer in 1997, Keith stepped up and provided the kind of support she had always given him, Ron recalls.

'Since Mum's illness, Dad has become a lot more domesticated. He does things for Mum that he never did before, like cooking, washing and ironing. I think he has become the father we never knew. He's a lot more at ease with himself, a more relaxed, more likeable person.'

To Derek and the others, the strengthening of their parents' relationship has been an unexpected bonus.

Recalls Derek: 'It was around the 1990s and you could see that they had rediscovered each other. It was like they were teenagers again. It was absolutely amazing to see them showing open affection and playfulness. Something had happened for them. I don't know where it came from, but it was beautiful to see.'

Together they attended functions and ceremonies all over the world. Keith was feted in London as a member of the Victoria Cross and George Cross Association and in the United States as a Distinguished Service Cross recipient. He and Flo located Anastacio Montez's name on 'The Wall', the memorial in Washington DC to the US military killed in Vietnam, and laid a wreath. They proudly represented Australia at the Victoria Cross 150th anniversary service at Westminster Abbey, and a year later were flown to Lincolnshire where Keith unveiled a plaque to honour thirty-nine Australians killed while flying missions over Europe in World War II.

One gathering of the Victoria Cross and George Cross Association in England proved particularly poignant.

'It was May 1978. Simmo was living in Japan and came over for the reunion. I remember one day we were having lunch outside under a marquee at the ancestral home of Lord De L'Isle, who was a Victoria Cross recipient. It was bloody cold and we were sitting next to these big braziers, trying to keep warm. It was all very proper and they brought out plates filled with the first pheasant of the season. Simmo took one look and said to the waiter, "Geez mate, that's a bloody big chicken you've got there". We flew back together and changed planes in Hong Kong. He was headed off to catch his flight to Japan and I was going back to Australia. I said to him, "Well, see you at the next one". He said, "No mate, that's it for me", and that was the last time I saw him. He knew he had leukaemia but he never said anything. He died six months later.'

And there was another trip that was even more memorable. In early 1995 Keith received a call from Paul Lockyer, a producer at Channel 9's *A Current Affair* program. They wanted to take him back to Vietnam for the first time in more than twenty-five years, retrace his steps at Pleiku and Ben Het, then film him attending the Anzac Day service at Long Tan. He agreed. The invitation was for Keith only, but the producers hadn't reckoned on the determination of Derek who insisted on going along.

'I thought it was pretty rude of them to be honest, to think they could just take my father back to Vietnam without any family support. Basically I just said "I will not allow you to take him over there to use him for your purposes without having any of us there to help him through it". I said "Screw this, I'm going". I made a call, they said okay. I guess there were three reasons I wanted to go. To understand him, to understand me, and to provide support. I'm so glad I did. It was a fantastic trip.'

Lockyer went over with Keith, Derek and the film crew. Interviewer Ray Martin met them in Vietnam a few days later. The trip coincided with the Paynes moving into their new home at Andergove. The morning Keith and Derek left was the morning Flo awoke to a house full of cartons to unpack, and reflected on how little had changed since the days when Keith was in uniform. Hours later, sitting in a Singapore Airlines jet coming in to land at Saigon, Keith was thinking exactly the same thing.

Recalls Derek: 'I was sitting next to my father when we flew in. He sat there in total silence, completely engaged. It was amazing to sit there beside him and look at him taking it all in. He didn't shed a tear, he was very pragmatic. After a little while he started reflecting on things. Everything was the same as when he had been there in the war – the bullet holes were still in the walls of the buildings at the airport. It was then that it really started to hit me; that I would be going with him to places that I'd heard so much about over the years, places that were so critical to our lives. I just thought, Oh God, this is going to be amazing.'

They went to Pleiku, where some of the Special Forces buildings were still standing and Derek could see where his father had slept and attended briefings before operations. It was a fascinating journey but merely a curtain raiser to the main event – Ben Het.

'That was where we began to lose it. It was the first time I had ever seen my father cry, and by then I was an emotional mess. We got out there and saw the bunkers and looked out to where they had to leave Montez. These were all the places I had heard about all my life. They were Dad's memories, but they were my memories too. I think for Dad it was so important to go back because in your mind a place is still the same until you go back and see that it is different but it was important for me to be there too. Dad and I shared something. The only regret I had was that my brothers couldn't share it as well because I don't think it will happen again.'

For Keith his initial feeling as he flew back into Vietnam was one of apprehension. It took him a long time to divorce the past from the present as Paul Lockyer and Channel 9's hired guides took them further into the Highlands.

'I was pretty edgy the whole time. Even driving along the road I'd be thinking, Why aren't we ducking? Don't get too close to that truck in front. During the war you'd never get too close to the vehicle in front in case it got hit by a rocket or went over a mine. In my mind I couldn't get away from that, and when we got to the Highlands it was worse, because it was so much like it was back in 1969. There were still bombs and shells lying around. They hadn't cleaned up a thing. One time the camera crew walked off the track to try to get some filming done and the guides started yelling at them. We didn't understand the words but we got the meaning. I said to them, "Okay, just retrace your steps, walk out backwards and get back on this bloody track". I was telling Derek to stick close to me and not go wandering off. It wasn't easy to relax.'

It was when they reached Pleiku that the memories came flooding back.

'It was strange because I remembered the Special Forces camp as this flourishing, busy place with people rushing around from one building to another, and now here it was this dilapidated place with everything falling down. The funny thing was, as I looked around I could still see all the blokes walking about. It took me a while to focus and see it how it really was. Back in the days when I came back from operations I liked to go over to the pilots' standby room at the airfield and play some cards and mingle with them. It gave me a relief to get away from the Special Forces camp and talk to some people who weren't directly part of what I was doing. When we went back I looked over at where those buildings had once been so neat and well maintained and thought, Oh God, it's all gone. One place that really stood out was the chapel. When I'd got back from the first operation at Ben Het, I'd wandered over to that chapel and walked in. There was no one else there, just the Australian padre Peter Dillon and we sat down and had a yarn. I needed someone to talk to then and he was there. We had our own little service. Looking over at that chapel, seeing it all falling down, brought back some memories, I can tell you.'

The group was able to get to the Special Forces camp at Ben Het but not onto the hill where the action of 24 May 1969 had taken place.

Keith said, 'It was too close to the Cambodian border. They wouldn't let us go there, but we could see it from where we were. That was where they did some filming, with us sitting there and the hill in the distance. When the filming was over I said to Paul Lockyer, "Mate, I'm going to need a bit of time to myself", and I just had to be there alone for a few minutes. It was very emotional, but I think everyone should go back, I really do.'

The bond between Derek and his father grew stronger because of that trip. Derek says his brothers have followed their own quests to get to know themselves and have a relationship with their father.

'I guess all we really want is to be seen by him, and respected by him. I remember in 1989 I was living in Goulburn and talking to him on the phone and at the end of the conversation he said, "Love you mate". I was dumbfounded, I nearly dropped the phone. We'd just had a very natural conversation for two or three minutes. It wasn't him putting his values on me, or talking down to me, and at the end of it he said that. That was a very warm, amazing moment for me. These days we can talk on the phone and there's no need to say "I love you". There's just an implied sense that things are okay. I think maybe it took my brothers longer to get over that boundary.'

Greg worked as an electrician in Mackay and is now a wardsman at Mackay Base Hospital. Colin and Ian have moved around over the years and are now both living in Townsville. Ronald runs his own successful tourism transport company in Adelaide. In 1978 he was again drawn back to the military, joining the Army Reserve. Older and more experienced, he was better able to cope with being the son of a famous soldier.

'I really enjoyed the service life and I wanted to give it another go. I went in knowing that there were times I was going to run into people who had served with Dad and this time I was ready. One time I was on a course run by a CSM who had been trained by Dad. I fronted up to him and said, "I'm Payne R.J., not WO2 Keith Payne. These are my boots and I have to fill them myself." There have been times I have had to put my foot down and say that I'm my own person. I'm not Dad; I'll make my own mistakes. I didn't manage to do it the first time in the navy but in the Army Reserve, I made my own mark.'

There was another legacy that Ron inherited from Keith's time in the military. In mid-2005 he filled in a questionnaire issued by the Vietnam Veterans' Counselling Service in Adelaide.

'They rang me two days later and asked if I could come in to see them. They said it was the worst case of PTSD they'd ever seen. They shunted me to a psychiatrist who put me on dope for a while but I chucked it all out in the end. I've learned to recognise the triggers and when I feel myself going down that path I just take myself out of the system for a few days. I'm pretty involved with the veterans community in South Australia these days. I help them where I can, providing buses and trailers and drivers when they need them. I'm pretty strong now.'

Just as for Ronald, no doubt the bad times have left scars on all of the Payne boys, but it seems they have found their own ways to deal with the past.

As Flo says, 'We don't think about the things that happened back then. We push on. We probably fared a lot better than some families. We're still together. We might fight from time to time but we're still a family and that's the important thing.'

22

A Cross to Bear

EARLY IN 2007 KEITH knocked on the door of R.D.F. Lloyd's home in Western Australia. He had something to tell him. He was selling his Victoria Cross.

'It had been something I had been thinking about for a long time. I wasn't getting any younger and I didn't want to just leave it to the family to sort out when I was gone. One thing I wasn't going to do was just give it to the Australian War Memorial museum in Canberra where my family would have to line up to see it like everybody else. The way I looked at it, the boys had given up a lot over the years. They could have lost their father and then when I came back there were some years when it was hard for all of us. I wanted the medal to go to all of them but what could I do? I couldn't split it five ways.'

To outsiders, particularly those who have never served in the military, the solution may have seemed obvious: sell the medal to the highest bidder and divvy up the proceeds. After all, the Victoria Cross was too valuable to wear anyway. Keith had been wearing a replica, with the original locked safely away in a bank vault, for years. But of course there was a lot more to it than that. Keith had never seen the Victoria Cross as an individual award, but rather one bestowed on behalf of everyone he served with. As one of his many duties in the lead-up to Anzac Day 2008, he opened an exhibition at the Queensland Museum titled *The Courage of Ordinary Men: Three Stories of the Victoria Cross*. Showcasing the medals and stories of Victoria

Cross recipients Patrick Bugden, Robert Beatham and Blair Wark, the display marked the 90th anniversary of the end of World War I. In his speech Keith made the point that recipients of the Victoria Cross had one thing in common: they had all been in the wrong place at the wrong time. Inevitably, he said, medals for bravery were the result of one man trying to get himself, and his mates, out of a jam.

And that, according to his son Derek, sums up Keith's take not just on the medal, but on his life as well.

'My father was always very aware of his duty. It took me a long time to come to grips with the fact that my father's job when he was in the military was to kill people but then I realised that there was another side to it. He was trained to kill, but at the same time, he was trained to protect, and there was that polarity. When Dad came back from Vietnam the peace movement was talking about our soldiers being baby-killers but in his mind he was protecting his fellow soldiers and the villagers and the wider community. When we went to Vietnam in 1995 I got an insight into that.'

In the TV interview conducted south of Saigon, Ray Martin had pushed Keith to admit that what he had done that day in 1969 had been madness, suicidal. Keith succinctly summed up his motivation.

'They were killing my soldiers, and it was my responsibility, damn it. I wasn't going to let them do it. Bugger 'em. Bugger 'em.'

It was that same sense of duty that saw Payne put down his beer and walk out of the Emieo Hotel in the late 1980s. A commitment to 'live for the dead'. People like Montez, Mick Gill and Supply Sergeant Pilkington hadn't come back from Vietnam. Keith had, and he saw it as his duty to wear the medal for them and all the other veterans.

But he had another duty as well. To his family. It was a quandary that caused countless sleepless nights. Keith knew selling the medal would help his sons and their children, but he also genuinely cared about how it would be perceived in the veteran, and general, communities. As someone who had taken the medal to the people for the best part of forty years and espoused the values it represented, the thought that he might be seen as mercenary, selling it for personal gain, was abhorrent.

A Cross to Bear

The turning point came in 2006 when West Australian media magnate Kerry Stokes bought the Victoria Cross awarded posthumously to Captain Alfred Shout following the battle of Lone Pine at Gallipoli in 1915. The last privately owned Gallipoli Victoria Cross, it was sold at auction, along with Shout's Military Cross, for $1.2 million. Stokes donated the medals to the RSL for display at the Australian War Memorial museum in Canberra. What was notable, other than the record price, was the public reaction to the sale.

It was by no means the first Victoria Cross sold. Many had found their way into the hands of private collectors and military museums over the years. In 1993 Stokes had also helped the RSL buy Dasher Wheatley's medal for $150,000. But while in many cases – Wheatley's included – the medals were awarded posthumously and the recipients' families were left to fend without the support of their main breadwinner, there were those who believed Victoria Crosses should not be sold under any circumstances. In 2006 when the three daughters of New Zealand dual Victoria Cross recipient Charles Upham announced they were considering selling their late father's medals, it elicited a scathing response in the British blog site *The Monarchist*. Correspondent 'Beaverbrook' quoted Captain Upham's comment on being offered £10,000 by his local council after the war: 'The military honours bestowed upon me are the property of the men of my unit as well as myself and were obtained at considerable cost of the blood of this country. Under no circumstances could I consent to any material gain for myself for my services.' Beaverbrook said the New Zealand government should 'cough up the cash because these three have obviously forfeited their right to hang such honour in their house'.

The anonymous correspondent made the point that 'the Victoria Cross is priceless. I submit that if there is one thing worse than cash for peerages, it is cash for VCs. Why should one man profit from another man's courage?'

It was precisely such a backlash that Payne was worried about. Like Captain Upham, he believed the medal was the property of the men of his unit, as well as his own, but by the same token he felt a responsibility to his family.

The reaction in Australia to the sale of Shout's Victoria Cross proved a watershed. Instead of outrage, there was appreciation that Stokes's philanthropy had allowed it to be kept in Australia and a feeling that Shout's grandson Graham Thomas had done the right thing for his family. Mr Thomas said he felt his grandfather would understand. Talkback radio callers and correspondents to newspaper letters pages agreed.

As always when a Victoria Cross was sold, reporters contacted Keith for his opinion. The obvious question was: 'Would you ever sell your medal?' For the first time he suggested he would consider it.

In the years since he had returned from Vietnam Keith's collection of medals had grown as new decorations and honours came his way. When the wearing of the US and Vietnamese medals was approved by the Australian government he was able to add the Distinguished Service Cross, Silver Star and Vietnamese Cross of Gallantry to his medal bar. The two medals he was awarded for his participation in the Dhofar campaign came afterwards, as did the Pingat Jusa Malaysia Medal. In 2006, he was awarded the Order of Australia Medal. With the order in which medals are worn strictly gazetted, from the Victoria Cross on the far left across to foreign awards on the right, every time a new decoration was added Keith's medal bar had to be reassigned. As he wore his medals more often than probably any other returned serviceman in the country, they also had to be regularly repaired, re-ribboned and reset.

The person chosen to carry out the maintenance of Keith's medals was Warwick Cary of Cary Corporation, regarded as Australia's leading expert in the mounting and presentation of military decorations. Cary, of Ramsgate in Sydney, was also a collector of medals and had bought the Victoria Crosses awarded to Royal Navy Able Seaman James Gorman for bravery during the Battle of Inkermann in the Crimean War, and Australian George 'Snowy' Howell for his action at Bullecourt, France, in 1917.

In 2002 Cary on-sold Snowy Howell's medal to John Meyers of the Maryborough Military and Colonial Museum.

Meyers and his wife Else had started the museum in 2005, with Howell's Victoria Cross as the star attraction. Located in a historical building in Wharf Street, it had been a labour of love for the couple. John had been partner in a successful sawmilling and hardware operation for many years but had also served in the Army Reserve and maintained a strong interest in colonial and military history. When he sold his share in the business, he immediately began making his dream of a museum a reality. It would give him a place to house and display his collection of artefacts, but more than that, it would give him and Else an opportunity to build a memorial.

John and Else had two children, Geoffrey and Karen. Geoffrey inherited his father's love of all things military and as soon as he finished school, enlisted in the army. In 1982 at the age of eighteen he came home on leave for a few weeks before leaving for his first overseas posting in Malaysia. To have some transport while he was at home he bought an old car and one day he took his sixteen-year-old sister for a ride. While they were on the open road Geoffrey's car was hit from behind by a semi-trailer. He and Karen were both killed. A small plaque on the wall near the front door dedicates the museum to their memory.

When John Meyers read that Keith would consider selling his Victoria Cross he contacted Warwick Cary whom he had known for more than twenty years and asked if he would speak to Payne on his behalf.

'I'd never even considered approaching him before because he had never shown any interest in selling,' Meyers said. 'In fact, from what I'd read in the past, he was actively opposed to it. Warwick asked Keith if he would mind if he gave me his number. He said that was fine and it started from there. Basically I asked him to name a price. He did, I met it, and that was that.'

Actually there was a bit more to it than that. A condition of the sale was that the price would remain undisclosed, but two of the boxes had been ticked. The price that Keith had settled on had been met and, almost as importantly, the medal would stay in Queensland.

'I'm a Queenslander and the first time I saw a Victoria Cross was when the Queen pinned it on my chest. I wanted the people of Queensland to see their Victoria Cross without having to leave the state,' he said.

There was still one very big box that needed ticking, and that was the approval of the family. The medal had had an enormous effect on all of them. At various times it had represented all that was good and all that was bad in their lives. It belonged to all of them. Keith called a family conference and he, Flo and the boys sat down to discuss his plans.

'Maybe I was being a bit selfish, but I wanted to have it all settled before I went. I wanted the boys to have some benefits and I wanted to see that happen. It just seemed to be the right thing to do. Interest rates were going up, no one was doing it too easy and I thought, Why should I deprive my family? I had the means to make their lives a bit easier so that's the way I decided to go.'

When Keith told a newspaper reporter on the day of the sale that 'my boys could have lost their father', he might not have been speaking literally. The boys nearly did lose their father in the years after he returned from Vietnam. Derek believes the sale of the medal may have been a way for Keith to say sorry.

'When we were in Vietnam Dad told Ray Martin during the interview that one of his regrets was that he hadn't spent much time with us boys growing up. That struck me because he'd never really said that to us. Maybe that was partly behind him selling he medal. It was a way to make reparation.

'Once again I think it was an example of Dad's courage because the VC had meant so much to him over the years. He was obsessed with it. It was the thing that held his life together. It represented so much – the army, the AATTV – and then he sells it. He didn't have to. It would have been easier for him not to, but once again there was that sense of duty. Of doing the right thing.

'I think one of the aspects was this fear over what would happen once he was gone. There's always this assumption that Dad will die first and I think he was worried about the pressure on Mum over what to do with the medal when it was just her and us. He would have been thinking, Can the boys hold it together?, and really, what he has done is the smart move. None of us encouraged him to do it. In the end we pretty much said, "If you choose to do that we'll support you", but ideally I wish we'd been rich enough as a family so we could hold on to it.

'It was a very big decision, a huge decision, and it was not taken lightly but it was made with all the best intentions. It was made with love, and that's a wonderful thing.'

Given how the boys had viewed the medal over the years, the thought that it would be leaving the family left them with mixed emotions.

'There had been times over the years when I'd thought, I wish you'd never won the bloody thing', said Ron. 'But in saying that, when Dad told us he'd made the decision to sell it, I was against it. It had become who he was. At first it was an intrusion into our family, something we had all had to adapt to because it was not going away. But it became an integral part of our family's life. It caused some problems, but it also brought us closer together and made us a stronger family.'

The decision made, Keith went to see the man whose opinion he valued most. The man who had written the words that the Queen's equerry had read out that day on the *Britannia* as Flo and the boys watched on. R.D.F. Lloyd.

If Payne hoped that the retired brigadier would slap him on the back and say 'Don't worry about it, mate. It's yours, you can do whatever you want with it', he was to be disappointed. Lloyd stayed true to the philosophy that the medal didn't belong just to Payne, or even just to Payne and his family. It belonged to everyone who had served with the Team, every Australian who had served in Vietnam in fact.

'I understand why he did it, but I can't accept it,' Lloyd said. 'I told him that to his face. He knows where I stand.'

And deep down Payne wouldn't have it any other way.

On the morning of 18 June 2007, Keith and Flo arrived in Maryborough with Keith's twenty-three medals, including the Victoria Cross, in a small carry case. They met John Meyers at the museum and walked with him to his bank.

'It was all set up for us,' Keith said. 'I signed a piece of paper and gave John the medals and the money was transferred from his account into mine. What can I say? It wasn't the nicest thing I've ever had to do in my life.'

Today a sign outside the Maryborough Military and Colonial Museum exhorts passers-by to come in and view the Keith Payne Victoria Cross display, but most who walk through the front door haven't needed a sign to tell them what is inside. They have come from all over Australia specifically to see the medal and share Keith's story.

In the twelve months before the medal was put on display 4000 people visited the museum. In the twelve months following, the number was 6500 and it continues to climb. Two couples hired a plane and flew the 250 kilometres from Brisbane.

For those who can't get to Maryborough, Keith Payne continues to go to them.

'I believe you have a responsibility for the decoration you wear,' he says. 'It's like R.D.F. Lloyd said to me that day in Saigon. You "have a cross to bear. Bear it well." That's it. That's all I've ever tried to do.'

He visits schools, talks to cadet units and parliamentary inquiries. He is at the opening of exhibitions and the naming of parks, at Anzac Day commemorations, from dawn to dark. Most of all Payne VC is just there, wherever he is asked to be, reminding Australians of the courage of ordinary men and women, and the sacrifices made in extraordinary times.

Lest we forget.

Glossary

AATTV: Australian Army Training Team Vietnam, known as 'The Team'. It was a small elite unit that trained South Vietnamese troops and operated with US Special Forces as part of the Civilian Irregular Defense Group program. It was the first Australian unit to arrive in Vietnam, the last to leave and the most decorated of the war.

Adoo: Collective term for rebel forces opposing the Sultan of Oman during the Dhofar Revolution

Adviser: Term given first to American and then to Australian military deployed to Vietnam whose mission was to train local troops only and not become involved in combat

Agent Orange: Defoliant sprayed from US aircraft during the Vietnam War. It was named after the orange bands painted on the canisters in which it was stored.

Airborne: Soldiers qualified as parachutists

AK-47: Soviet-manufactured Kalashnikov semi-automatic and fully automatic combat assault rifle. Standard weapon of the North Vietnamese Army

ARVN: Army of the Republic of Vietnam; the South Vietnamese Regular Army

B52: US Air Force high-altitude bomber

Bailey bridge: Prefabricated steel panel bridge

Base camp: Resupply base for field units and a location for headquarters of brigade or division-size units. Also known as the rear area

Glossary

Batman: Also known as an orderly, a soldier assigned to a commissioned officer as a personal assistant

Battalion: Made up of four companies plus headquarters, around 1200 soldiers

Battery: Artillery unit

BDA: Bomb Damage Assessment. Written report of the effectiveness of a bombing mission

Bird: Helicopter or any aircraft

Blood trail: Trail of blood left by a fleeing man who has been wounded

Body bag: Plastic bag used to transport dead bodies from the field

Braino: Episode of anger, temper tantrum, brought on by the effects of post-traumatic stress disorder

Bren gun: Light machine gun used by Commonwealth forces from the 1930s to the 1990s. It could be fired hand-held or prone on the ground, using a two-legged stand.

Brigade: Three battalions plus headquarters, around 3800 soldiers

Bronze Star: US military decoration awarded for valour or meritorious service

Burp: Type 50 submachine carbine used by the Chinese during the Korean War

C-130: Large propeller-driven planes that carry people and cargo, known as Hercules

Cache: Hidden supplies

Charlie: Viet Cong or North Vietnamese Army

Chinook: CH-47 cargo helicopter

Choofer: Heating device made using a discarded artillery shell. Burned aviation fuel

Chopper: Helicopter

CIA: Central Intelligence Agency, the US government intelligence-gathering organisation. Instigator and initial financier of the Civilian Irregular Defense Group operation

CIDG: Civilian Irregular Defense Group. American-financed, irregular military units led by members of the US Special Forces. Usually members of Vietnamese ethnic minorities

Glossary

Communications trench: Trench linking front-line trenches to headquarters, allowing messages to be sent from one to the other via runners

Concussion grenade: Hand grenade filled with extra explosive but no shrapnel

Clacker: Small hand-held firing device for a claymore mine

Claymore: Anti-personnel mine. It propelled small steel projectiles in a 60-degree fan-shaped pattern to a maximum distance of 100 metres.

CMF: Citizens' Military Force. Now known as the Army Reserve

Cobra: AH-1 attack helicopter, armed with rockets and machine guns

Company: Four platoons plus headquarters, around 135 soldiers

Compound: Fortified military installation

Concertina wire: Coiled barbed wire with razor-type ends

Contact: Firing on or being fired upon by the enemy

Counter-insurgency: Anti-guerrilla warfare

C-rations: Combat rations. They usually consisted of a canned main meal, canned fruit, packet dessert, powdered cocoa, sugar, powdered cream, coffee, cigarettes, two pieces of chewing gum and toilet paper.

CSM: Company sergeant major

CT: Communist Terrorists. Irregular forces operating in Asia during the 1950s and 1960s

Distinguished Service Cross: The United States' second highest medal for valour

Division: Three brigades, up to 20,000 soldiers

Dust-off: Medical evacuation by helicopter

DVA: Department of Veterans' Affairs

Entrant: Point of entry and return for patrols through a gap in the wire

Fatigues: Standard combat uniform, green in colour

Feature: Hill

Firefight: Battle or exchange of small-arms fire with the enemy

Flare: Illumination projectile; hand-fired or shot from artillery, mortars or the air

Forward observer: Person attached to a field unit to coordinate the placement of direct or indirect fire from ground, air and naval forces

Green Berets: US Special Forces

Glossary

Gunship: Armed helicopter

Highlands: An area some 300 kilometres north-east of Saigon known as Trung Nguyen, or the Central Highlands. It was home to many ethnic minority communities living outside small towns from Dalat to Danang.

HO: Home Only. Stamped on military papers to signify a soldier was not to serve overseas

Hot: Area under fire

HQ: Headquarters

Huey: Nickname for UH-1 series helicopters

In country: Term used by soldiers to signify arrival and presence in country of conflict

Insert: To be deployed into a tactical area by helicopter

Irregulars: Soldiers involved in a conflict but not part of the main regular armed force

K-Force: Australian volunteer force recruited to fight in the Korean War

KIA: Killed in action

Konfrontasi: Indonesian term for the Indonesia–Malaysia Confrontation from 1962 to 1966

The Line: Front line of military action

Litter: Stretcher to carry the wounded

LZ: Landing zone. Usually a small clearing secured temporarily for the landing of resupply helicopters

M16: Standard US military rifle used in Vietnam from 1966

Magic Dragon: AC-47 propeller-driven aircraft. Originally designed as a transport, it was armed with three rapid-fire machine guns.

McGuire Rig: Rope with harness used to extract soldiers by helicopter

Medevac: Medical evacuation from the field by helicopter

MID: Mentioned in Dispatches. Recognises meritorious conduct that warranted a written report by a superior officer. While not awarded a medal, soldiers MID receive a certificate and are entitled to wear a silver oak leaf on the ribbon of their campaign medal.

Mike Force: Mobile Strike Force; also called M-Force. Indigenous soldiers led by US or Australian commanders under the auspices of the US Special Forces

Glossary

Montagnard: French term for tribes of mountain people inhabiting the hills and mountains of central and northern Vietnam

Mop-up: Clean-up operation after battle, retrieving weapons, the wounded, and bodies

Mortar: Consists of a steel tube, base plate and tripod. A round is dropped in the tube, striking a firing pin, causing the projectile to leave the tube at a high angle.

MSF: Montagnard Special Forces. Indigenous soldiers serving under the command of the US Special Forces

Napalm: Jellied petroleum substance which burns fiercely, used against enemy personnel

Nashos: Nickname for those who took part in Australia's National Service Scheme of compulsory military service

NCO: Non-commissioned officer

NVA: North Vietnamese Army

Occupation Force: The British Commonwealth Occupation Force, including 16,000 Australians, occupied Japan from 1946 to 1951.

Operation: Troops involved in a mission to engage or harass the enemy or gain information

Patrol: Short operation with a specific aim, such as reconnaissance, ambush or capture of the enemy

Perimeter: Outer limits of a military position

PIR: Pacific Island Regiment; generic nickname for a Pacific Island soldier

Platoon: Three sections plus headquarters, 33 soldiers

Police action: Military action undertaken without a formal declaration of war

Potato masher: German-style World War II hand grenade on a handle, used by Communist forces in Korea

PTSD: Post-Traumatic Stress Disorder. Psychological disorder triggered by a traumatic event or life-changing experience. Officially recognised in Australia in the early 1990s

Punji stakes: Sharpened bamboo sticks used in pit trap. They were often smeared with excrement to cause infection.

Purple Heart: US military decoration awarded to members of the armed forces wounded by enemy action

Glossary

RAR: Royal Australian Regiment, the parent regiment for regular infantry battalions of the Australian Army. Each battalion is numbered in relation to its position in the regiment. First Battalion Royal Australian Regiment is 1RAR, Second Battalion is 2RAR etc.

R & R: Rest and recreation. A holiday from armed service. There were two types during the Vietnam War: three day in country and seven-day out of country.

Re-entrant: Area at the base of a hill between two spurs

Recon: Reconnaissance. Going out into the jungle to observe for the purpose of identifying enemy activity

RPG: Rocket-propelled grenade. Russian-made portable anti-tank grenade launcher

Routine orders: Regular orders from headquarters outlining the requirements of missions

SAS: Special Air Service Regiment. Australian special forces regiment based on the British model and drawing on the traditions of Australian World War II Z Force commando unit

Section: Group of ten soldiers with specific skills and duties within a platoon

Shakedown exercise: Routine operation to allow officers to assess strengths, weaknesses and capabilities

Shrapnel: Pieces of metal sent flying by an explosion

Silver Star: US military decoration awarded for gallantry in action

Sitrep: Situation Report. Summary notes taken while on operation and submitted to military intelligence on return

SKS: Simonov 7.62 millimetre semi-automatic carbine

Smoke grenade: Grenade that released brightly coloured smoke. Used to signal helicopters. Yellow indicated a safe landing zone; red was a hot landing zone.

Special Forces: Elite special operations unit of the US Army. Known as Green Berets

Spooky: AC-47 cargo plane fitted with machine guns. Also known as Magic Dragon

Spur: Ridge of rock jutting down into a valley

Standdown: Infantry unit's return to base camp for refitting and training

Glossary

Strobe: Hand-held strobe light for marking landing zones at night

Tiger fatigues: Camouflage fatigue uniforms worn by US Special Forces

TPI: Totally and Permanently Incapacitated. Classification of veteran disablement as a result of active service

Tracheotomy: Making an opening into the windpipe to facilitate breathing

Triage: Procedure for deciding the order in which to treat casualties

38th Parallel: Circle of latitude 38 degrees north of the Earth's equatorial plane. Line used to divide North and South Korea in 1948

Unit: In Australian terms usually refers to a battalion

VC: Victoria Cross

Viet Cong: South Vietnamese Communist

Viet Minh: Liberation movement that fought the occupation of Vietnam by the French, and later the Japanese. Formed the first North Vietnamese government in 1954

Vietnamese Popular Forces: South Vietnamese local military groups charged with protecting homes and villages from infiltration and attack. Originally known as the Vietnamese Civil Guard

Vietnamization: US policy initiated by President Richard Nixon late in the Vietnam War to turn fighting over to the South Vietnamese Army during the phased withdrawal of American troops

WIA: Wounded in action

WO: Warrant officer; the most senior non-commissioned officer in the Australian Army

WRAAC: Women's Royal Australian Army Corps

XO: Executive officer; the second-in-command of a military unit

Yard: Nickname for Montagnard

Index

Adoo 188, 190, 193–4
Affiliation Parade 52–3
Agent Orange 211–12
air mobility 93–4
Allen, Dave 80
Alvarado, Alberto 125
Army of the Republic of South
    Vietnam (ARVN) 77, 92, 106,
    135
Auhl, Bob 36
Auriemma, Paul 1, 137–9, 141–2,
    144, 146, 148, 150
Austin, Art 88, 96–7, 134
Australian Army Training Team
    Vietnam (AATTV) 49, 61,
    77–81, 92, 154
Australian Women's Weekly 163

Badcoe, Peter 125
Baluchistan 190–1
Battle of Kapyong 41
Battle of Long Tan 65
Battle of Maryang San 13
Beale, Pat 72
Beatham, Robert 226
Ben Het 101–3, 105–6, 127, 132–51,
    221–2

'Big John' 94, 113, 140, 142
bin Nafl, Mussalim 187
bin Said, Qaboos 188–91
bin Taimur, Said 187–8
Black, Corporal 56
Borneo 58
Bracken, George 4–5
Brackenbridge, Arthur 4, 71
Breen, Gus 26–7, 30–6
Brennan, Pat 67–8
Bright, John 36
Britannia 176–80
Bruce, Jean 163
Bugden, Patrick 226
Buick, Bob 66
Burgess, John 36
Byrne, Clarence 178

Cairns, Dr Jim 170, 183
Cameron, Don 86, 88
Campbell, Wally 74
Canungra 45, 49, 58, 61, 82
Caracciolo, Dave 200
Cary, Warwick 228–9
Charfield, Albert 33–4, 36–7
Civilian Irregular Defense Group
    (CIDG) 86, 124–5

Index

Clarke, Rex 185–7, 190
CMF 10–11, 14
Cold War 45–7, 69
Collier, Dave 166
Courier-Mail 165, 167, 172, 188–9
Crawford, Jimmy 74–6
Crisp, Billy 4
Crisp, Grassy 4, 143, 184–5, 200
Crosby, Lieutenant 'Bing' 74
Current Affair, A 220–3
Cutler, Roden 217–18

Dak To 152
Daly, Tom 31–2, 45
Deighton, John 178
Dellwo, Gerard 'Gerry' 1, 103–5, 113, 115, 117–20, 123, 134–42, 144, 146–51, 169
Dhofar 186–7, 190–1
Diem, Ngo Dinh 49
Dillon, Peter 223
Doe, Sergeant 138
Donnelly, Eric 'Bluey' 14, 38–9, 167
Duc Lap 89–91
Dugger, Elder 134, 149–50
Duntroon 171–6, 183–5
duodenal ulcers 164

Enoggera 14–15, 42–3

Fischer, Tim 65
Flora 30–1, 33
Forbes, Dr David 202–3, 216–17
Fox, Russell 173
Freudenberg, Graham 170
Fuge, John 74

Gill, Mick 74, 86, 88, 127–9, 226
Goldspink, Norm 67–8
Gorman, James 228
Green, Captain 88, 129–30

Grey, John 85

Harris, Peter 128–9
Hay, R.A. 131, 159
Hill 355 (Little Gibraltar) 22, 26, 28, 36, 38
Hines, Allan 161
Hiro 16–17
HMAS *Terra* 57
Hogbin, Ronald 138
Holiday Hill 20–1, 25
Holmberg, Peter 127, 130
Hook, the 21, 37
Howell, George 'Snowy' 228

Ibo, George 73
Indonesia 54–7, 70–1
Indonesia–Malaysia Confrontation (*Konfrontasi*) 56–8, 70
Ingham 3–11, 15–16, 42–3, 71, 167–9
Ingleburn 15, 64

Jackson, Laurie 90
Jackson, O.D. 80–1
Jaegles, Major 147, 149
Jebelis 186–8
Johnson, President Lyndon 81, 168
Johnston, Frank 159
Jones, Lord Mayor Clem 165
Juliana, Queen of the Netherlands 54

Kavanagh, Sergeant 36
Keith Payne VC Botanical Gardens 182
Keith Payne VC Club 182
Keith Payne VC Park 182
Keldie, John 178
Kelly, Jock 86, 88, 129–30
Kenna, Ted 71, 217–18
Kennedy, President John F. 86
Kennett, Jeff 65

Index

Keyes, Bill 183
K-Force 14, 69
Khan, Colin 'Genghis' 26–7
Korean War 17–40
  background 11–13
Kure 39–40

Latham, Kev 2, 88, 91, 93–4, 96, 98–9, 105–7, 109, 111–16, 118–19, 122–3, 137, 140–2, 145, 149–50, 169
Lee, Arthur 183
Levis, Arthur 4
Lewis, Laurie 73
Lloyd, Russell 'R.D.F.' 71, 85, 124–32, 145, 152–7, 159, 163–4, 177, 225, 231–2
Loan, Nguyen Ngoc 169
Lockyer, Paul 220–3

MacArthur, Douglas 12
McKay, Gary 66
McLachlan, Marty 151–2, 157
McNeill, Ian 77, 80–1
McNulty, John 'Mac' 25–7, 36
Malaya 45–53, 56–8
Malaysia 53–4, 56, 58, 70
Manila 16
Mann, A.S. 'Joe' 30, 32, 35–6, 77
Martin, Ray 221, 226, 230
Maryborough Military and Colonial Museum 228–9, 232
Matthews 38
Menzies, Prime Minister Robert 81, 177
Meyers, Else 228–9
Meyers, Geoffrey 229
Meyers, John 228–9, 231
Meyers, Karen 229
Mike Force (M-Force) 79, 85–9, 126–9, 134, 155
Millett, Lewis 181

Moffitt, Frank 152
Montagnards ('Yards') 62–4, 78–9, 82, 86–7, 89–102, 104–7, 109, 113, 115, 117–18, 122, 126, 128–30, 132–5, 137–8, 140–2, 144, 146, 149, 157
Montez, Anastacio 1, 89, 92, 106–7, 111, 113, 118, 122, 132–41, 146–8, 222, 226
Morgan gallup poll 170

nashos 45, 46, 58
National Front for the Liberation of South Vietnam 49
National Service Scheme 45–6, 58–9
Neville, Danny 78
New Guinea 55, 67–76
Nixon, President Richard 102
North Vietnamese Army (NVA) 66, 81, 84–5, 90, 92–3, 106, 108–9, 116–17, 124–5, 127–8, 134, 136–7, 142–3, 150, 167

Oman 186–95
Operation Fauna 30–7
Oven 190, 192–3

Pacific Islands Regiments 70–2
  2PIR 72
Papua New Guinea *see* New Guinea
Payne, Colin 47, 162, 173, 176, 179, 224
Payne, Derek 47, 76, 167, 172–3, 176, 203–8, 214–15, 217–18, 220–3, 230–1
Payne, Florence 'Flo' (nee Plaw) 42–5, 49–53, 57, 60, 64–5, 74–6, 80, 83–4, 114, 157–8, 160–3, 166–7, 170–1, 178–82, 184–5, 197, 199, 204, 207–9, 214–16, 218–21, 224, 230–1
Payne, Frank 8, 166–7

Index

Payne, Greg 47, 75, 161, 173, 176, 224
Payne, Gwenda 8
Payne, Henry 3–6, 8–9, 168–9
Payne, Ian 47, 173, 176, 197, 207, 224
Payne, Janice 166
Payne, John 3
Payne, Keith
  childhood 3–10
  Duntroon Royal Military College 171–4, 183–4
  Korean War 17–40
  Malaya 49–58
  meeting Florence Plaw 42
  New Guinea 69–76
  Oman 186–95
  post-traumatic stress disorder 197, 200–3, 206, 208–9, 211–12, 217
  Victoria Cross, awarding of 154–63
  Vietnam War 81–151
Payne, Merle 8
Payne, Remilda 'Millie' 3, 8–9, 11, 15–16, 43, 169
Payne, Ron 45, 47, 83, 114, 158, 161–2, 172–3, 176, 184, 204–5, 218–19, 224, 231
Payne, Toby 4, 7–10, 16
Pearson, Sandy 174–5, 177
Petersen, Barry 61–4, 78–9, 86, 99–101
Pilkington, Supply Sergeant 120, 226
Pipeline Ambush 51
Plaw, Florence 'Flo' *see* Payne, Florence 'Flo' (nee Plaw)
Pleiku 88–97, 221–2
Porto, Ron 33–7
post-traumatic stress disorder (PTSD) 194, 197–8, 200–3, 206, 208–9, 211–12, 214, 216–17, 224
Prince Charles 177
Prince Philip 179
Princess Anne 177

Puckapunyal 14–15
Pusan 17

Queen Elizabeth II 174–80
Quetta, Tommy 5

Ramsay, Don 'Jock' 71–2
regimental cadets 9–10, 14
rice wine 99–101
Ridgway, Matthew 12
Roberts, Betty 16, 42–3
Robson, Frank 198–9
Rootes, Ron 35–7
Rothwell, Peter 128–31
Royal Australian Regiments (Korea)
  1RAR 18, 27, 37
    B Company 18–19, 29–30
  2RAR 14–15, 21, 37
  3RAR 18, 21, 41, 52
Royal Australian Regiments (Malaya)
  1RAR 47
  2RAR 47–8, 51
  3RAR 47–8, 52, 56, 58–9
    A Company 53
  4RAR 58
Royal Australian Regiments (Vietnam)
  3RAR
    A Company 66
  5RAR 26
  6RAR 174
    D Company 65–6
Ryan, Raymond 178

Salmon, John 33, 35–6
Savage, David 89–90
Scheyville 59, 64–8
Scrub Hill 15
Searchlight Hill 38
Seaton, John 25–6, 36
Seoul 17
Serong, Colonel F. 80–1

Index

Sharp, Gordon 65–6
Shelley 207
Shout, Alfred 227–8
Silver Star 123, 180–2, 228
Simpson, Ray 'Simmo' 88, 125–32, 154, 157–60, 163, 220
Singapore 56–7
Small, Sammy 27, 36
Smith, Geoff 90
Sparkes, James 178
Stack, Daphne 160
Stanley, Regimental Sergeant Major 60
Star Mountains 72–3
Stewart, Jock 133, 152
Stokes, Bevan 79
Stokes, Kerry 227
Suharto, General 70
Sukarno, President 54–6, 70
Sunday Sun 198–9
Swanton, R.J. 'Butch' 124–5
Sydney Morning Herald 177

Taylor, Don 105–7, 111–20, 123, 132–3
Telegraph, The 162
Tet Offensive 84
Thomas, Graham 228
Toget, R'Com 90–1, 94–5, 98–9, 101, 118, 138
Tolley, Barry 88–90, 92, 96, 105–7, 111, 113, 116, 118–19, 121–3, 132–6, 138, 142, 148–9, 151
Townsend, Colin 174
Townsville 42–3
Truong Son Force 78–9

Upham, Charles 227
US Special Forces 85–6, 132, 134
USS *Harpers Ferry* 182

Victoria Cross 37, 71, 124–5, 153–64, 205–6, 225–32
Viet Cong *see* North Vietnamese Army (NVA)
Viet Minh 48, 92
Vietnam Veterans Association 212, 214
Vietnam War 84–164
 background 48–9, 58–9
Vietnamese Cross of Gallantry 109, 228
Vietnamization 102–3, 117–18
von Kurtz, Alex 67

Wacol 81–2
Walsh, Brian 129–31
Wark, Blair 226
wasp sting 51–2
water divining 5, 192–3
Watts, Don 74
Wewak 71–6
Wheatley, Kevin 'Dasher' 124–5, 227
White, J.F. 166
Whitlam, Prime Minister Gough 170, 183–4, 199
Wiggans, Rex 74
World War II 5–9

Yards *see* Montagnards